Economic Biology and Behavioral Economics

Economic Biology and Behavioral Economics: The Prophesy of Alfred Marshall explores the prophesy of Alfred Marshall, the grand synthesizer of neoclassical economics, that the "Mecca of the economist lies in economic biology".

The book presents the proof of that prophesy through examination and establishment of the fundamental biological science necessary and then applying that science to the examination of current economic theory. In doing so, the book focuses primarily on the fundamentals of neoclassical economic theory—which is the reigning theory and the general framework of which is taught as "science" in first courses in college economics. These courses are at best an idealization, if not an ideology, of the discipline—presented to fresh minds misleadingly as confirmed science. The book examines the bases and the history of these idealizations, points to the sources of their error from the biological perspective and suggests a path forward for the discipline. Through this process, the book demonstrates the power of the biological perspective anticipated by Marshall.

This book provides invaluable reading for anyone interested in the future of economics and economic theory, and particularly those interested in behavioral economics and neuroeconomics.

Gerald A. Cory Jr., Former Senior Fellow, Graduate Studies and Research, San Jose State University (Retired)

Routledge Advances in Behavioural Economics and Finance
Edited by **Roger Frantz**

Traditionally, economists have based their analysis of financial markets and corporate finance on the assumption that agents are fully rational, emotionless, self-interested maximizers of expected utility. However, behavioural economists are increasingly recognizing that financial decision makers may be subject to psychological biases, and the effects of emotions. Examples of this include the effects on investors' and managers' decision-making of such biases as excessive optimism, overconfidence, confirmation bias, and illusion of control. At a practical level, the current state of the financial markets suggests that trust between investors and managers is of paramount importance.

Routledge Advances in Behavioural Economics and Finance presents innovative and cutting-edge research in this fast-paced and rapidly growing area, and will be of great interest to academics, practitioners, and policy-makers alike.

All proposals for new books in the series can be sent to the series editor, Roger Frantz, at rabeandf@gmail.com.

The Art of Experimental Economics
Twenty Top Papers Reviewed
Edited by Gary Charness and Mark Pingle

Behavioural Sports Economics
A Research Companion
Edited by Hannah Josepha Rachel Altman, Morris Altman and Benno Torgler

Behavioural Economics and Regulation
The Design Process of Regulatory Nudges
Maria C. de Campos

Economic Biology and Behavioral Economics
The Prophesy of Alfred Marshall
Gerald A. Cory Jr.

For more information about this series, please visit: www.routledge.com/Routledge-Advances-in-Behavioural-Economics-and-Finance/book-series/RABEF

Economic Biology and Behavioral Economics

The Prophesy of Alfred Marshall

Gerald A. Cory Jr.

Routledge
Taylor & Francis Group
LONDON AND NEW YORK

First published 2023
by Routledge
4 Park Square, Milton Park, Abingdon, Oxon OX14 4RN

and by Routledge
605 Third Avenue, New York, NY 10158

Routledge is an imprint of the Taylor & Francis Group, an informa business

British Library Cataloguing-in-Publication Data
A catalogue record for this book is available from the British Library

Library of Congress Cataloging-in-Publication Data
Names: Cory, Gerald A., author.
Title: Economic biology and behavioral economics : the prophesy of alfred marshall / Gerald A. Cory Jr.
Description: 1 Edition. | New York, NY : Routledge, 2023. |
Series: Routledge advances in behavioural economics and finance |
Includes bibliographical references and index.
Identifiers: LCCN 2022014456 | ISBN 9781032300467 (hardback) |
ISBN 9781032300481 (paperback) | ISBN 9781003303190 (ebook)
Subjects: LCSH: Neoclassical school of economics. | Science–Methodology. |
Biology, Economic. | Neuroeconomics.
Classification: LCC HB98.2 .C673 2023 | DDC 330.15/7–dc23/eng/20220519
LC record available at https://lccn.loc.gov/2022014456

ISBN: 978-1-032-30046-7 (hbk)
ISBN: 978-1-032-30048-1 (pbk)
ISBN: 978-1-003-30319-0 (ebk)

DOI: 10.4324/9781003303190

Typeset in Bembo
by Newgen Publishing UK

Contents

1 Introduction 1

PART I
The Biological Fundamentals 9

2 Foundations: Evolutionary Brain Science in the 21st Century 11

3 Our Mammalian Heritage: A Dual Motive Neurobehavioral Model 29

4 The Dynamic Algorithms of Social Behavior 40

5 The Physiology of Social Behavior 47

6 The Organic, Homeostatic Equation of Our Neural Architecture 53

7 Physics vs. Social Science: Some Differences 59

PART II
Biological Linkages to the Discipline of Economics 65

8 Family, Gift, and Market 67

9 Adam Smith and the Market 76

10 The Invisible Hand as a Neural Algorithm 81

11 General Equilibrium Theory: From Newtonian Physics to Organic Dynamics 90

12 The Social Brain and the Idealized Version of Price Theory 97

13 Calculus and Neural Algorithms in Price Theory 104

14 Further Application of the Basic Homeostatic Equation to Economics 107

15 Self-Interest and the Fallacy of Self-Reference 113

16 Hayek: Wishful Thinking and a Not So Spontaneous Order 119

17 Nash: Modeling Equilibrium with Beautiful Minds, Beautiful Equations 127

PART III
The Wider Context 135

18 The Emergence and Promise of Neuroeconomics 137

19 The Larger Context: The Stiff Upper Lip, Original Sin, and Western Science 141

20 Evolutionary Neuroethology and Inclusive Fitness 152

21 Social Exchange and the Structure of Society 157

22 Conclusion 169

References 172
Index 184

1 Introduction

As the title of this book states, my purpose is to explore the linkages between economic biology, or the biology of socio-economic exchange, and behavioral economics. This responds to the famed but yet unfulfilled prophesy of the grand synthesizer of neoclassical economics Alfred Marshall (1842–1924).

Marshall famously prophesied that the "Mecca of the economist lies in economic biology". Unfortunately, the science of his time did not exist to develop or fulfill that prophesy. As a result, in part, there is now wide-ranging concern among economists and observers from related disciplines that economic theory has hit a stone wall. Many, understandingly, feel that new approaches are needed. Some have gone so far as to call the modern age of economics an age of delusion.(Clower & Howett 1997: 31; Kirman 2006: 275). I share their concerns.

The challenge of this book is to fulfill Marshall's prophesy by presenting both the proof and the power of his prophesy. This proof will be achieved by examination and establishment of the fundamental biological science necessary and then applying that science to the examination of current socio-economic exchange theory. In doing so, I will focus primarily, but not exclusively, on the behavioral fundamentals of neoclassical economic theory—which is the reigning theory and the general framework of which is taught as "science" in first courses in college economics. These are the courses for those who seek a basic familiarity as a part of a general education—for instance, business and humanities students. These courses also set the basic and often lasting framework for students pursuing graduate degrees preparing them to be professional economists, teachers, and professors.

What these students learn can have lasting effects. And when what they learn is wrong or poor science, the effects can be harmful to their lives, to their later careers, and to society. These courses are at best an idealization, if not an ideology, of the discipline—presented to fresh minds misleadingly as confirmed science. I will examine the bases, and to some extent the history of these idealizations, point to the sources of their error from the biological perspective, and suggest a path forward for the discipline and the larger context in which it is embedded. By this process I will also demonstrate the power of the biological perspective anticipated by Marshall.

DOI: 10.4324/9781003303190-1

My approach will be from the perspective of *consilience*, the effort to unify the sciences, both natural and social. E. O. Wilson of Harvard issued the most recent call for this approach of antiquity in is his *Consilience: The Unity of Knowledge* (1998). Seeking the unity of the sciences, the consilient approach works to establish actual *linkages* among the sciences, not analogies or metaphors—although the latter two may sometimes be useful as guides to identifying the sought-after linkages.

The book will confront two challenges in identifying, clarifying, and establishing the needed linkages.

The first challenge, in pursuit of Marshall's undeveloped insight, will be to draw from two disciplines or sciences that economic theory has yet to connect with meaningfully. They are the biological subdisciplines of evolutionary brain science and general physiology. From the perspectives of these neglected disciplines I will examine two key foundational features of present economic theory that have been referred to as the crown jewels of economics.

These reputed jewels are:

First, the sole primary motive of self-interest—the so-called first principle of economics—which nobelist George Stigler called "the crown jewel of *The Wealth of Nations*" in reference to Adam Smith's foundational work (1976: 3).

And, second, general equilibrium theory (GET)—the foundational belief that market forces will be driven by some unspecified inherent force to achieve a general equilibrium. Economic historian Mark Blaug has called GET "that jewel in the crown of neoclassical economics" (1990: 226).

As the second challenge, I will confront the misuse by economics of two other sciences or disciplines—physics and math—that it does connect with. Physics is a science that economics understandably, but erroneously, modeled itself after. As French economist Thomas Piketty (cf. 2014: 574; 2020: 1039–40) and others have recently noted, math is a tool of science that economics often applies to obscure inherent flaws and enhance a credibility it does not deserve. I will discuss the misuse of the physico-mathematical approach from the beginning of economic theorizing in the 18th century to the modern-day use of top-down modeling with no connection to market realities.

Finally, I will place economic thinking in a wider context, suggest the unity of economics with the other social sciences, and point the way forward hopefully free of the delusional aspects that have led the discipline down a wrong path into a theoretical impasse or dead end.

Part I consists of Chapters 2 through 7 that establish the fundamental biological science linkages foundational to understanding of the social sciences.

Chapter 2 proceeds from an insight by 19th-century British scholar, Alfred Marshall, one of the chief architects of present-day neoclassical economic theory. Marshall's famed but yet undeveloped insight was that "The Mecca of the economist lies is in economic biology" rather than the traditional metaphors drawn from Newtonian and later 19th-century physics. From this starting point the chapter moves to resolve the contested areas of the evolutionary neuroscience of the human brain that have been an obstacle to consilience—the unification of the natural sciences and socio-economic theory. In acknowledged response to criticism by the present author, distinguished comparative neurobiologist Ann Butler, recently of George Mason University, has published a modified and updated version of Paul MacLean's well-known triune brain concept that resolves the contested areas of human brain evolution in that more fundamental biological science of comparative evolutionary neurobiology.

Thus, the three-phase evolution of thc human neural architecture, proceeding from self-surviving ancestral amniotes to the appearance of nurturing behavior in mammals to the self- and other-preserving *social brain* (a term now widely accepted in psychology and psychiatry) of humans, is firmly established science. By proceeding from established evolutionary neuroscience, then, we can move from *metaphors* to the actuality of scientific *s*—a major step forward in the unification of the natural with the social sciences.

Chapters 3 and 4 develop the Conflict Systems Neurobehavioral (CSN) Model to express the dynamic of our essentially conflicting dual motive mammalian neural architecture that combines both self-preserving and other-preserving circuitries. At a high level of cognitive integration our self-preserving circuitries are expressed as self-interest or Ego whereas our other-preserving circuitries are expressed as other-interest or Empathy. The tug-and-pull of these essentially conflicting circuitries sets us up for internal as well as interpersonal behavioral tension that must be managed by our higher evolved executive neural circuitry. The range of the Ego/Empathy dynamic of our *social brain* is offered as the primary source of most, if not all, other motives postulated in the literature.

Algorithms describing the interaction of the Ego/Empathy dynamic are developed as testable empirical statements. Reciprocity in social behavior emerges as an outcome of the Ego/Empathy interaction.

The scale of inclusiveness is offered as a fundamental concept to reflect the fact that our neural architecture evolved to function in small kinship groups and requires socialization and education to expand the Ego/Empathy dynamic to increasingly larger social groupings.

Chapter 5 relates social exchange or economic behavior to physiology. Homeostasis, or the maintenance of a steady organic state, is the foundation of modern physiology. Homeostasis has been the inspiration and the model for the high-tech sciences of cybernetics and control theory that led to the computer age. The brain, as a physiological organ, likewise operates to maintain a homeostatic or steady state not only on a purely physiological level, but also on a behavioral basis. Homeostasis requires standards, the ability to monitor and evaluate, sensors and effectors, and, of course, feedback. Our social behavior, then, is an expression of the physiological processes as they interact with the social environment.

Our archetypal neural circuits driving Ego and Empathy seek to maintain a steady state both in our internally experienced as well as our externally expressed social behavior. Behavioral tension is the generic regulator. As we deviate from the steady state of dynamic balance in our social behavior toward the extremes of either Ego or Empathy behavioral tension increases within us and externally—between us and others. The higher level circuits express a considerable degree of plasticity or learning. That is, interaction with the environment can modify gene expression of the behavioral circuitry. But plasticity has its limits—it cannot change the fundamental nature or biology of the circuitry. Overall, our social life is a homeostatic success reflected in our spectacular, if not planet threatening, population growth.

Chapter 6 develops an equation representing and expressive of the homeostatic dynamic of our archetypal, conflictual neural architecture. It is an organic, not physics, equation. The contrasting features and special characteristics of the equation are discussed from the perspective of history, thermodynamics, and complexity theory. Chapter 7 discusses some important differences as well as linkages between physics and the social sciences.

Part II consists of Chapters 8 through 17. These chapters analyze, develop, and demonstrate the effectiveness of the biological linkages developed in Part I to the discipline of economics.

Chapter 8 focuses on the family, gift, and market to begin the process of demonstrating that the reciprocal architecture of the social brain founded in evolutionary neuroscience is the proper model for economics, not the model of Newtonian mechanics and later nineteenth-century physics. It begins with the ubiquitous norm of reciprocity long studied in anthropology and sociology and more recently in economics.

The prevalence of reciprocity means that in society, everywhere we look, we find social relations of give and take.

The CSN Model, developed in Part I goes to the heart of the question of brain circuitry substrating reciprocity. The social brain, driven by the tug-and-pull of Ego and Empathy or self- and other-interest, is the motive source of human reciprocity. It is the motive source driving the evolution of the market from reciprocal behavior within the family and larger kinship groups to the gift-giving economy to the emergence of the commercial transaction in larger nonfamilial communities.

Chapter 9 focuses on a re-evaluation of Adam Smith, the acknowledged founder of economics. Smith has long been misinterpreted as considering self-interest as the sole primary motive for market exchange. When properly understood, Smith's concept of market exchange as developed in his two volumes—*The Wealth of Nations* and *The Theory of Moral Sentiments*—intuits, without knowledge of evolutionary neuroscience, the tug-and-pull of Ego (self-interest) and Empathy (other-interest or, in his words, *fellow-feeling*). In describing an offer of exchange in Book I, Chapter 2 of *The Wealth of Nations* he writes: "Give me what I want, and you shall have what you want, is the meaning of every such offer." In that phrasing, which we intuitively call win-win, Smith virtually states the algorithms of reciprocity and the tug-and-pull of Ego and Empathy.

Chapter 10 takes on that icon of economic lore—the Invisible Hand, also known as the doctrine of unintended consequences. One school of thought following Hobbesian logic saw as it motivated by pure self-interest. A second school followed more in the footsteps of philosophers Locke, Hume, and others who held that mankind had an innate concern or sympathy for others that led to a moral sense. Smith, when properly understood, followed the Lockean tradition in his emphasis on self-interest and sympathy or fellow-feeling. Smith went on to develop the famous principles of Demand and Supply (or provisioning) as the dynamic forces that drive the market. These principles, now inappropriately elevated to the status of laws, have served as the foundation of economics up to the present day.

The chapter goes on to develop the case for Demand and Supply as expressions of the social brain or the archetypal circuitry of the human neural architecture. Demand expresses our egoistic, survival-centered needs whereas Supply, or providing, proceeds from Empathy and is fundamentally an act of mammalian nurturing. As we move from the gift economy to the commercial or transactional market the dynamic tug-and-pull of Ego and Empathy becomes expressed as Demand and Supply. The behavioral tension driving toward a proper reciprocal balance between Demand and Supply in the marketplace accounts for the basic motive force for the Invisible Hand. The very structure of the market is the institutionalized product of the Ego/Empathy dynamic. The chapter, further, develops an important distinction between structure and behavior in the marketplace that draws upon an insight by Milton Friedman.

Chapter 11 discusses the evolution of general equilibrium theory (GET) from its initial modeling of Newtonian physics through its outright copying from late nineteenth-century physics to the top-down formalization based on the work of von Neumann and Morgenstern. None of these approaches was successful in meeting the essential elements of proof for GET. The failure to achieve proof of GET has led many prominent economic thinkers to declare it utopian or even dead. The so-called God model (according to nobelist Thomas Sargent) or natural law model analogous to physics does not exist in economics. It is a chimera chased in vain for some two centuries by some of the best minds in economic theory. The neural algorithms of Ego and Empathy expressed as Demand and Supply likely provided an intuitive motivational basis for the search for laws and patterns, but they are too weak and variable—too subject to blockage and frustration in the complexities and distances of the greater market—to ever assure us of getting to an unassisted equilibrium that is unique or stable. We must give consideration to Sargent's "intelligent design" suggestion to direct the organically motivated market to a desirable equilibrium.

Chapters 12 through 13 take the biological analysis to greater depths. They move from large-scale generalizations of the theoretical interplay of Supply and Demand, the Invisible Hand, and general equilibrium theory to the nitty-gritty of microanalysis. These chapters demonstrate how well the dynamic of our mammalian neural architecture can account for and further illuminate the essentials of price theory.

Chapter 12 challenges the foundational premise of traditional price theory that self-interest is the sole primary motive of economic exchange. In traditional price theory, economists present and interpret theoretical demand curves, supply curves, and the combined form, illustrating their intersection at the equilibrium price, from a self-interested viewpoint. Two functions: Demand and Supply. One motive: self-interest. The presentation seems superficially ok. The interpretation, however, is schizophrenic. The two functions, Demand and Supply, are themselves the motives of Ego and Empathy, given new names from an economic vocabulary. In reality, we have two primary motives disguised as functions—with one disguised to the point of denial. The disconnect from reality in economics, like the disconnect from reality in the mental condition, is not harmless. It creates problems. Applying the organic homeostatic equation developed in Part I, it is easily demonstrated that each curve represents a give-and-take or Ego/Empathy interaction.

Demand and Supply can be substituted for Ego and Empathy in the equation, correcting the schizophrenic condition and clearly demonstrating that the market dynamic expresses a biological, homeostatic algorithm—not an algorithm of physics. Chapter 13 repeats the analysis using the functions of calculus. Chapter 14 extends the microanalysis and presents a consistency proof of the application.

Chapter 15, following the microanalysis of the three preceding chapters, sums up the case against self-interest as sole primary motive in economics. After all, economics is about social exchange. And social exchange requires Empathy. You cannot be socially engaged without the capacity to put yourself in the other's moccasins—see things from their viewpoint. Self- and other-interest, Ego and Empathy, the archetypal circuits of our mammalian brain, are the very essence of social exchange. Without the dual motives there would be no exchange.

When faced with the increasing evidence for Empathy, cooperation, and even altruism among humans, economists grudgingly acknowledge the interlopers but do not give them full status. Self-interest remains the only primary motive. The "softer" human qualities (soft-headed some might say) are called preferences or tastes. Economists maintain the primacy of self-interest by shifting from *self-interest* to *self-reference*. The confounding of *self-reference* with *self-interest* is, in fact, a fundamental fallacy of the entire traditional economic approach. Taking the individual as the starting point, microeconomic theory mistakenly transforms this individual or self-referential perspective into an all-inclusive motive of self-interest. From this logically unwarranted transformation any other motive, like Empathy, is thus obscured or swallowed up in self-interest. The distortions produced by this fallacy are further examined. This fallacy was foreseen and discussed by nobelist Amartya Sen in his well-known article *Rational Fools*.

Chapter16 examines the thought of Friedrich Hayek from the perspective of the social brain dynamic. At the beginning of the 21st century Hayek is among the most influential theoretical economists in the Western world. Of special interest is Hayek's concept of spontaneous order. It sounded similar to Smith's Invisible Hand and Hayek acknowledged that. However, the two concepts are significantly different. There was no place in his concept for Smith's fellow-feeling or sympathy. Hayek's concept was an order based on law and the rules of civil society. He acknowledged that humans had moral instincts, but he saw these instincts as injurious to the production of wealth and its equitable distribution. Close examination in light of the social brain dynamic reveals that he sets by law and civil behavior the essential implicit and structural empathetic framework for the neural dynamic to function.

Chapter 17 turns the searchlight of the social exchange dynamic on the work of John Nash. It is important to recognize that Nash equilibria, as conceived by Nash, apply to human social interactions. Nevertheless, in keeping with standard acceptable and publishable economic theory, Nash's modeling proceeds on his explicitly announced assumption of rational self-interest as the primary motive. On close inspection, however, Empathy is shown to be a foundational but unclarified assumption of the Nash equilibria. An analysis of his noncooperative, cooperative, and bargaining games reveal clearly the interplay of Ego and Empathy, self- and other-interest. His equilibria, then, unwittingly depend on and display the social neural dynamic.

Part III consists of Chapters 18 through 21 dealing with the emergence of neuroeconomics and the wider context within which economics functions with other social sciences.

Chapter 18 discusses the emergence and development of neuroeconomics. The emergent discipline has been motivated largely by the new imaging techniques of medical neuroscience. In truth it seems governed by the well-known law of instrument—that is, "give a kid a hammer and he will find something to nail". It has been criticized for its fascination with and overuse of *fmri* (functional magnetic resonance imaging) and other issues. It shows no connection with or knowledge of evolutionary neuroscience which has been around considerably longer and has long been influential in medicine. It may, however, if done with care, help to fill out the detail of the social brain's neural circuitry relevant to economics upon which this work has been based.

Chapter 19 shifts from a primary focus on the market and economics to the larger context of Western science within which economics exists and from which it draws perspective if not inspiration. There is, of course, no real separating of the subject matter across the social sciences. Our academic disciplines, our departmented university systems, force artificial divides upon the seamless texture of society as well as the consilient unity with the natural sciences. It also traces the evolution of the concept of "scientific" economics over the past two centuries and challenges that misleading expression of original sin in biology—the selfish gene theory.

Chapter 20 discusses a major shift of scientific interest in human behavior that emerged in the last quarter of the 20th century. The previously neglected domains of human cognition, emotions, and consciousness were opened up to scientific study. The impact of Darwinian theory fueled the emergence of evolutionary biology, evolutionary psychology, and ultimately, evolutionary neuroethology. The concept of inclusive fitness resolved the pesky question of how cooperation, even altruism, could have been etched into the human genome.

Chapter 21 pushes the analysis of the social brain dynamic into disciplines of sociology and political science. The social brain equation from evolutionary biology provides a metric of sociobehavioral tension and inequality. As the ratio of inequities of Ego and Empathy expressed as dominance and submission or differentials of power and wealth approach homeostatic dynamic balance, the tension of such differentials or inequalities tends to be reduced. As the ratio diverges from homeostatic balance to the extremes, the equation indexes the behavioral tension in the society. It gives us insight into the important issues of social stratification which can be viewed as structured sociobehavioral tension. Society is analyzed as an overall Social Exchange System inclusive of a Politico-Legal Exchange System plus an Economic Exchange System. The two systems should ideally interact correctively and importantly to maintain homeostatic balance in the greater society. When that the imbalance is allowed to go to extremes it will tend to motivate change or even revolution.

Chapter 22, as the closing chapter, sums up the evidence that the so-called crown jewels of neoclassical economic theory—the sole primary motive of self-interest and general equilibrium theory—are flawed gems that, combined with the wrong mathematics, took us down a long and tortuous path to a theoretical dead end. Proceeding from Marshall's original, but undeveloped insight that the Mecca of economics is to be found in biology, we have laid an alternative foundation and dynamic for social exchange and economics in the biological subdisciplines of evolutionary neuroscience and human physiology. Economics can now hopefully move forward along this new path in fulfilling its promise for a better society.

Part I

The Biological Fundamentals

2 Foundations

Evolutionary Brain Science in the 21st Century

The first relevant science that economics doesn't connect with is evolutionary brain science. Adam Smith (1723–1790), the acknowledged founder of economics, had no access to the findings of evolutionary brain science. The discipline simply didn't exist in his day. The model of science at that time was the physics of Isaac Newton (1643–1727) describing the forces driving the workings of a clocklike mechanical universe.

Nor did Smith's followers—throughout the 19th and early 20th centuries—have access to evolutionary brain science as they sought to make economics a true science modeled along the lines of Newtonian mechanics plus later developments in nineteenth-century physics in which vectors of invisible law-like forces of nature led to a state of universal equilibrium.

Along Came Marshall

British scholar Alfred Marshall (1842–1924) has long been acknowledged as a leading architect of neoclassical economic theory—that theory built mainly upon a mechanical metaphor drawn from Newtonian mechanics and later 19th-century physics. Neoclassical theory prevails today and is the foundation of economic theory as presented in standard introductory college textbooks.

Biology as "Mecca" of Economics

Despite his reliance upon the mechanical metaphor in his development of neoclassical theory, Marshall sensed that economics dealt with a more complex reality and required a more complex dynamic. His intuited but undeveloped assertion that economic biology is the "Mecca" of economics (1947: xiv) has nevertheless resonated through the succeeding decades dominated by the mechanical metaphor.

Neither he nor his followers, however, ever developed a theory that exploited the full potential of the biological Mecca. As Hodgson (1993) has so thoroughly explicated and discussed this subject, I will not replicate his efforts here.

DOI: 10.4324/9781003303190-3

Metaphors vs. Linkages

Marshall's followers in institutional and evolutionary economics drew primarily upon *metaphors* taken from biology in their failed efforts to achieve influential theory. They avoided the task of establishing *linkages*—not metaphors—that are necessary to the true unification of the sciences anticipated by the ancients as well as Herbert Spencer and E. O. Wilson. In the unification of the natural and social sciences, then, *linkage rules*—not metaphor or analogy.

Marshall as Synthesizer Not Innovator

Marshall was not a great innovator of new thinking but rather a great synthesizer. He pulled together the parts of the emerging neoclassical approach and framed them well. He also intuited the weaknesses of the essentially mechanical metaphor upon which the neoclassical edifice was built.

That is, he saw the so-called laws of economics as *tendencies* rather than the precise laws of Newtonian mechanics. He also saw useful metaphors for economics in the organic hierarchy of interrelated parts and their growth, development, and evolution. Although some later scholars, such as Veblen and other institutionalists, made use of the biological metaphors of organic growth and evolution, they never succeeded in achieving an integrated body of theory to challenge the dominance of neoclassical economics.

In these next few chapters I will develop the case for evolutionary brain science as a proper foundation for economics.

Background: The Three-Phased Evolutionary Transition to Humanity

Evolutionary brain science, or more formally, evolutionary neuroscience, emerged meaningfully on the scene in the last decades of the twentieth century.

Before dipping into the evolutionary findings about the human brain, it may be helpful to make a few comments about how research is done and how conclusions are drawn. One of the first constraints on research is that unlike bones, brains are soft tissues that do not fossilize. Endocasts, internal artificial casts made by natural causes or intentionally by researchers of the inside of the fossil skull, have historically been very helpful. Endocasts are limited, however, since they depend on impressions left on the inner skull and the detail must be inferred from those impressions plus other factors such as size and shape of the cranial cavity. One of the most useful methods is the comparative study of living species. Common ancestry can often be inferred from similar neural structures appearing in the end product of divergent evolutionary lines such as the divergent lines that produced mammals and reptiles.

In accounting for the evolution of the human brain, comparative neurobiologists have generally followed a three-phase transitional framework.

This framework generally begins with the appearance of amniotes, one group among those vertebrates that ventured out of the sea onto land about 350 million years ago.

So What Are Amniotes?

Amniotes are those four-legged terrestrial vertebrates that evolved a tough membrane cover of the reproductive DNA carried by eggs (and later in placentas internal to the mother) that facilitated the survival of DNA-bearing eggs on land. This was a protective membrane covering called the amnion that was not needed in the home environment of water.

The amnion may be thought of as capturing a portion of the watery environment for the safe development of the reproductive DNA into embryos, fetuses, and ultimately living offspring. The watery environment within the amnion is called the amniotic fluid. It is called a serous or benign fluid in physiology. This protective membrane was given the name *amnion* from the Greek word *amnus* meaning lamb and referring later to the bowl which captured the blood of sacrificial lambs.

So Who Are Amniotes?

Amniotes are the ancestors of mammals, reptiles, and birds.

As descendants of ancestral mammals, we humans are also amniotes. The fact that we are all amniotes is important to remember because subsequent terminology often is the source of confusion.

As amniotes evolved differing characteristics along two divergent lines, we gave them different names: the many diverse names given to the various species of mammals, reptiles, and birds. Sometimes this re-naming has led to a forgetting or obscuring of our fundamental ancestral amniotic identity.

Back to Framework: The First Phase: Self-Survival

This framework, then, considers, first, the basic self-survival neural structures of ancestral amniotes before the split of that ancestral line into two divergent amniote lines: the first (synapsid) line leading to early mammals and the second (diapsid or sauropsid) line leading to reptiles.

The Point of Divergence: Last Common Ancestor of Mammals, Reptiles, Birds

The point of divergence marks the last common amniote ancestor of the mammalian (synapsid) and reptilian (diapsid) lines. The two divergent amniote lines continued to evolve independently over millions of years, modifying and expanding the neural structure inherited from the ancestral amniotes.

For Human Brain Evolution: Follow the Synapsid Line

In considering human brain evolution the synapsid amniote line leading to mammals and ultimately to primates and humans is of primary interest. The diapsid amniote line went its own way to become reptiles and, later, birds. The diapsid line did not contribute to mammalian or human brain evolution. It is of interest to human evolution chiefly on a comparative basis.

Point of Divergence Ends the First Transitional Phase: Cold-Blooded Self-survival is the Key

The original point of amniote divergence marks the end of the first transitional phase leading to human brain evolution and the beginning of the second phase. At the point of divergence, our ancestral amniotes were creatures who were structured neurally for self-survival. They laid eggs and left them to hatch alone, showing little or no capacity for parental care. They were ectothermal or cold-blooded depending on the environment and behavior for the warmth necessary to survival and reproduction.

The Second Phase: Evolution of Parental Care, Social Bonding

The second phase considers the subsequently evolved mammalo-amniote neural structures that brought parental care, social bonding, and endothermy or warm-bloodness. The appearance of these mammalian neural structures depended on modification, diversification, and elaboration of rudimentary neural structures inherited from the amniote line before the point of divergence.

The Third Phase: Evolution of Higher Primates and Homo Sapiens

The third phase considers the most recently evolved neural structures of the higher primates and homo sapiens with the appearance of dramatically expanded social and cognitive abilities.

Paul MacLean and Ann Butler

In discussing the positions of scholars articulating the three-phase evolutionary transition of the human brain, I will limit myself to work of pioneer evolutionary neuroscientist, Paul MacLean, and the re-work of his three-phase concept by comparative evolutionary neuroscientist, Ann Butler.

Paul MacLean: The Triune Brain Concept

Paul MacLean (1913–2007), long-time head of the Laboratory of Brain Evolution and Behavior of the National Institutes of Health, was one of the first evolutionary neuroscientists to propose a three-phase evolutionary transition to the appearance of the human brain. He was one of the most notable pioneers in the emergent field.

I first met Paul on February 5, 1991, when, at his invitation, I visited him at the laboratory in Poolesville, Maryland. We became friends and stayed in regular contact through e-mails, telephone calls, and an occasional visit until shortly before his death in 2007.

In July 1999, with Russell Gardner, then Professor of Psychiatry at the University of Texas, I co-sponsored a symposium on Paul's work in Boston, Massachusetts. Among the many prominent scholars participating was Karl Pribram (1919–2015), who worked with Paul at Yale University in the late 1940s and 1950s. Karl, whom, I had met in the 1970s at Stanford, where he was Head of Neuroscience, was also one of the leading pioneers in evolutionary neuroscience. His presentation set the historical stage for the meeting. The outcome of this symposium was reported in *The Evolutionary Neuroethology of Paul MacLean: Convergences and Frontiers* (Cory & Gardner 2002).

The Mismeasure of MacLean's Triune Brain Modular Concept

MacLean's well-known triune brain concept is not only one of the earliest efforts to articulate the three-phased evolutionary transitions leading to the human brain, it is also one of the earliest modular concepts of the brain.

Since its initial publication in the mid-1960s, the concept has been well-received in the field of medicine. As recently as 1992, it has been acknowledged to be the single most influential idea in brain science since World War II (e.g., Durant in Harrington 1992: 268). Nevertheless, it has largely been overlooked by academic neuroscience, cognitive psychology, and other social sciences, including economics.

Faulty Reviews in Key Journals

This anomalous situation—in which the pioneering three-phased modular statement of brain organization coming from neuroscience itself and providing a natural match with aspects of the modular cognitive approach—has been brought about in part by a couple of seriously flawed reviews of MacLean's (1990) masterwork that appeared in the influential journals *Science* (1990) and *American Scientist* (1992).

The effect of these faulty reviews has been to deny the use of MacLean's very significant research and insights to researchers in the psychological as well as the social science community, who relied upon the authority of these prestigious journals.

In fact, Steven Pinker, a popular academic writer, bases his unfortunate, mistaken rejection and virtual caricature of MacLean's thought solely on a reference to the review in *Science* which is the most prejudicial and grossly inaccurate of the two (Pinker 1997: 370, 580). If Pinker had done proper scholarly due diligence and studied MacLean's work closely, he would have discovered that it provided a foundation supportive of much of his own thinking.

The detailed and documented rebuttal of these faulty reviews is reported in Cory 1999, 2000, 2002, 2004.

A Resurgence of Interest

A considerable, well-deserved, and important resurgence of interest in MacLean's work has occurred in very recent years. For example, the reader is referred to Damasio 1999; Lieberman 2000; Cory 1999, 2000, 2004; Cory and Gardner 2002; Panksepp 2002; Lambert and Gerlai 2003. The latter scholars edited an entire issue of the journal *Physiology and Behavior* devoted to MacLean in which leading scholars discussed the importance of his work to modern neuroscience and medical physiology; see also Wilson and Cory 2008; Newman and Harris 2009.

In the more popular science field Michio Kaku, a prominent physics scholar, in his *The Future of the Mind* (2014) acknowledges the importance of MacLean's evolutionary concept of human brain development (see especially pp. 18–21).

It is also significant that the development of molecular genetics in recent years has brought new support to MacLean's concepts. Molecular genetics, like MacLean, emphasizes the remarkable conservation of evolved brain architecture from our ancestral vertebrates.

As Tom Insel, Director of the US National Institutes of Mental Health (NIMH), significantly and appropriately stated in a New York Times obituary, MacLean's research opened the door for neuroscience to "ask big questions about consciousness and philosophy, instead of the more tractable questions about vision and movement" (*NYT*, January 10, 2008). Such overdue and well-deserved acknowledgment of MacLean's pioneering work is indeed welcome.

MacLean's concepts of the limbic system and the tri-level modular brain, when properly represented, are soundly grounded in evolutionary neuroscience, and with some clarifications, are among the most useful concepts for linking neuroscience with the more highly integrated concepts of the social sciences. The presentation that follows here is adjusted to accommodate criticisms that raise valid questions.

The Interconnected Three-Phase Human Brain

In his thoroughgoing, encyclopedic summary of the previous 50 years of brain research, MacLean (1990) documented the human brain as an evolved three-level, interconnected, modular structure (Figure 2.1).

MacLean, unfortunately, and perhaps overdramatically, contributed to the misunderstanding of his own triune brain concept by presenting it graphically as "three-brains-in-one"—as if there were separate, independent parts combined loosely together. The *three-brains-in-one* plus the well-known accompanying graphic, was popularized by Carl Sagan (among others) in his Pulitzer

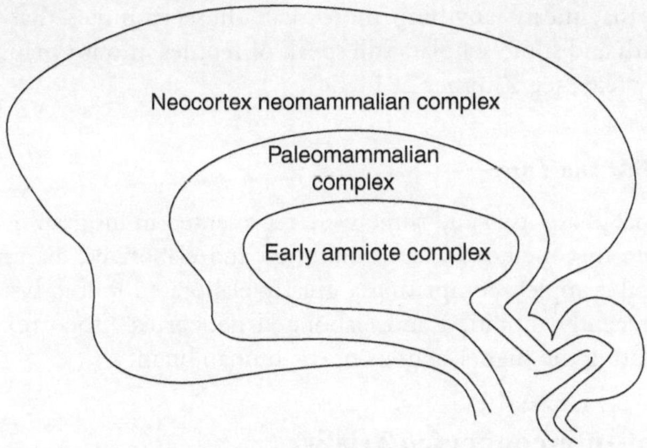

Figure 2.1 The tri-level brain modified from MacLean.
Source: Cory 2004, 2012; Wood, et al. 2015: 147.

Prize-winning *Dragons of Eden* (1977). The overpopularization led to simplistic interpretation and confusion in both the popular and scholarly communities.

The well-known graphic was, of course, oversimplified—even though the detailed discussion in his 1990 masterwork was much more comprehensive. Butler referred to this oversimplified graphic as the "mammalian chauvinist" version since it focused primarily on mammalian brain evolution and omitted components also rudimentarily present in what she called the "reptilian chauvinistic" version (2009: 1186, figures 1 & 2).

When understood properly, which MacLean attempted to clarify in his 1990 classic, the tri-level structure includes—rather than separate brains—interconnected and elaborated neural circuitry from major periods of human evolution.

The tri-level structure includes a component of self-preservational circuitry reflecting gene-based continuity from our ancestral stem amniotes. We split off from these stem vertebrates, as did the dinosaur ancestral line, during the Permian period some 300+ million years ago. Based on new scientific thinking since MacLean formulated his concept, it is appropriate to call this the early amniote neural complex rather than the reptilian or protoreptilian complex.

Current Thinking on the Timing of the Point of Divergence

It is currently thought that the synapsid-mammalian ancestral line diverged from the ancestral amniote line some 320 mya—about 10 million years prior to the divergence of the diapsid-reptilian line—and before that line produced development of anything like a modern reptile (from which dinosaurs and birds diverged much later) (Butler & Hodos 2005: 80–81; Evans 2000: 109–111).

A yet perplexing problem among scholars is that there is no definable group of "reptiles" that means anything more than those amniotes that are not mammals or birds and some scholars still speak of reptiles in our synapsid/mammalian ancestry (e.g., see Zimmer 2014: 84).

MacLean's Phases Two and Three

MacLean's transitional phases two and three were represented in his graphic by the tri-level structure that included a later modified and elaborated mammalian affectional neural complex comprising a greatly elaborated limbic system topped by a most recently modified and elaborated neocortex (isocortex or neopallium) representing the higher centers of the human brain.

The Evolution of Interconnected Triality

As brain evolution continued in the branching synapsid amniote line leading to humans, simple ancestral amniote or early vertebrate brain structure was not replaced.

Genes and Continuity

As noted earlier, in keeping with what we have learned recently from gene molecular studies, evolution always builds upon preexisting structures. Genes reflect continuity. They don't just pop out of nowhere to create new structures. They usually experience minor variations that lead to modification and elaboration of existing structures.

In control genes, however, which direct the activity of other genes, minor modifications may occasionally lead to significant change—even the appearance of new species (see Gehring 1998; Pollard 2009; Hubisz & Pollard 2014).

Early Amniote Structure Master Routines of Life Support

The early amniote structure, then, gave us the DNA-directed substructure or gene-based continuities (called homologues) for later brain development. It did this while largely retaining its basic character and function. The mammalian modifications and neocortical elaborations that followed reached the greatest development in the brain of humankind.

We must understand the qualitative differences of the three interconnected levels to appreciate the dynamics of human social experience and behavior.

The stem amniote neural circuits in humans mainly do the same job they did in our ancestral vertebrates. They run the fundamentals, or daily master routines, of our life-support operations: blood circulation, heartbeat, respiration, basic food getting, reproduction, and defensive behaviors.

These were functions and behaviors also necessary in the ancient ancestral amniotes as well as earlier amphibians and fishes. These earlier vertebrates had to do these things to stay alive, reproduce, and become our ancestors.

Early Mammals Warm-bloodedness, Parental Care, Play and Social Bonding

The next developmental stage of our brain comes from rudimentary mammalian/amniotic life. This set of circuits is also known collectively as the limbic system. These limbic tissue clusters developed from gene-based continuities and homologues preexisting in the ancestral amniote neural complex. They included significant elaboration of such physiological structures as the hypothalamus, the amygdala, the insula, the hippocampus, the thalamus, and the probable innovation of the limbic cingulate cortex.

Behavioral contributions to life from these modified and elaborated paleomammalian structures or limbic system included, among other things, the mammalian features (absent in our ancestral amniotes) of warm-bloodedness, nursing, infant care, socially interactive play, and extended social bonding. These new characteristics were then neurally integrated with the life-support functional and behavioral circuitry of the stem amniote circuits to create the more complex form of amniotic mammals. Even basic texts acknowledge the well-established differences that mammals evolved (cf. Zimmer 2014: 390).

The Neocortex and Greater Complexity of Behavior

The neocortex, which MacLean called the neo- or "new" mammalian brain, is the most recent stage of brain modification and elaboration. This great mass of bi-hemispherical brain matter dominates the skull case of higher primates and humans. It gained its prominence by elaborating the preexisting gene-based continuities present in the brain of earlier ancestral amniote vertebrates.

Gradually—perhaps more precipitously in the gap between chimpanzees and humans (see Pollard 2009)—it overgrew and encased the earlier ("paleo") mammalian and ancestral amniote interconnected neural tissues. It did not, however, replace them.

As a consequence of this neocortical evolution and growth, these older brain parts evolved greater complexity and extensive interconnected circuitry with these new tissue clusters. In that way, they produced the behavioral adaptations necessary to life's increasingly sophisticated circumstances.

Butler and the Three-Phased Transition

Ann Butler, a prominent comparative neurobiologist of George Mason University, has recently offered a revised version of MacLean's triune brain concept (2009).

As a Motivated Response: A Replacement Generalization

This revision is motivated by an acknowledged need to respond to criticisms that I made (2002), especially of the *Science* article by Reiner (1990).

In her own words:

> As someone thus already involved in the continuing dispute, I will endeavor to be as objective and dispassionate as possible in presenting MacLean's triune brain concept and also the objections to it raised by comparative neuroscientists, recognizing that my own background and knowledge of brain evolution unavoidably influence and inform my perspective. Also, since Cory characterized Reiner's criticisms as 'destructive' rather than 'constructive,' in that Reiner did not offer a 'replacement generalization,' I will do so here.
>
> (2009: 1185)

Butler then lists two alternative concepts to characterize her replacement generalization:

1. An objective terminology model for amniote brain evolution.
2. An evolutionarily accurate model of mammalian brain evolution.

She states these will clarify why most comparative neurobiologists view the triune brain concept as they do.

Of Profound Importance for Consilience

Further on, she makes what I consider the profoundly important statement from the perspective of consilience (unifying the natural with the social sciences).

> Of great importance for those whose research is focused on human behaviors—including *social, psychological*, and *economic* as well as pathological conditions such as those of the basal ganglia – is that the 'replacement generalizations' … the objective-terminology model for amniotes and the evolutionarily-accurate model for mammals, *do not contradict or undermine any of their findings or theoretical base.* These models simply rectify the conceptual approach with the full range of comparative evolutionary data on brain evolution.
>
> (2009: 1185–86, italics are mine)

An Objective Terminology

Let's consider the first of Butler's alternative concepts to characterize her replacement generalization.

1. The use of term *nonlimbic pallium* to refer to the developing cerebral cortex.
2. The Common Amniote Formation or A-Complex to replace and expand MacLean's Reptilian Brain or complex.
3. The Stem Mammalian Formation to replace and modify MacLean's Paleo-mammalian Brain or complex.
4. The Therian Formation to replace and modify MacLean's Neomammalian Brain or complex.

An Evolutionarily Accurate Model

Butler's replacement generalization, then, as an evolutionarily accurate model of mammalian brain evolution would be graphed from top to bottom as follows:

Therian Formation

Therian mammals: Include the marsupials as well as the eutherians (placental mammals). These mammals have additional association neopallia areas, an expanded prefrontal cortex, and the corpus callosum fiber tract connecting the two hemispheres of the brain

Stem Mammalian Formation

Stem mammals: These early mammals possibly see the addition of the thalamocingulate component to limbic system with the neopallial cytoarchitecture of the cingulate gyrus; expanded sensory, motor, and association pallial areas, including prefrontal cortex with all with neocortical cytoarchitecture.

Common Amniote Formation or A-complex

Common amniote ancestor: The neural architecture of the common amniote ancestor included basal ganglia, major limbic system components, primary sensory, motor plus a few association pallial areas.

The higher primates and, of course, we humans have the greatest expanded areas of the neopallial or neocortical areas of the eutherian brain providing for the high level of parental care, social bonding, and cognitive skills that we display.

The main disagreement of comparative evolutionary neuro-biologists with MacLean's triune brain graphic is that it did not recognize or include major limbic system and pallial components of our common amniote ancestor in his concept of the Reptilian Brain or complex.

I will not attempt here to reconstruct a triune graphic in the style of Butler (2009: 1191) because it also is a simplified representation of a more complex process. If I were to modify the graphic I presented previously in Figure 2.1., I would have to, as a minimum, significantly increase the area covered by the early amniote complex.

A Welcome "Replacement Generalization"

I welcome this revised version or "replacement generalization" offered by Butler. It corrects perceived difficulties with MacLean's triune brain concept and affirms the three-phase evolutionary transition leading to the evolution of the human brain. As noted previously, she stated that it is of great importance that her alternative representation *does not undermine or contradict the theoretical basis of those scholars who applied MacLean's concept to social and economic behavior.* Her additions and corrections "simply rectify the conceptual approach with the full range of comparative evolutionary data on brain evolution" (2009: 1185–1186).

The path is clear, then, to proceed with the theoretical analysis that follows in this book and that was presented in a number of my previous publications (1992, 1999, 2002, 2004, et al.).

Cautionary Pitfalls

But wait! There are a few cautionary pitfalls to acknowledge before going forward with our analysis.

No Ancestral Dragons

First: Unfortunately, stimulated by MacLean's presentation of the Reptilian Brain (or Complex), popularizers like Carl Sagan in his Pulitzer Prize-winning *Dragons of Eden* (1977), and followed by some others, the reading public was lead to believe erroneously that there were giant reptile-like dragons in our evolutionary ancestral line. Of course, based on more recent findings this is clearly not true.

It is now generally held that our synapsid line split off from the ancestral amniote line several million years before the diapsid (sauropsid) line that eventually produced what are now defined as reptiles and later dinosaurs and birds. By the revised chronology and definitions, reptiles (dinosaurs) and birds are not in our ancestral line.

Our amniote ancestor was more likely a small, rather unimpressive creature. It took about 100 million years or so from the Upper Carboniferous (320 million years ago) appearance of the synapsid line to the appearance of the first mammaliaforms in the upper Triassic Period (237–201.3 million years ago). According to T. S. Kemp such a span of time indicates how long it took to evolve from "a scaly, ectothermic (cold-blooded), sprawling-limbed, small-brained, and simple-toothed amniote to a fur-bearing, endothermic (warm-blooded), parasagittally-gaited, large-brained, complex-toothed, and behaviorally complex mammal" (Kemp 2016: 117, parenthetical terms added).

Emphatically then, there are no reptilian dragons in the Eden of our ancestry! It is notable, however, that some recent texts on evolution still refer to reptiles in our ancestral line (e.g., see Zimmer 2014: 84).

No Scala Naturae or Great Chain of Being

Secondly: Focusing on a single line of evolution leading to humans tends to suggest or evoke reminiscences of the now discredited *scala naturae* or great chain of being—an idea going back to Aristotle and still dominating much evolutionary thinking until recent times. The scala naturae was essentially a teleological concept that saw evolution as a predestined process leading from simple lifeforms to the ultimate grand appearance of that end point in evolution—the human species.

The current concept of evolution is not a predestined great chain of being or scale of nature but an essentially random process generating great diversity and best represented by a tree diagram with many branches than a straight line or chain.

At this point it may also be cautionary to note that whatever parental caring and higher cognitive abilities that are expressed in birds proceeded on different evolutionary paths from humans at the point of divergence from the ancestral amniotes and are of interest primarily from a comparative neurobiology standpoint.

Scholars generally accept that mammals and birds followed different paths of encephalization (an evolutionary increase in the complexity or relative size of the brain, involving a shift of function from nonpallial parts of the brain to the pallium).

The Rise of Epigenetics: Avoiding Simple-Minded Genetic Determinism

In broadest terms epigenetics is the study of changes in organisms caused by modification of gene expression without alteration of the DNA sequence of genetic code itself. The "epi" part means "above" or "on top of." Therefore the word means on top of or above genetics. It is an emerging discipline with a yet fluid definition and set of parameters and accompanied in the popular literature by a lot of hype and exaggeration.

For some researchers it includes all changes in the phenotype of the individual brought about by environmental experience (Blumberg, Freeman, & Robinson 2010).

And that environmental experience can range from hunger, deprivation, learning, education, and socialization (Kolb & Gibb 2011).

Other researchers define it to include only heritable changes that can be passed across generations (Berger, et al. 2009).

At its broadest definition epigenetics, then, is part of the nature/nurture conundrum that has always preoccupied science. It is phrased, however, from the biological perspective rather than the sociological or philosophical perspectives that have sought to avoid strict genetic determinism. If stretched to its definitional limit, epigenetics could subsume all of what we think of as *nurture*.

Some Special Characteristics to Keep in Mind

Since epigenetic changes by definition do not alter fundamental DNA passed in the genome, for our purposes it can be thought of as concerning superficial or surface changes to fundamental genetically prescribed neural architecture and other human physiology that was laid down over millions of years of evolutionary adaptation.

Epigenetic changes may be helpful or harmful. They have been found to underlie certain medical disorders to include some forms of cancer. Some epigenetic changes seem to be heritable; others such as learning are not.

Epigenetic changes are reversible. Fundamental DNA prescribed neural architecture is not—that is, not without serious invasive genetic intervention.

Nevertheless, *expression* of aspects of the fundamental neural architecture can be affected by epigenetic changes—that is what long-term memory or learning is all about. Both require gene expression, the creation of new proteins, to record the long-term memory or learning (e.g., see Kandel, et al. 2013: ch 66; Fioriti, et al. 2015). In the broader definition of epigenetics, education and proper socialization are included. And that is why they are so important! They help to direct our neural architecture into desirable homeostatic balance and social expressions.

A Final Important Thought

As a final important thought, we should not feel overwhelmed by the presently seemingly sweeping definitions and claims of epigenetics. This is a new discipline still searching for its proper parameters. It is essential to keep in mind the fundamental fact that our neural architecture, like other aspects of our physiology, evolved in the environment of evolutionary adaptation—an environment that covered millions of years of evolution. The human species presently occupies practically every terrestrial clime on the planet—some long isolated from others—and we still recognize them as one of us.

Epigenetics does not change our fundamental humanity and our fundamental mammalian neural architecture is an essential component of that humanity.

The Concept of Niche

The concept of niche has in recent years become a growing area of interest in evolutionary biology and biological anthropology (e.g., see Whittaker, Levin, & Root 1973; Odling-Smee, Laland, & Feldman 2003; Wells & Stock 2007; O'Brien & Laland 2012; Fuentes 2012, 2014).

There has been a tendency since the modern synthesis in evolutionary biology took root about mid-20th century to measure species reproductive success in terms of adaptation to a niche. One expression of this is the claim that there are no primitive species on the planet today. They have all evolved new capabilities out of ancestral heritage to adapt to running changes in the niche environment. This position has led to a sort of species egalitarianism that, in the extreme, views all present-day species as equally advanced and equally important within the planetary environment. Such views encourage us to avoid being anthropocentric in thinking about the products of evolution.

But most of us cannot avoid being at least a little anthropocentric in the area of niche discussion. After all, we *are* humans and, from our view, niches are not all equal. The main social and political issues that concern us are essentially anthropocentric: global climate change, overcoming economic inequalities, nuclear proliferation, world peace. Even the concern for loss of biological diversity by advance of civilization into pristine forests and other environments so well-articulated by E. O. Wilson of Harvard has anthropocentric overtones—we could lose valuable sources of new medicines yet undiscovered.

So properly understanding our niche becomes important—perhaps to our species survival—even planetary survival. The human niche, as I see it, is the planet and as we are expanding into space—the solar system, and even potentially the galaxy. If we accept responsibility for our expansive niche, then we cannot avoid being somewhat anthropocentric in viewing our evolutionary future.

My Goal in This Book

My purpose in this book draws in from the discussion above. We need to follow the consilient approach of unifying our natural and social sciences in order to more fully understand ourselves, our evolutionary constraints and possibilities within our niche—so that we may become a truly planet-preserving custodial species ready to expand our niche into the territories of space.

My goal in this book is, in part, to contribute to that effort.

Refining and Defining Human Uniqueness

The unique features of our human brain were refined over a period of several million years in a mainly kinship-based foraging society where sharing or reciprocity was necessary to our survival. Such sharing and reciprocity strengthened the adaptive evolution of the now combined mammalo-amniotic characteristics of self-preservation and affection.

Ego and Empathy, self-interest and other-interest, are key features of our personal and social behavior. To connect these features to MacLean's as well as Butler's modified three-phased concept we need to include at this point a behavioral vocabulary rather than a neurophysiological one.

We need a vocabulary that will express what the presence of our ancestral amniote self-preserving mechanisms and our stem mammalian affectional brain structures mean for our day-to-day, subjectively experienced, behavioral initiatives and responses to one another and the world we live in. I will draw the behavioral vocabulary from analogy with information and computer technology.

The Self-Preserving and Affectional Programmed Circuitry

Our early amniote ancestors were ectothermic or cold-blooded and they did not have brain structures for any extended parental caring. Their care of offspring was, in most cases, limited to making a nest or digging a hole to lay eggs in. The eggs were, then, left to hatch on their own.

The eggs and hatchlings were easy marks for predators. Further, some stem amniotes, not knowing their own offspring, would cannibalize them. It was not much of a family life. But the early amniotes continued to exist because they produced large numbers of eggs—enough to make sure some offspring survived to reproduce again and continue the species line.

Of Snakes, Geckos, and Sharks

This basic ancestral amniote complex thus contained little or no neural circuitry for parental care and social bonding of the later evolved stem mammals. From the mainly survival-centered promptings of these ancestral amniote circuits, as elaborated in our human brain, arise the motivational source for egoistic, surviving, self-interested subjective experience and behaviors.

Here we have the cold-blooded, seemingly passionless, single-minded, self-serving behaviors that we have generally associated with the present-day lizard, the snake, and that most maligned of fishes, the shark.

And intuitively, we call our fellow humans who behave this way such names as snakes, geckos, and sharks.

> *Here is a world revolving almost exclusively around matters of self-preservation. The stem amniote brain structures, then, will be called, following our high-tech vocabulary, our self-preservation programming or circuitry.*

Of Caring and Playful Mammals

But we humans are mammalian amniotes. We not only got the self-preserving circuitry of our early amniote ancestors, we also got the programmed circuitry for infant nursing, warm-blooded, passionate, body-contacting, playful, and social behaviors that we share with the lion, the wolf, the primates. The motivational source for nurturing, empathetic, other-interested experiences and behaviors arises from such circuitry.

> *Here is a world in which nearly single-minded self-preservation is simultaneously complemented and counterpoised by the conflicting demands of affection. The early mammalian modifications, then, will be called our affectional programming or circuitry.*

Our Evolved Networked Brain and Behavioral Conflict

These core behavioral programs within us are built up of many contributing subroutines of our neural architecture. Neuroscientist Jaak Panksepp calls such core programs global-state variables since they sum up the effect of many subroutine circuits. He states that a network doctrine is needed to grasp such system-wide emergent dynamics (2002: xiv; see also Schulkin 2002; cf. Rolls 2016: 4, 10, 40–71).

Energized, Global-State Circuits

These global-state circuits act as dynamic factors of our behavior. They are energy-driven by our cellular as well as overall bodily processes of metabolism, or energy production, as mediated by *hormones*, *neurotransmitters*, and *neural architecture*. And each is an inseparable part of our makeup, because each is "wired into" our brain structure by the process of evolution.

The degree of gene control, however, does vary. Older brain parts, like the brain stem and parts of the limbic system, long established and necessary for survival, are under tighter gene control. Other, more recent tissues, especially the higher centers of the neopallium or neocortex, depend a lot on epigenetic development and experience.

We are set up for behavioral conflict simply by the presence of these two global-state, energy-driven circuits in our lives—up and running, perhaps, even before birth. Their mere physical presence sets us up for a life of inner and outer struggle, as we are driven by and respond to their contending demands.

Conflict External and Internal

Conflict is more than an externally observed, objective ethical, moral, or decision-making dilemma, as much modern science tends to see it. We also feel it very strongly within ourselves.

That is, inwardly or *subjectively*, we get feelings of satisfaction when we can express our felt motives. On the other hand, we get feelings of frustration when we cannot express our self-preservation or affectionate impulses in the behavioral initiatives and responses we wish to make.

The Rise of Behavioral Tension

Behavioral tension then arises. We experience such behavioral tension as frustration, anxiety, or anger. And it arises whenever one of our two fundamental behavioral circuitries—self-preservation or affection—is activated but meets with some resistance or difficulty that prevents its satisfactory expression.

This subjective tension becomes most paralyzing when both circuits are activated and seek contending or incompatible responses *within a single situation*. Caught between "I want to" and "I can't"—for example, "I want to help him/her, but I can't surrender my needs"—we agonize.

Whether this tension arises through the blocked expression of a single impulse or the simultaneous but mutually exclusive urgings of two competing impulses, whenever it continues unresolved or unmanaged, it leads to the worsening condition of behavioral stress.

The Blessing of Tension and Stress

The evolutionary process by which these two opposite global-state promptings of self-preservation and affection were combined in us gave us a great survival advantage. Their combined dynamic binds us together in social interaction and provides us with a wide range of behavioral responses to our environment—a range much wider than species lacking our dual motive circuitry.

Conflict: A Mitigated Curse

Our naturally conflicting programs are a curse, then, only to the extent that we fail to recognize them as a blessing. Our self-preservation and affection circuits allow us a highly advanced sensitivity to our environment. They impel us into social action and serve to keep our interactive social behaviors mostly within survival limits by giving us the ability to understand and appreciate the survival and affectional requirements of others.

Behavioral Tension/Stress an Internal Emotional Compass

Ironically, the accompanying behavioral tension—*even the stress!*—is an integral part of this useful function. It allows us to more quickly evaluate our behavior and the effect it is having on ourselves and others.

> *Behavioral tension serves as an internal emotional compass that we can use to guide ourselves through the often complicated and treacherous pathways of interpersonal relations.*
>
> *Behavioral stress tells us that we are exceeding safe limits for ourselves and others, and even for our larger social, economic, and political structures.*

3 Our Mammalian Heritage

A Dual Motive Neurobehavioral Model

Evolutionary brain science is an emerging discipline. It, therefore, offers new opportunities for research in the fine detailing of our mammalian neural heritage.

A mountain of research, however, some old and some very recent, has established beyond doubt a couple of fundamental characteristics of the human brain.

First, the brain is a physiological organ.

Second, it is an organ evolved for social interaction. I will look at both characteristics in more detail.

The Human Brain: A Physiological Organ

Like other organs of the body—hands, feet, heart—the brain developed over many millennia to its present form in *homo sapiens*. It evolved out of accumulated mutations—including mutations of the highly influential master control genes that can in some instances produce dramatic change by single mutations (Gehring 1998; Pollard 2009; Hubisz & Pollard 2014).

Such mutations were confirmed by natural selection—that is, they generally helped us survive and reproduce—in the genetic information repository of our DNA. The brain, then, develops in each individual under the prescriptive guidance of DNA that, despite a considerable amount of developmental and experiential plasticity, assures a high degree of fidelity in the replication of fundamental brain architecture.

The main features of our brain, like the main features of our human body plan (head, trunk, arms, legs), are expressed in common across our human species.

The Social Nature of the Brain

Physiologically, the human brain is also an organ supporting *social* life. The social brain concept necessarily emphasizes both the self-preservation (self-interested) and affectional (other-interested) mammalian components necessary to social interaction.

DOI: 10.4324/9781003303190-4

The Social Brain: An Organizing Concept

The *social brain* is an organizing concept heralded in a number of recent publications—*Human Evolution* (Dunbar 2016), *Consilience, Brains, and Markets* (Cory 2010a), *The Evolutionary Epidemiology of Mania and Depression* (Wilson & Cory 2008), *Attachment and Bonding: A New Synthesis* (Carter, et al. 2006), *Textbook of Biological Psychiatry* (Panksepp 2004), *Foundations in Social Neuroscience* (Cacioppo et al. 2002) and *Handbook of Affective Sciences* (Davidson, Scherer, and Goldsmith 2003; see also Cory & Gardner 2002).

Slightly earlier but related volumes include *Descartes' Error: Emotion, Reason, and the Human Brain* (Damasio 1994), *The Integrative Neurobiology of Affiliation* (Carter, Lederhendler, & Kirkpatrick 1997) and *Affective Neuroscience* (Panksepp 1998). Recent years have thus brought great advances in detailing the many complex and interrelated pathways of interactive social circuitry in the brain.

Hunting, Gathering, and Sharing

The genes specifying social circuitry were selected over millions of years of evolutionary history in small kinship groups that required a cooperative interactive dynamic for survival. In fact, our survival strategy as an emerging species was not only hunting and gathering but also essentially *sharing* of the fruits of these activities. These dynamic social circuits motivate human social interaction and social exchange at all levels of our lives today. (e.g., see Humphrey 1976; Isaac 1978; Knauft 1994; Erdal & Whiten 1996; Boehm 1999).

On Choices and Meaning

As scientists we don't know for certain whether kindred mammals—cats, dogs, elephants, dolphins, chimpanzees, and others—with paleo-mammalian brain structures, with self-preservation and affectional circuitry, just act on preset neuronal priorities. Or whether they experience conscious conflict and must choose among such conflicting behavioral priorities.

We may suspect that these mammals do have conflict. Or we may protest from the perspective of *homo arrogance* that they do not. It's a tough question for scientists. Science has not yet developed good interviewing techniques for these other mammals.

There is, however, absolutely no doubt about us humans. We certainly do. We can reflect and generalize not only upon our choices, but upon the meanings they have for our personal lives as well as our species' existence and significance.

Executive Circuitry and Language

And it is in that capacity to reflect, to self-consciously experience, generalize, and decide upon the tug-and-pull of our conflicting urgings, that we come to third stage of brain development in both MacLean's and Butler's models. That is, the "new" mammalian or neopallium brain structures—what I call the executive programming or circuitry.

As well, our elaborated neopallium or neocortex provides us with the evolutionarily unique and powerful ability to use verbal and symbolic language. We can, thus, create concepts and ideas by which to interpret our consciousness. We can describe the feelings, motives, and behaviors that arise within us and in response to our social and environmental experiences.

It is with this so-called executive circuitry or programming, then, that we acquire the ability to name, to comment upon, to *generalize*, and to *choose* between our contending sets of behavioral impulses.

Higher Cognitive Integration: Self- and Other-Interest

Self-preservation is commonly called, at a high level of cognitive integration, "egoistic" or "self-interested" behavior.

We call affection, at an equally high level of cognitive integration, "empathetic" or "other-interested" behavior.

Empathy allows us the critical social capacity to enter into or respond emotionally to another's self-interest as well as other emotional states.

CSN Complex vs. CSN Model: Physiology vs. Function

I developed the forerunner of The Conflict Systems Neurobehavioral (CSN) Model (introduced in Figure 3.1 below) in my multidisciplinary doctoral thesis at Stanford University (1974).

In my thesis, I drew heavily upon biology, psychology, general systems theory, and cybernetics in an effort to integrate these disciplines with the social sciences. Although my multidisciplinary thesis was anchored in the political science department where I was primarily interested in comparative politics (to include political economy), I was supported in my integrative effort by distinguished scholars in biology, psychology, and other disciplines. For example, Donald Kennedy, then chair of biology and later head of the FDA, read my papers on biology; Daryl Bem, a distinguished psychologist, most recently at Cornell, chaired my PhD orals committee.

I believe I may have produced one of the earliest dissertations in the field that E. O. Wilson of Harvard has more recently called *consilience*, the unification of the natural with the social sciences (1998).

My academic efforts and numerous publications over the 40 years since have been devoted to this process of integration of the natural and social sciences.

The CSN Model as a Functional Representation of Physiological Circuits

The CSN Model is a functional neurobehavioral representation of the underlying Conflict Systems Neurobehavioral (CSN) Complex. The CSN Complex refers to the actual physiological structures or circuits of the brain—the brain stem, basal ganglia, limbic system, and the neopallium or neocortex. The CSN Model, then, is a functional schematic of that underlying physiology.

The functional schematic of the CSN Model also represents the now scientifically well-established evolutionary transition from a primarily self-preserving ancestral amniote to a both self-preserving and other-preserving mammalian amniote to the highly social, cognitively powered human amniote species.

The Functional Approach May Avoid Future Minor Technical Disagreements

By approaching the all-important three-part evolutionary transition from a functional perspective, The CSN Model attempts to avoid some of the minor rather technical disagreements that may yet arise among comparative evolutionary theorists. As Butler (2009) has so helpfully noted, the three-part evolutionary transition, first represented by MacLean's triune brain theory and more recently modified by herself, is not itself in question.

Lateralization vs. Integration

Although the positioning of Ego and Empathy in Figure 3.1 (facing the reader) is primarily for illustrative purposes only and is not intended to suggest a definitive lateralization, there is evidence to suggest that the right hemisphere is favored somewhat for emotion and the left for more analytical self-preserving behaviors (e.g., see Damasio 1994; Tucker, Luu, Pham, & Pribram 1995; Brownell & Martino 1998; Henry & Wang 1998; Stuss & Knight 2002).

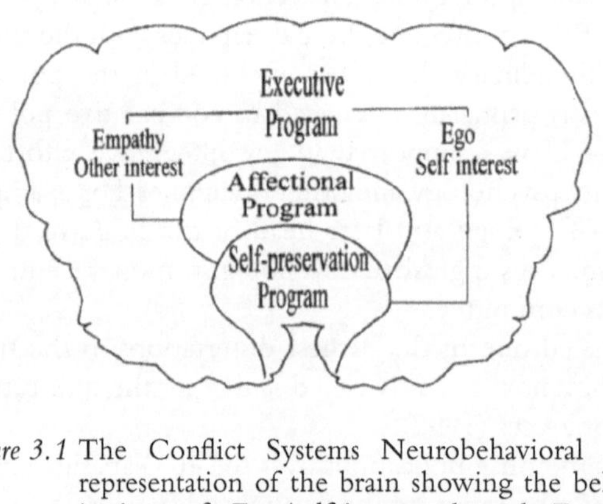

Figure 3.1 The Conflict Systems Neurobehavioral Model. A simplified cutaway representation of the brain showing the behavioral programs and the derivation of Ego/self-interested and Empathy/other-interested motives and behaviors. I should note that earlier models, e.g., Freud (Id, Ego, and Superego) postulated three-part conflictual models. Freud, however, was unable to tie his model to brain circuitry and it remained ungrounded in neural science because brain research had simply not advanced to that point.

Source: Cory after MacLean, see Cory 1992, 1999, 2000ab, 2001ab, 2002, 2004, 2006ab, 2010.

However, the total experience of emotion is not lateralized but involves dynamic interactions between forward and posterior regions of both hemispheres as well as subcortical (limbic) structures (Heller, Nitschke, & Miller 1998). Therefore, such complex, highly integrated capacities as Ego and Empathy should more safely be thought of as engaging the interaction of both hemispheres (Beauregard & O'Leary 2007; Decety & Ikes 2009).

In other words, our executive programming, especially our frontal cortex, has the capability and the responsibility for cognitively representing these ancestral limbic and stem amniote brain connections and inputs and making what may be thought of as our moral as well as rational choices among our conflicting, impulsive, and irrational or nonrational motivations.

This self-conscious, generalizing, choosing capacity accompanied, of course, with language, is what differentiates us from even closely related primate species and makes findings in primate behavior, although highly interesting and unquestionably important, insufficient in themselves to fully understand and account for human behavior.

Executive Circuitry and Neural Networks

The frontal neocortex has long been recognized to be involved in executive functions (Pribram & Luria 1973; Fuster 1980, 2008; Stuss & Knight 2002; Leh et al. 2010). However, the more inclusive concept may be that the neural substrate of executive functions is a neural network that includes the synchronized activity of multiple regions, both cortical and subcortical.

Interconnected Neural Networks Subjectively Drive Objective, Observable Behavior

Our early vertebrate and limbic circuits are interconnected neural network circuits that *subjectively* generate and drive specific, and *objectively* observable behaviors. These core motivational (and emotional) circuits are connected largely through the thalamocingulate gateway to the executive frontal circuitry as well as other neocortical regions. In these higher regions, they are respectively represented as self-preserving Ego and species-preserving Empathy cognitions (e.g., see Berridge 2003; cf. Saarela, et al. 2006; Tankersley, Stowe, & Huettel 2007; Ward 2013).

The neural substrate for self-survival Ego mechanisms likely proceeds from circuits in the brain stem, basal ganglia and rudimentary limbic structures (ancestral amniote complex) through connections with the elaborated amygdaloid and other limbic circuits to include an emergent cingulate cortex (early mammalian amniote complex), and probably other subcortical circuits, such as the insula, which add emotion or passion, ultimately to be gated into the frontal cortex by thalamocortical circuitry (see Jones 2007; Sherman & Guillery 2001; Devinsky & Luciano 1993).

Likewise, the mammalian nurturing (affectional) substrate and its associated motivation, a fundamental component underlying Empathy, may originate in the septal and medial preoptic limbic areas. It may, then, proceed through hippocampal and amygdaloid circuitry, the insula, as well as other limbic structures (Carter, et al. 2006; Morgane, Galler, & Mokler 2005; Numan & Insel 2003; Carter & Keverne 2002; Taylor 2002; cf. Porges 1998).

Ultimately, and in turn, the affectional circuitry will largely be gated into the orbital, frontal, and other areas of the cortex by neuromodulating thalamocortical circuits (to include the cingulate cortex), where the conflict with egoistic inputs is resolved in the executive or global workspace of conscious self-awareness.

Additionally, and more recently the temporoparietal junction (TPJ) of the neocortex has also been shown to be an important node within the social brain. A number of studies indicate that the TPJ may host or control representations of the self and/or other and be a significant player in the neocortical expression of Empathy and other sociocognitive processes (e.g., see Santiestaban, et al. 2012; for more recent research and discussion from an evolutionary perspective of the neural circuitry underlying self-survival and affectional behaviors and their gating into the frontal executive see Loonen & Ivanov 2016; Rolls 2016; Sherwood et al. 2012; Abiotiz & Montiel 2012).

The Gating of Dual Motives

As noted above, the dual motives of self-survival and affection are largely gated into the neocortical executive by a structure known as the thalamus. The neuromodulating and gating of *affect* as well as cognition by the thalamocortical circuitry is a function well known to medical neuroscience. The role of the thalamus as the essential gating structure of the myelinated cables passing from the subcortical motivational circuitries, into the higher cortical areas, has long been established (e.g., see Devinsky & Luciano 1993; Jones 2007; Ward 2013).

It was these fiber tracts that were cut in the well-intended, but now notorious psychosurgical procedures of the 1930s–1950s. Lobotomies, leukotomies, and other similar procedures were deliberate efforts to disconnect the frontal cortex from the lower archetypal motivating circuitries. The objective was to reduce anxiety, violence, and other unwanted behaviors.

Psychosurgery as Clear Evidence for Dual Motive Theory

The psychosurgical procedures were largely effective in achieving their objective. They regularly produced what medical science euphemistically called "flat affect." That is, reduced or no Ego and Empathy. Some critics to this day complain that the current drugs used in treating such symptoms have the same intention and effect—deactivation of the emotional and motivating circuitries (Breggin 2008).

The psychosurgical practices of the 1930s through 1950s provide some of the clearest physiological evidence for dual motive theory. The archetypical neural circuitries, their thalamocingulate gating mechanisms, and their frontal connections were known facts of physiology. The work done on humans had previously and since been confirmed by experiments upon other primates (Fulton 1951; O' Callaghan & Carroll 1982; Valenstein 1986, Housepian 1998; Pressman 1998).

Ego and Empathy Clarified

As noted earlier, Ego as used here is not the Ego of Freudian psychoanalysis although there are some similarities. Ego, as indicated in Figure 3.1, is defined as deriving from self-preserving circuitry. It closely matches the standard definition of Egoism in philosophy and as referenced in literary terms such as "self-focused," "self-absorbed," "self-interested," or "narcissistic."

Empathy, on the other hand, includes the affectional feelings of sympathetic attachment reinforced by cognitions added in the course of neocortical assessment and representation (e.g., see Hoffman 1981, 2000). Empathy and sympathy, despite their rather distinct meanings in medical-psychiatric settings, are otherwise and especially in recent citations, more often posited inclusively (Wilson & Cory 2008; Eisenberg 1994; Batson 1991).

Recent research has further indicated that Empathy has both emotional and cognitive components activated by different but overlapping areas of neural circuitry (Singer 2006; Blair 2003). Perhaps mirror neurons, recently reportedly found in humans (Rizzolatti 2011) as well as other primates, serve as switches to activate and access the rather wide-ranging but overlapping areas of neural circuitry. This overlapping is summed in the CSN Model, with its varying mixes of Ego and Empathy across a spectrum of behavior.

For the reasons cited above and to indicate the most inclusive and customary use of the term suggesting other-interest/other regard plus shared affect and sympathy, the variant *Empathetic* is used as distinct from the more specific term, *empathic*.

The Electrochemical Physiology of Dual Motives

Although it is beyond the scope of this chapter to deal with the as yet incompletely understood detailed electrochemical physiology of such egoistic/empathetic conflict, it is appropriate to acknowledge that such behavior is made possible, in part, by the complex electrochemical excitatory and inhibitory interactions among groups of interconnected neurons and neural networks. A more detailed discussion is contained in Chapter 3 of Wilson and Cory (2008).

The role of hormones, neurotransmitters, and neuroreceptors must also be acknowledged in any complete analysis. For instance, from the egoistic perspective, testosterone is associated with competitiveness and power urges. Serotonin levels in humans seem related to confidence and self-esteem. On the empathetic side, oxytocin, arginine vasopressin, and prolactin are important to pair bonding and maternal as well as paternal caring behavior. Opioids (endorphins and enkaphalins) seem important to positive social relationships. Donaldson and Young (2008) have recently reviewed the social bonding effects of oxytocin and vasopressin. Zak (2012) has presented a thorough-going analysis of the effects of oxytocin on social relationships. The authors note that these ancient mammalian neuropeptides display a marked conservation in gene structure and expression.

Of course, without the corresponding receptors within the neural circuitry, the hormones and neurotransmitters would lack their effect.

The Major Ranges of Reciprocal, Conflict Behavior

The two master archetypal programs of self-preservation and affection that have been wired into our brain structure operate dynamically according to a set of behavioral rules or algorithms.

We experience the workings of these algorithmic rules internally. We also express them externally in our interpersonal behavior. We need to understand the workings and applications of these algorithms to grasp the role of conflict, tension, and stress in our personal and interactive lives.

The major ranges of the CSN Model (Figure 3.2) show graphically the features of this Ego-Empathy dynamic. In the display, both internally felt as well as overt interpersonal behavior is divided from right to left into three main ranges. From right to left, they are the egoistic range, the dynamic balance range, and the empathetic range.

The Source of All Motives

Each range represents a varying mix of egoistically and empathetically motivated behaviors. The solid line stands for Ego and pivots on the word "Ego" in the executive program of the brain diagram. The broken line stands for Empathy and pivots on the word "Empathy" in the diagram.

Before going further, I wish to emphasize an important, but not necessarily obvious point. That is, all behavioral motives emerge from and are expressive of our mammalian neural architecture. Ego and Empathy are the most fundamental of motives. All other motives—and an endless proliferation of them appears in the both scientific and popular literature—derive from the Ego/Empathy dynamic. All the expressions of Ego/Empathy included across the spectrum—some of which are listed above each range of the behavioral spectrum in the graph above—can be viewed as motives. After all, they are energized expressions of behavior derived from our archetypal neural architecture.

The Egoistic Range

The egoistic range indicates behavior dominated by our self-preserving circuitry. Since the two behavioral programs are locked in inseparable unity, Empathy is present here, but to a lesser degree.

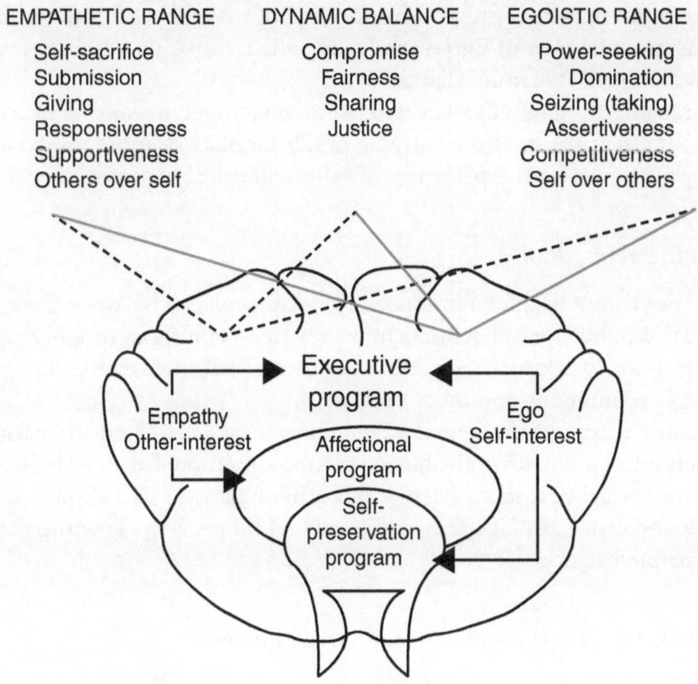

Figure 3.2 The Major Ranges of Reciprocal, Conflict Behavior (Cory 1974–2012). The dynamic of the model, the tug-and-pull of Ego and Empathy, allows the expression of the mix of motive and behavior as a range or spectrum. The usual dichotomizing of self-interest and altruism is seen only at the extremes of the spectrum. For a neural network modeling of the dynamic see Levine (2006), Levine & Jani (2002).

Behavior in this range is self-centered or self-interested. It may tend, for example, to be dominating, power-seeking, or even attacking, where Empathy is less. When Empathy is increased, Ego behavior will become less harsh. It may, then, be described more moderately as controlling, competitive, or assertive.

As Empathy is gradually increased, the intersection of the two lines of the diagram will move toward the range of dynamic balance. That is, Ego behavior will be softened as Empathy is added.

But the defining characteristic of the egoistic, self-interested range is *self-over-others*. Whether we are blatantly power-seeking or more moderately assertive, in this range we are putting ourselves, our own priorities, objectives, and feelings, ahead of others.

The Empathetic Range

The empathetic range represents behavior weighted in favor of Empathy. Ego is present, but is taking a back seat. When Ego is present minimally, empathetic behavior may tend to extremes of self-sacrifice and submission.

When Ego is increased, empathetic behaviors are moderated. We can then describe them as supportive, responsive, or any of a variety of "others first" behaviors. As the influence of Ego is gradually added, empathetic behavior will approach the range of dynamic balance.

In the empathetic range, the key phrase to remember is *others-over-self* or others first. Whether we are at the extreme of self-sacrifice or more moderately responsive, we are putting the priorities of others ahead of our own.

The Dynamic Balance Range

The range of dynamic balance represents a working balance between Ego and Empathy. At this point our behavioral circuitries are operating in roughly equal measure. I speak of "working," "rough," or "dynamic" because the tug-and-pull between the two programs continues ceaselessly.

The dynamic nature of the neural architecture means that "perfect" balance may be a theoretical point, unattainable in practice. Our more balanced behavior tends to express equality, justice, sharing, and other behaviors that show respect for ourselves and others. In fact, respect for self and others is the keynote of the range of dynamic balance.

Energy or Activation Level Escalation and De-escalation

The extent to which the circuits of self-preservation and affection are out of balance, or pulling against each other, is a measure of behavioral tension. We experience this behavioral tension both internally and between ourselves and others in any relationship or interaction.

But that is not all.

Excessive, unmanaged, or unresolved tension engenders behavioral stress along a range of behavior. But the amplitude of escalating or de-escalating energy we invest in the interaction or the relationship is an equally important factor affecting behavioral stress and its multiple physiological manifestations.

Much of this arousal occurs automatically by activation of the HPA (hypothalamic-pituitary-adrenal) axis. Nevertheless, it is also under cortical control to a significant degree. We can put more energy into activities and responses for which we feel enthusiasm—less into others.

In highly competitive sports or contests, qualitative differences in energy are easily observed. In intellectual contests, like chess, the energy may be intense, but less obvious.

Such arousal level—or escalation/de-escalation—is applicable across the Ego-Empathy spectrum, giving us two essential axes of social behavior. Gray (1987) has indicated that the brain may moderate behavior for both inhibition and reward-seeking. Witter and Groenewegen (1992) and Gloor (1997: 325–496) report a comparator role for the hippocampus, a prominent limbic structure, in the routing of internal and external stimuli in relation to previous affective experience (cf. Vinogradova 2001; Iidaka, et al. 2003).

The Ego-Empathy and escalation/de-escalation axes, thus, are two of the most essential axes of social behavior. For an alternative graphic representation of these axes, see Wilson and Cory (2008: ch. 10).

From the descriptions of these two axes given above I can put together the reciprocal algorithms of our social behavior. These algorithms are detailed in the next chapter.

4 The Dynamic Algorithms of Social Behavior

Although unfamiliar to many of my generation, the word *algorithm* has come into popular parlance with the rise of computers and information technology. In a sense it is a buzzword, a word of currency and sophistication. When you use it, you let everyone know that you are "in the know"—technologically "cool," perhaps. Let's look deeper.

Algorithmic Origins

Because of its recent and current celebrity, some people think of algorithm as a new word. Some even see it as a possible acronym put together from parts of other words.

A Gift from Persia

Looking back into the history books a couple of millennia, however, we find that the honors must go to a Persian mathematician of the ninth century. His name is recorded as Mohammed al-Khowarizmi. Through twists and turns of fate plus the vagaries of translation, his name has come down to us in the present form that the venerable Persian would probably not recognize today.

Formal Procedures for Solving Math Problems

But al-Khowarizmi gave us the formal procedures for solving standard problems of arithmetic: addition, subtraction, multiplication, and division. Procedures or processes that every schoolchild takes for granted today. At the time, however, it was a significant achievement.

Algorithm, then, originated as a way or method of solving math problems, usually by breaking them down into simpler sequential steps. Its usage, however, has now become extended. In computer science we use the word to describe the various step-by-step procedures for solving problems so that they can be programmed into computers.

DOI: 10.4324/9781003303190-5

Extended Applications

Some writers, however, have taken the meaning even further. David Harel (1987) of the Weizmann Institute of Science in Israel, for instance, applies algorithms to human decision-making in most areas of life.

Harel sees algorithms applicable not only in business, science, and technology, but also to such ordinary things as looking up a telephone number, filling out a form—even cooking. Algorithms have, in fact, been compared to recipes that provide a step- by-step process for making dishes for the family dinner.

Algorithm: A Flexible Term Taming Variable Processes

Algorithm, then, has become a flexible term that can tame many variable processes. That is why I have chosen to use it in describing the interactive dynamic of our neural architecture.

In an earlier 1992 publication, *Rescuing Capitalist Free Enterprise for the Twenty-First Century*, I called the neural dynamic the *laws* of reciprocal behavior. This was, of course, by analogy with the laws of the physical sciences.

Although the laws of physics and the interactive dynamic of our neural architecture are undoubtedly linked (see Cory 2000, 2009), the neural dynamic as the product of organic evolution is more variable. This variability makes the use of the word *laws* somewhat misleading.

Algorithm, then, offers the better choice to reflect the variability of the neural dynamic.

The Algorithmic Neural Dynamic

From Figure 3.3, representing the major ranges of behavior, we saw the dynamic of our neural architecture displayed graphically. Here, I will supplement that visual reference by a precise verbal description of that global-state, interactive dynamic.

From the dynamic interplay of Ego, Empathy, and activity or escalation/de-escalation level come a series of algorithmic rule statements.

The First Rule Describes the Egoistic Range

1. *Self-interested, egoistic behavior, because it lacks Empathy to some degree, creates tension within ourselves and between our selves and others. The tension increases from low to high activity levels. And it increases as we move toward the extremes of Ego.*

   Within ourselves, the tension created by the tug of neglected Empathy is experienced as a feeling of obligation to others or an expectation that they might wish to "even the score" with us.

Within others, the tension created by our self-interested behavior is experienced as a feeling of imposition or hurt, accompanied by an urge to "even the score."

In the Behavior of Children

Children often reveal the dynamic of such behavior in a clear, unsophisticated form. Imagine two children playing on the living-room floor. One hits the other. The second child hits back, responding in kind. Or the children may not hit each other at all.

One might instead call the other a bad name. The second child reciprocates, kicking off a round of escalating name-calling. One child may eventually feel unable to even the score and will complain to a parent to intervene. Most of us have experienced such give-and-take as children. Surely, we have seen it countless times in our own children and grandchildren.

In the Behavior of "Grownups"

Similar behavior is embarrassingly observable among adults. It can be seen in husband-and-wife arguments, bar fights, hockey games, political campaigns, even in sophisticated lawsuits. The rule operates not only in such highly visible conflict situations, but also in very subtle interactions—in the small behavioral exchanges, the ongoing give-and-take of all interpersonal relations.

Expressive of the underlying conflictual excitatory/ inhibitory dynamic of the neural architecture, we can say that

> The reactions that build in ourselves and others do so potentially in proportion to the behavioral tension created by egoistic, self-interested behavior.

That is, the harder I hit you, the harder you hit me in return. Or the fouler a name you call me, the fouler a name I call you in return. Or perhaps with more sophistication, I resolve the tension in me by an act of visible "superiority." I ignore you—although I *could* call you an even fouler name, if I chose.

The Second Rule Describes the Empathetic Range on the Other Side of the Scale

2. *Empathetic behavior, because it denies Ego or self-interest to some degree, also creates tension within ourselves and others. This tension, likewise, increases as activity levels increase and as we move toward extremes of Empathy.*

   Within ourselves, the tension created by the tug of the neglected self-interest (Ego) is experienced as a feeling that "others owe us one" and a growing need to "collect our due." This tension, especially if it continues over time, may be experienced as resentment at being exploited, taken for granted, not appreciated, or victimized by others.

   Within others, the tension created is experienced as a sense of obligation toward us.

The reactions that build in ourselves and others, again, are in proportion to the behavioral tension created. And again, the unmanaged, or excessive tension is experienced as behavioral stress.

"Thank you" as Payback There Is No Free Behavioral Gift

When we do things for others—give them things, make personal sacrifices for them—it can make us feel righteous, affectionate, loving. But we *do* want a payback. At least a *thank you* or other expression of appreciation. That's the tug of self-interest. It can be very slight, hardly noticeable at first. But let the giving, the self-sacrifice, go on for a while, unacknowledged or unappreciated (that is, without payback to the Ego), and see how we begin to feel.

The tension, the stress, starts to show. We complain that others are taking advantage of us, taking us for granted, victimizing us. Self-interest cannot be long short-changed without demanding its due. We may eventually relieve the stress by blowing up at those we have been serving—accusing them of ingratitude, withdrawing our favors, or kicking them out of the house.

Or we may sandbag the stress, letting it eat away at our dispositions, our bodies.

Goodness, Gift-giving and Reciprocity

On the other hand, when we do things for others, they often feel obliged to return the favor in some form to avoid being left with an uneasy sense of debt. Gift-giving notoriously stimulates the receiver to feel the need to reciprocate.

Think of the times when you have received a holiday gift from someone for whom you had failed to buy a gift. Sometimes the sense of obligation prompted by the empathetic acts of others can become a nuisance.

E. O. Wilson plus Sapolsky vs. Ghiselin

The no-free-behavioral-gift, described by the interactive dynamic of Ego and Empathy circuits, has been sensed by some leading scholars but without a full grasp or articulation of the neural dynamic. Famed sociobiologist and student of ant behavior, E. O. Wilson, for instance, cites the evolution of cooperative behaviors in humans that contain elements of both selfishness and altruism (2012: 17, 248).

Robert Sapolsky, a prominent primatologist, for another example, asks about the self-interested reputational rewards of being altruistic, and, further, questions if the element of self-interest is ever truly absent? In closing his discussion, he refers (without attribution) to Michael Ghiselin's much quoted comment about scratching an altruist to see a hypocrite bleed. And he asks us to ease up a bit on the application of that observation. He justifies the easing up by asserting that the bleeding altruist is merely the product of altruism and reciprocity being evolutionarily inseparable in human behavior (2017: 545–552).

Michael Ghiselin, a prominent biologist, made his widely quoted altruist/hypocrite comment near the conclusion of his work on the economy of nature (1974: 247). In the last paragraph of the same work, however, he modified the earlier statement by suggesting that self-interest and common welfare are not fundamentally beyond reconciliation (p. 263). In a later work he refers to the "altruist as a bleeding hypocrite" statement as piece of widely quoted hyperbole that he really didn't mean (1989: 83).

The Third Rule Statement: The Range of Dynamic Balance Between Our Contending Motives

3. *Behavior in the range of dynamic balance expresses the approximate balance of Ego and Empathy. It is the position of least behavioral tension. Within ourselves and others, it creates feelings of mutuality and shared respect.*

For most of us it is an especially satisfying experience to interact with others in equality, with no sense of obligation, superiority or inferiority. To work together in common humanity, in common cause, is to experience behavioral dynamic balance.

Of course, there are many versions of the experience of dynamic balance: the shared pride of parents in helping their child achieve, the joy of athletes in playing well as a team, the satisfaction of coworkers in working together successfully on an important project.

Reciprocity Through Conflict

These algorithms of behavior operate in the smallest interactions, the vignettes, of everyday personal life. The dynamic of behavioral tension provides that for every interpersonal act, there is a balancing reciprocal. A self-interested act requires an empathetic reciprocal for balance. An empathetic act, likewise, requires a balancing self-interested reciprocal. This reciprocity goes back and forth many times even in a short conversation.

Without the reciprocal, tension builds, stress accumulates, and either confrontation or withdrawal results. If not, and the relationship continues, it becomes a tense and stressful one of inequality or domination/submission, waiting and pressing for the opportunity for adjustment.

These, then, are the basic interpersonal algorithms of our three-level brain. These algorithms show how we get to reciprocity through conflict. They shape the conflict and reciprocity, the give-and-take, at all levels of our interactive social lives.

Overemphasis on either self-interest or Empathy, exercise of one program to the exclusion of the other, creates tension and stress in any social configuration—from simple dyadic person-to-person encounters up to and including interactions among members of the workplace, society at large, social groups, and entire economic and political systems.

The Scale of Inclusiveness

The reciprocal algorithms of our neural architecture, the tug-and-pull of Ego and Empathy, apply at all levels of social exchange.

However, the intensity of empathetic bonding tends to vary with proximity and related factors creating a varying scale of inclusiveness. The scale of inclu siveness is an important factor in fully understanding the nature of human bonding created by the Ego/Empathy dynamic.

The Family Connection

A basic feature of our evolutionary development is that we evolved to full humanity in small family kinship groups. Our neural architecture is, therefore, designed primarily to work most effectively in such small face-to-face, closely knit groups. Empathy bonds us most tightly and securely in the family, Ego is reined in by love and care for parents, children, mates, cousins.

And we feel the depth of love and passion most keenly to those in close physical proximity—those we live and work with on a daily basis. With distance the intensity of Empathy tends to become increasingly rarefied.

In Africa, our brain developed over millions of years in such small group circumstances. Dynamically-balanced, essentially egalitarian, social behavior characterized such groups. A leader, or Alpha, did not dominate through brute Ego force, as some traditional lore would have it. The leader emerged as the one who could engage alliances and provide the most in wisdom, survival skills, and affection. Providing such is the essence of mammalian Empathy.

Our survival strategy as a species, thus, was *sharing, reciprocity*—not *domination and submission.* All this, and the neural circuitry supporting it, was essentially cast in DNA/protein concrete—hard-wired—long before we entered into larger social groupings. Long before we developed agriculture and settled down. Long before we grouped into early cities and kingdoms, creating civilization.

And long before the barely five to ten thousand years ago (a very short and recent time in our human development), when we created writing and made recorded history possible.

Present-Day Mismatch and the Importance of Socialization and Education

Our evolution of Ego and Empathy in small family groups means that this architecture is in somewhat of a state of mismatch with our current mass impersonal environment.

Empathy for others weakens, as they are more distant from us—creating the scale of inclusiveness. We feel Empathy most strongly for family and those most close to us, less to those more distant.

This scale of inclusiveness is a consistent and perennial problem for larger societies. It is only resolved by socialization or education which extends and universalizes the archetypal motivational circuitries.

Our Sense of the Mismatch

Historically, we have sensed this mismatch and attempted intuitively to overcome it by appeals to kinship terms. Secularly, we have used such terms as: the family of man, brotherhoods, sisterhoods, mother- or fatherlands.

Without the basic architecture, such appeals would be groundless. They are clearly intuitive efforts to extend and universalize the fundamental Ego and Empathy dynamic.

Predictability and the CSN Model

The scientific worth of a model is often said to be its ability to make predictions.

Given an appreciation of the algorithmic rules of behavior and the scale of inclusiveness, the CSN model meets that standard. Each of the algorithmic rule statements can be phrased as a testable prediction.

As a homey example, try behaving in an egoistic, domineering manner toward a family member or friend. That is, if you dare to risk the consequences.

The CSN model predicts that both you and the family member or friend will experience behavioral tension and will report such feelings. This has been tried many times and has produced consistent results. It's really not recommended. If, on the other hand, you prefer to try empathetic, serving behavior, especially over a period of time, you may find the model's predictions of behavioral tension likewise hold.

Despite the qualifications of the scale of inclusiveness, the CSN model's predictive and explanatory powers go far beyond such straightforward or intuitive proximal examples. The predictive power will be explicit in the extraordinary range of its explanatory power in social exchange and economic theory demonstrated in the following chapters of this book.

5 The Physiology of Social Behavior

In this chapter I introduce the second science that economics has failed to connect with effectively. That is, basic human physiology.

Basic physiology has been the inspiration and model for the modern sciences of cybernetics or information control theory. Cybernetics and General Systems Theory are often used synonymously. Norbert Wiener, a mathematician at MIT, wrote *Cybernetics* in 1948. Ludwig von Bertalanffy, a biologist, then at the University of Alberta, authored *General Systems Theory* (GST) in 1968. Bertalanffy considered cybernetics a subfield of GST (1968: 17). According to Wiener the term *cybernetics* was adapted from the Greek word for steersman and dates back no further than 1947 (1948: 19). Both men drew upon biology for their concepts.

The Biological Inspiration

As both Wiener and von Bertalanffy observed, living things, from the single cell on up, have remarkable regulating mechanisms. They must. If they didn't, they would fall apart. They would simply die and breakdown into their many component parts.

Bernard and Cannon the Discovery of Homeostasis

In physiology, this ability to regulate, to keep all parts working together within set limits, was first described by Claude Bernard, a French physiologist of the 19th century. However, it was Walter B. Cannon, an American physiologist, who gave these regulating processes the name "homeostasis."

The year was 1929 and the name stuck. The word Cannon chose comes from two Greek words. *Homeo* means similar and *stasis* means standing. As used by Cannon, and other scientists who followed him, homeostasis does not mean something rigidly set in concrete, unshakable, or immovable.

DOI: 10.4324/9781003303190-6

Homeostasis as the Foundation of all Modern Physiology

Homeostasis, then, describes a condition that varies yet at the same time is relatively constant. For the organism it describes a condition that is kept within survival limits. When the homeostatic limits are exceeded, the mechanism either self-corrects or the organism gets dysfunctional. That is, it either gets out of whack, sick, or dies.

Like all other creatures, our human vital processes are homeostatic. Built-in controls keep them generally within healthy and, ultimately, within survival limits. As a recent edition of a well-known college text on anatomy and physiology states: "The principle of homeostasis is the central theme of this text and the foundation of all modern physiology" (Martini, et al. 2015: 7).

Examples of Homeostasis

Familiar examples of homeostasis are our body temperature which must be kept within a rather narrow range around 98.6 degrees Fahrenheit. Above that we have a fever. Below that we risk hypothermia. Our body must act to correct both indicated conditions to stay healthy or alive. Another example is our blood pressure which varies rather widely to accommodate our changing levels of physical activity. Nevertheless our blood pressure must remain within limits or we're in for big trouble.

The list of homeostatically controlled physical processes is very long indeed. I could go on and on. Practically every bodily process is regulated within certain varying limits. Even the hormones and neurotransmitters that mediate behavior within our neural architecture are regulated homeostatically. When the regulation fails, our moods, our feelings, and ultimately our behaviors get out of sorts.

A huge pharmaceutical industry exists to help us keep our bodily and behavioral processes in relative homeostasis—from blood pressure medications, to diet pills, to mood regulators.

These homeostatic processes, from the vital activities of the smallest cell up to the integrated functions of our body as a whole, can all be described by algorithms. They can likewise be represented by mathematical equations. Despite sometimes mind-boggling complexity, they all function within necessary survival limits.

Homeostasis, Cybernetics, and Information Theory

As noted, the discovery and study of homeostasis in the vital processes of living organisms led to the science of cybernetic control systems, information theory, and GST.

Biological systems gave us both the model and the inspiration for these technological advances. The computer or information revolution depends upon modeling of our physical regulating processes.

Computers, Software, Information Control Systems: Manmade Analogs of Ourselves

When we build computers, software, and information control systems, we are creating partial analogs of ourselves out there. And then we're interacting with them to support our daily lives. Information, computers, controlled mechanical processes—all model the organic algorithms that regulate living processes.

Essentials of Homeostatic Systems

Homeostatic systems, whether biological or fabricated, require certain essentials. At a minimum, they must have standards or limits, the ability to monitor and evaluate those standards and limits against performance, and the capacity to initiate corrective action. They must also have sensors to get input for comparison, and effectors that can act to carry out the needed adjustments.

The concept of feedback is one of the most important ideas to come out of the study of homeostasis and its human-made information control sciences. Feedback refers to the information for comparison and evaluation that sensors both internal and external bring us. Homeostatic systems need feedback to tell them how they are doing. When to start corrective action. When to stop it.

Homeostasis of the Social Architecture

The word homeostasis usually refers to the regulation of the internal environment of living organisms. Can we legitimately apply the concept to the workings of our social neural architecture?

Absolutely, We Can

As stated above, homeostasis is the foundation of all modern physiology. The brain is, of course, a physiological organ. Therefore, it should not come as a surprise that the social behavior of our neural architecture is also homeostatically regulated. All the elements for homeostatic regulation are present—standards, the ability to monitor and evaluate, sensors and effectors, feedback.

In fact, our autonomic nervous system through its connections with the hypothalamus has primary involvement in behavioral homeostasis. The hypothalamus is closely linked with neural structures in the both the affectional and self-preservational circuitry located in the limbic system and the brain stem (e.g., see Herbert & Schulkin 2002; Kandel, Schwartz, & Jessell 2000: 871–997; Nelson 2000, esp. pp. 447–494).

Like other bodily processes, our social neural architecture is regulated within limits. All the sensory systems of our body feed information into the monitoring neural centers. Many cues—from happy, sad, angry facial expressions to vocalizations of tenderness, frustration, surprise, and anger—are genetically wired and fine-tuned epigenetically through development and experience. The muscles of our body act to carry out adjustments to our social as well as physical environment.

Behavioral Tension: Generic Regulator of Our Social Architecture

What we experience as behavioral tension is the generic regulator.

Behavioral tension tells us when we are deviating from balance. Behavioral stress warns us that we're exceeding safe limits for ourselves and others (e.g., see Przewlocki 2002).

The behavioral spectrum set out in Chapter 3 illustrates the necessary behavioral range and limits. The algorithmic rules of reciprocity in Chapter 4 describe the social regulatory process. The social equation to be formulated in Chapter 6 represents the process mathematically.

Homeostatic Variability, Neural Plasticity, and Learning

Homeostatic regulations, as noted, can vary quite a bit in the ranges permitted. Some are tighter, some are looser. Our social architecture is one of the looser kind. This is to be expected.

The brain, in its higher centers, is the most plastic of our organs. It is designed for learning—to respond to new experience. Learning plays an important role in the development and variability among individuals of the neural dynamic. This was discussed previously under the topic of the emerging science of epigenetics in Chapter 2.

My friend and colleague John Tomer, a leader and former President of the Society for the Advancement of Behavioral Economics (SABE), feels that I did not emphasize enough the importance of learning and experience in some earlier works and thoughtfully sought to correct that perceived deficit in a recent article in the *World Economic Review* (2012). The reader may also wish to consult the following scholars on neural plasticity: Chalupa, et al. 2011; Kolb and Gibb 2011; Kolb, Gibb, & Robinson 2003; Shaw and McEachern 2001; Kolb 1995; Greenough and Chang 1989.

Executive Brain Centers: Considerable Control, But not Absolute

In addition, the higher executive centers of the brain can also assert considerable control. Such control can never be absolute, but it can be strengthened or weakened by learning or experience. If this were not so, there would be no point in writing this book.

By self-consciously exercising our executive neural architecture we can vary the expression of our behavior across the spectrum of Ego and Empathy quite widely. As long, that is, as we can handle the behavioral tension we create in the process. That is to say, to a considerable extent, we can control the heat in our own kitchen.

But Variability Has Its Limits

Despite the variability our social architecture is, nevertheless, set within clear outer limits.

When we act too egoistically. When we nearly totally suppress Empathy. For instance, when we engage in attacking behavior, we approach the outer limits. And clearly somebody can get hurt or killed. Perhaps we even get hurt or killed ourselves.

Behavior at the extremes of either Ego or Empathy can be life-threatening. We see examples of the egoistic extreme in street crime, gang wars, bar fights, and even in domestic violence.

We see the relentless and deadly reciprocity of extremes at a societal level—in war, in the conflict between Israel and the Palestinians, between Pakistan and India over Kashmir. The examples are countless.

On the other hand, we see the empathetic extreme when parents sacrifice themselves for their children. We also see it when firefighters rush into blazing, collapsing buildings to rescue trapped citizens.

In the summer of 2002 Empathy was demonstrated on television for all to see as extraordinary efforts were made to save trapped miners in Somerset, Pennsylvania. Also the world rejoiced in Empathy when in the summer of 2010 a group of 33 Chilean miners were rescued after being trapped underground for 69 days.

Human Social Life: A Resounding Homeostatic Success

In the face of so much violence reported daily in the news, we may seem mostly inclined to exceed homeostatic limits and create mainly death and destruction in our social world.

This, however, is a distortion—perhaps based on our natural tendency to see the disturbing exception, rather than the comforting rule. It is an illusion encouraged by mass media reporting in a global society.

In Spite of Media Emphasis on Violence we Mostly Cooperate

Much more often the controls of behavioral tension and stress keep us well within survival limits. Mostly we cooperate, help each other out, obey the law. Mostly we live together in reasonable harmony or dynamic balance.

Over history, despite the emphasis on violence in the written record, cooperation has prevailed overwhelmingly. In truth, we seldom exceed homeostatic limits. The historical evidence speaks to us loudly in confirmation. Our homeostatic neural social architecture is an undeniable success. It has brought us to a population success or explosion of over six billion.

Is the Human Species a Suicidal Success?

Crispin Tickell, a longtime advisor to British prime ministers and former president of the Royal Geographical Society, deals with this point in a well-read article titled *The Human Species: A Suicidal Success?*

Of course, this collaborative success of our social brain has created other challenges to the maintenance of social homeostasis that we must yet confront adequately—like overpopulation, exhaustion of resources, pollution, climate change.

Nevertheless, there is no denying the evidence of success so far.

6 The Organic, Homeostatic Equation of Our Neural Architecture

The previous chapter discussed the homeostatic regulation of our social neural architecture. Earlier chapters presented the dynamic of our neural architecture in two forms: the CSN model of the major ranges of behavior and the descriptive algorithmic rules of reciprocal behavior.

The Third Form of the Neural Dynamic

Here, I will introduce a third form—the mathematical expression or equation that represents the homeostatically regulated dynamic.

If math is not your favorite subject, don't let the math I use intimidate you. I will keep it simple. I won't use a lot of the usual confusing math symbols or Greek letters. Instead I will use abbreviations of the actual English words. You won't have to hold a bunch of numerical abstractions in the higher part of your neural architecture while you try to follow the reasoning.

Math Represents Reality Symbolically

Keep in mind something that is easy to forget. The math is *not* the dynamic. Nor is it the reality. Math *represents* the dynamic and the reality. Math is a tool we invented that helps us clarify and simplify. Symbols are used because they are easier to manipulate than word descriptions. They also help us to see relationships more sharply.

In the equation, I will *represent* the previous graph of the major ranges of behavior as well as the written description of the algorithms. I will try to capture very simply the dynamic of our social neural architecture.

Here goes:

$$\begin{aligned} \text{BT} &= \frac{\text{Ego}}{\text{Empathy}} \text{ or } \frac{\text{Empathy}}{\text{Ego}} \\ &= \pm 1 (\text{dynamic balance, approx. equilibrium, or unity}) \end{aligned}$$

DOI: 10.4324/9781003303190-7

There it stands: the dynamic homeostatic equation of our social brain expressed as a dynamically-balanced equation, an equation approaching equilibrium, or an equation expressing optimal homeostasis.

Pretty straight forward really.

BT as a Function of Magnitude

In the equation BT stands for behavioral tension and is a function of the ratio of Ego to Empathy or vice versa. It represents our self-preservation and affection circuitry tugging and pulling against each other.

Because of the self-correcting homeostatic nature of the dynamic—the varying tug-and-pull of forces against each other—we can make either Ego or Empathy the numerator or denominator as needed. We can do this because it is the *magnitude* of divergence or convergence between the two self-correcting forces that we are interested in expressing by the equation.

This short equation gives basic mathematical expression to the social architecture of our evolved brain structure. As the conflicting circuits of our social brain approach equilibrium, dynamic balance, or optimal homeostasis, behavioral tension/stress are minimized.

I use the symbolic notation, ± 1 (plus or minus one) to represent dynamic balance for two reasons:

First, the plus or minus notation represents approximate, but not perfect unity, equilibrium, or dynamic balance. Perfect unity, equilibrium, or balance, would be 1 or unity without the plus or minus. Perfect unity is a theoretical point impossible to attain because of the ongoing tug-and-pull of the dynamic circuitry.

Second, the notation represents the minimal range for behavioral tension. Since the dynamic tug-and-pull goes on ceaselessly, there is never zero tension. Also there is never zero Ego or Empathy because they are locked together in inseparable unity in our neural architecture.

An Organic Equation Zero Equals Death

Zero is impossible as a value in the numerator or denominator because that would indicate organic death. At death the organic homeostatic equation would decompose into a Newtonian or non-organic equation. Physics nobelist Ilya Prigogine and others have identified this quality of organic systems, which are called dissipative systems or far from equilibrium systems as opposed to inorganic systems (e.g. see Prigogine & Stengers 1984). Equilibrium, as used in the latter work, refers to thermodynamic equilibrium not homeostatic (organic) equilibrium. As Harry Teitelbaum, a medical doctor and PhD, earlier observed in an article "Homeostasis and Personality" in the *Archives of Neurology and Psychiatry* (1956): "When homeostatic failure occurs, then the organism goes into thermodynamic equilibrium with its environment: or, to put it more simply, it dies. The organism becomes an inorganic system and reacts like other inorganic systems" (1956: 317).

Divergence to Extremes Due Warning of Survival Danger

On the other hand, as the ratios diverge more and more toward the extremes of Ego or Empathy, behavioral tension increases. In proximity to either extreme, our behavior becomes life-threatening, we may kill or self-sacrifice. Behavioral tension gives us due warning.

As a moderate example, however, if we have an Empathy magnitude or numerical value of 8 and an Ego magnitude of 4, or vice versa, we have a behavioral tension magnitude of 2.

The neural dynamic works generally to keep our social behavior within survival limits. This is its most important function and that is the reason for its Darwinian selection into our genome.

Optimal Function: A Measure of Health and Happiness

On the other hand, at the level of optimal functioning, the contending algorithms, driven by behavioral tension, tend to move us toward dynamic balance of Ego and Empathy or self- and other-interest—that is, toward balanced reciprocity, or equality.

The equation, therefore, is very simple, but deceptively so, because it can be quite variable and can ramify in many ways.

For instance, we can experience, even control or direct, by effort of our frontal executive, a different mix of Ego and Empathy in every one of our relationships and interactions. Some of our relationships may be quite dynamically-balanced or harmonious. Some may be tension-filled. Some may be quite unbalanced and stressful.

In one day—even in one hour of an exciting day—we may be jerked reactively back and forth all over the Ego-Empathy spectrum. Or we may move back and forth more self-consciously. Perhaps the average of all our relationships and interactions is a measure of our personal social health or happiness.

A Historical Note on Mathematics in Social Sciences

The issue of magnitudes in economics as opposed to precise numerical calculation has been acknowledged at least since the time of the French economist Jean-Baptiste Say (1767–1832).

What Say Had to Say

Concerning the application of mathematics to economics Say wrote:

> The *values* with which political economy is concerned, admitting of the application to them of the terms *plus* and *minus*, are indeed within the range of mathematical inquiry; but … they are not susceptible of any rigorous appreciation, and cannot, therefore, furnish any *data* for absolute

> calculations. In political as well as in physical sciences, all that is essential is a knowledge of the connexion between causes and their consequences. Neither the phenomena of the moral or material world are subject to strict arithmetical computation.
>
> (italics in the original, 1855: xxvi)

Cournot and Walras on Math Elaboration of Form and Structure

Another French mathematician and economist, Antoine Augustin Cournot (1801–1877), considered by some to be the first to apply mathematics successfully to political economy, had thoughts similar to Say.

Cournot affirmed that simple numerical calculation of magnitudes is not the point of mathematization in economics. The purpose of such presentation is the elaboration of form and structure.

Cournot was concerned with the demonstration of functional relationships that could be expressed by the functions of calculus. He was not concerned with numerical calculation and felt some events were resistant to precise numerical calculation except in trivial situations or games of chance.

He wrote:

> those skilled in mathematical analysis know that its object is not simply to calculate numbers, but that it is also employed to find relations between magnitudes which cannot be expressed in numbers
>
> (1838: 2–3)

Later on, French economist Léon Walras (1834–1910) attempted to solve the issue by dividing economics into three classes: *pure science, applied science, and practical science.*

In the first two, mathematical formulas should be abstract and general in order to apply to all cases. Pure theory is concerned with the relationships and functions of magnitudes, not precise numerical calculation. On the other hand, in practical economics, under limited conditions, one can hope to achieve instances of precise numerical calculation (Jaffe 1983: 27–28; see also Walras 1954: 63–64).

The Neural Social Equation: Some Differences

The neural social equation is not a simple reciprocal. Don't let this confuse you.

Simple reciprocals, which we see a lot of in math, merely show a proportional relationship. They compare the amount of something to the amount of something else. Or they compare a part to a whole.

Simple reciprocals have no dynamic similar to the social equation. There is no behavioral tension. On the contrary, the social equation is dynamic. It is driven by tension. The numerator and denominator tug-and-pull against each other, straining toward dynamic balance or equilibrium.

Don't confuse the equation with the resultant or outcome of a simple intersection of forces like you see often in the physical sciences. Such forces impact each other but they do not varyingly tug-and-pull against each other dynamically.

The organic equation is different. It represents a homeostatic, dynamic, living process. And that difference makes all the difference in the world.

The Equation and Complexity Theory

At this point it may be clarifying to say a few words about the equation from the perspective of physics and complexity theory. The equation is repeated here for ready reference.

The equation:

$$BT = \frac{Ego}{Empathy} \text{ or } \frac{Empathy}{Ego} = \pm 1$$

In thermodynamic terms of chaos/complexity theory, an organic, homeostatic equation such as the above can never be 0 at the point of force equilibrium. This is because, in keeping with complexity theory and the theory of dissipative systems, organic processes or algorithms are kept at a state far from thermodynamic equilibrium.

Thermodynamic Equilibrium as Organic Death

Therefore as long as the self-correcting dynamic of homeostasis is doing its job, there will never be zero in either numerator or denominator. Thermodynamic equilibrium for living things is death. This would occur only when homeostatic forces fail or exceed survival limits. The self-correcting forces while organically alive, or at a state far from thermodynamic equilibrium, will always have a ratio of 1:1 at perfect force equilibrium, representing their dynamic presence in balance.

In the CSN Model Death or Zero At or Below Extremes of Ego or Empathy

In the behavioral spectrum of the CSN Model, death or 0 is represented at or below the extremes of Ego and Empathy, which are out of survival limits. Anywhere in between represents degrees of behavioral tension motivating homeostatic self-correction in the direction of dynamic equilibrium or balance—at 1 in the unlikely case of perfect equilibrium, or ± 1 representing dynamic homeostasis.

Any equation representing the organic, homeostatic process must be consistent with the premises of chaos/complexity and dissipative systems. It must also recognize and maintain the distinction between thermodynamic equilibrium which is total entropy or chaos and organic, homeostatic equilibrium which reflects the equilibrium of processes/forces far from thermodynamic equilibrium (see Gribbin 2004; Prigogine & Stengers 1984).

For a consistency proof of the equation through the calculus process of differentiation and integration, you may wish to consult several of my previous works (e.g., Cory 2006a, 2006b, 2010) or perhaps later chapters in this book. Of course, a proof of consistency does not mean that the equation exactly matches the reality it purports to represent. That is a separate question that math itself cannot address.

Simple, but Powerful

Indeed the equation is simple. But it does what has not been done before. It captures in simple form the central dynamic of our social neural architecture. It captures a vitally important living, organic algorithm in very simple terms.

The equation allows us to see and express relationships in many areas of our lives. Relationships we have seen only dimly and, perhaps, as fragmented up to now.

In the chapters that follow I will show these relationships. They extend from our social relationships to the dynamics of the market to the workings of our social worlds.

Scientists use the words *elegant* and *beautiful* to describe such equations. There are a number of them in physics. There are none so far in the social sciences. If you choose to follow me through to the end, you too may judge it to be the elegant or beautiful equation of our social neural architecture.

7 Physics vs. Social Science

Some Differences

The major ranges of behavior, the algorithmic rules of reciprocal behavior, the social equation—all describe *global* or *central behavior tendencies* of our social brain. That is, they don't explain all the detail about our behavior but only the general homeostatic dynamic at a high level of physiological integration.

Organic Algorithms Are Variable

Such central behavior tendencies also operate rather *imperfectly*. I suspect that this will be true of any behavioral algorithms or principles we try to describe at this level of integration. As Maynard Smith has observed, such variability is characteristic of organic algorithms (2002). These behavioral algorithms, then, can only approximate, but not fully match, the precision of the laws of classical physics or even quantum mechanics.

Organic Evolution Inherently Variable

This is partly because they come about through the process of organic evolution. Organic evolution is by its very nature quite variable in its outcomes. It involves some random change and shuffling of DNA, some mixing up of the DNA-bearing gene packets themselves, all acted on in an unpredictable way by natural selection. Epigenetic effects also enter into the picture.

Even if we could track DNA changes as they happen, we could not be sure what changes natural selection would eventually choose to keep.

If the falling objects of Galileo's famous experiments acted like these organic algorithms, his findings would not be so mathematically neat and specific. Instead gravity may vary from moment to moment. Objects may fall fast at times, slower at others, and sometimes take short detours, before finally reaching the ground.

Getting to the ground would be the outcome of a general tendency to fall.

DOI: 10.4324/9781003303190-8

Marshall and Economic Laws as Tendencies

It should be noted that some economists have also referred to the so-called laws of economics as *tendencies* rather than strict laws of physics. The noted economist Alfred Marshall, for example, at the close of the 19th century, wrote:

> Now there are no economic tendencies which act as steadily and can be measured as exactly as gravitation can: and consequently there are no laws of economics which can be compared for precision with the law of gravitation.
>
> (1892: 23)

The reciprocal algorithms of our social brain, therefore, cannot operate as immutable universal physical laws but as generalized algorithms with degrees of variation. Probability gets into the calculus.

Newmarch: Statistics Has No Laws Comparable to Physics

Even the early developers of the application of statistics to economics were aware of the limitations of such application. For example, William Newmarch, of Yorkshire, England, wrote in 1861 that in statistics there was no body of laws comparable to the physical sciences.

He commented that statistics as applied to man in society amounted to no more than carefully recorded observations of events that take place under certain conditions. He considered that the element of free will (or perhaps choice as presented by the dynamic of the reciprocal algorithms) would prevent the appearance in the social sciences of regularities or laws comparable to physics (1861: 451–467).

Sources of Probability and the CSN Model

The CSN model, then, because of its organic, homeostatically, variable nature, depends on probabilities for a great deal of its predictability. The idealized, or rather statistically generalized, tug-and-pull of Ego and Empathy may be further probabilized in actuality by other contributing factors.

Among such factors are: genetic variation, gender and developmental differences, individual experience and learning, as well as other environmental shaping and reinforcing influences that have been noted in the discussion on epigenetics.

In other words, *genetically speaking*, given the individual differences in genetic inheritance that we see in such obvious things as in hair, skin, or eye color, some individuals *behaviorally* may be more or less as strongly wired for self-preservation and affection as others.

Nevertheless, granting *gender*, *developmental*, *experiential*, and *learning* differences, every human being is similarly wired with the fundamental brain architecture unless he/she has very serious genetic defects indeed.

We Take Our Compatibility for Granted

We generally take the commonality of our human brain architecture for granted. We interact with each other socially without questioning our general compatibility. Indeed, without a common architecture our social life would be impossible. A good deal of early childhood research backs this up.

Influential developmental psychologists like Jean Piaget of Switzerland (1932, 1965) and Lawrence Kohlberg of Harvard (1984), operating from a behavioral perspective, have built and tested theories of childhood moral development. In the theories of both scholars, moral stages of development emerge much the same in all cultures when the child experiences anything approaching a normal family life.

Such generalized moral stages could not be found across cultures if they were not genetically based on the species-wide brain structure and its associated behavioral potentialities.

Development and Learning Interact with Our Genes

From the standpoint of *individual learning*, *socialization*, and other *environmental* factors, modifications in gene activity and expression occur in early development and throughout life (see Tomer 2012 and the earlier discussion of epigenetics).

The higher brain centers, especially, develop in an interactive social context producing some variation in gene expression. Our *individual* life experiences may epigenetically facilitate, suppress, strengthen, or otherwise modify the expression of these DNA based neural circuits.

Other environmental factors, to include the physical conditions under which we live, as well as our socially and scientifically accepted institutions and paradigms, may also epigenetically shape and reinforce the expression of the evolved algorithmic dynamic. As noted previously, recent research has revealed considerable plasticity in our neural development.

Individual learning, experience, or environmental factors of our individual lives *cannot*, however, *eliminate* the fundamental gene-based structure and programming of the brain.

That is, not without radical injury, surgical, or genetic intervention. And the behavioral tension of our dynamic architecture will be there to both resist the changes and to shape the experience, even shape the environment itself, in a dynamic manner. That is, we resist radical manipulation of the human genome and we work assiduously to support and create physical and social environments for our healthy gene expression.

Physics, Genes, and Behavior Precision vs. Statistical Probability

Because of these factors, the behavioral algorithms are *statistical*—much in the same way as are the second law of thermodynamics and quantum theory of physics.

That is, they *generally do not allow precise* prediction of specific behavior at the basic unit of analysis—the individual, molecular, or subatomic levels respectively—but only on the aggregated basis of statistical probability.

The algorithmic rules of reciprocal behavior may, nevertheless, very well prove to be *equally* as valid and useful to social science as the laws of physics are to physical science.

They do not and cannot, however, have the immutable quality of physical laws such as gravity. As products of organic evolution and developmental processes, they inevitably involve *more probabilities* because of individual differences, genetic and learned, in the evolved basic units.

The Behavioral Wave Function Simularities with Quantum Physics

We can make an admittedly loose, but interesting, analogy between the inclusive spectrum of possible behaviors of the CSN model and the particle wave function of quantum physics. The wave function of a particle is defined to include all the possible values of a particle according to probability.

Similarly, we can think of the "wave" function of behavior as including all possible internal and interpersonal behavioral probabilities (mixes of Ego and Empathy) spreading across the egoistic, empathetic, and dynamic balance ranges.

We could write a mathematical wave formula to represent this, but predictability on an individual basis would be challenging because of the high rate of individual variability. I will avoid the temptation of such a detour from my main undertaking and get on to developing the insights and applications of the dynamic equation of our global-state neural algorithms for economics and social science theory.

But first a few final observations. Viewed from the outside, behavior is predictable from the CSN model, as is quantum behavior—only on a probability basis specified by the metaphorical wave function.

The behavioral "wave" function, like that of particle physics, collapses or reduces to one behavior in a decision, action, or observation. If it doesn't collapse, we may see frustration and indecisiveness—ambiguous behavior stalled in uncollapsed waveform.

Upon observation by an external observer, the wave function of behavior can be said to collapse to a specifically observable behavior by the individual and that is the end of it. But this would be an overly simplistic "objective" perception somewhat more characteristic of the now largely superseded perspective of radical behaviorism.

Internally, subjectively, we experience a much more complex process because we have conscious access to the dynamic. We know in our conscious self-awareness the tension, the difficulty, the struggle we go through in important issues of Ego and Empathy conflict.

Even yet, in the surely much simpler processes of quantum physics we still do not fully understand what set of dynamics leads to the wave function collapse.

In behavior, the dynamic lies in the complexities of subjective preconsciousness and/or self-aware consciousness.

That is to say, in physics it is not known exactly why and how wave function collapses or reduction occurs and how eigenstates (those having a determinate fixed value) are determined (e.g., see Hameroff & Penrose, 1996: 311). The standard Copenhagen Interpretation sees collapse as occurring at randomly measured values when the quantum system interacted with its environment, was otherwise measured, or consciously observed (e.g., see Stapp's (1972) well-known article on the Copenhagen Interpretation).

Penrose (1994) and Hameroff and Penrose (1996) introduce a new physical ingredient they call objective reduction (OR) which becomes guided and tuned into orchestrated OR, in which quantum systems can self-collapse by reaching a threshold related to quantum gravity.

Part II

Biological Linkages to the Discipline of Economics

8 Family, Gift, and Market

This chapter begins the process of demonstrating that the reciprocal architecture of the social brain founded in evolutionary neuroscience is the proper model for economics, not the model of Newtonian mechanics and later nineteenth-century physics.

Our social brain is structured for give and take—for social exchange. The graphic of the CSN model, its descriptive algorithms, and the equation of our social brain represent a dynamically reciprocal neural architecture. In this chapter I show how the market evolved from this dynamic.

Reciprocity: The Ubiquitous Norm

Anthropology and sociology have long studied the norm of reciprocity. Economists have picked up the theme more recently. This universally observed norm is found in all societies, primitive and modern.

An Extensive, Still Growing Literature

The literature on reciprocity is extensive and still growing. L. T. Hobhouse (1906: 12) called it "the vital principle of society." Richard Thurnwald (1932: 106) described it as a principle "which pervades every relation of primitive life." Anthropologist Bronislaw Malinowski (1922, 1926) and sociologist Georg Simmel (1950: 387) have considered it the sine qua non of society.

Harvard sociologist Talcott Parsons (1951: 21) viewed it as "inherent in the nature of social interaction." Alvin Gouldner (1960) wrote an extensive review article in the *American Journal of Sociology* citing much of the previous literature.

French anthropologist Claude Levi-Strauss (1969: 98) has referred to it as a "trend of mind." J. van Baal (1975: 12) has considered it a "part of the human condition." More recently reciprocity has become of interest in economics (e.g., see Fehr & Gachter, 2000; Cory, 1999, 2002, 2004; Bowles & Gintis 1998: esp. Ch. 17; Gintis 2000).

DOI: 10.4324/9781003303190-10

A Long Suspected Biological Origin

So universally has reciprocity been observed that leading anthropologists and sociologists have long suspected that it must have a psychological or biological origin (e.g., see Levi-Strauss 1969 & Homans 1950; 1961: 317). That is, reciprocity must ultimately rest upon mechanisms within the human brain.

The dynamic of our evolved neural architecture provides these mechanisms. A closer look at some of the dynamics of exchange will bear out the empirically observable workings of these algorithmic processes.

The prevalence of reciprocity means that in society, everywhere we look, we find social relations of give and take. The relations are sometimes informal, sometimes formal. But spoken or unspoken, written or not, they tell each member that what is received must be returned in some form, at some time.

The tension binding these give-and-take relations produces the web work of obligation that holds the society together.

Mixed Evolutionary Thought on Reciprocity

In evolutionary theory, scholars account for reciprocity by such concepts as kin selection, inclusive fitness (Hamilton 1964), reciprocal altruism (Trivers 1971, 1981; Alexander 1987), and game theory (Maynard Smith 1982; Axelrod & Hamilton 1981; Bendor & Swistak 1997). These accounts draw upon so-called selfish gene perspectives, which see such reciprocity as basically selfish.

More recently, however, researchers have reported widespread reciprocity in the behavior of rhesus monkeys and chimpanzees based not upon selfishness, but Empathy. Two excellent books that present the extensive evidence for Empathy among primates are de Waal (1996) and Boehm (1999).

The observation of Empathy in our primate cousins is a welcome approach that tries to escape the selfishness of traditional approaches. All these approaches, however, are based on the outside observation of behavior. They have not tried to identify or even speculate about the neural circuitry within the animal that must necessarily have been chosen by the evolutionary process to accomplish the work of motivating, maintaining, and rewarding such observed reciprocal behavior.

The CSN model, building upon evolutionary neuroscience goes to the heart of the question of brain circuitry substrating reciprocity. The social brain, driven by the tug-and-pull of Ego and Empathy, is the motive source of human reciprocity. The circuitry lies within the self-preservation and affection structures of our evolved neural architecture. From these insights, we can easily understand the evolution of market exchange.

The Evolution of the Market

To understand the behavior of the modern-day free enterprise market as it is shaped by the circuits of our social brain, it helps to go back to early times—to reconstruct as best we can the days before the market appeared.

The Family or Group Bond

In those times, when our ancestors consumed what they produced, the excess that they shared with, gave to, or provided for the needs or demands of the family or community was in the nature of natural affection or Empathy. The reward for the empathetic, supplying act was emotional—there was not a specific, but a diffuse value assigned to it.

Social Dynamic Effects and Diffuse Reciprocity

It also had social effects. The givers, providers gained status in the group. The emotional and the social effects were both directly governed by the reciprocal algorithms of behavior.

Let us look more closely. The provider, say the warrior, brought meat from the hunt or the mate brought berries and fruits from the field, tanned skins, and so on, to give to the family or group. The act of providing created behavioral tension in the giver, who, acting with Empathy, denied Ego to some degree. This Ego denial required a response of acknowledgment—an expression of gratitude, respect, affection, or some other reaffirmation of Ego.

This providing or giving also created behavioral tension in the receivers. It was a service to their Ego, their needs or demands—to their own preservation. The tension created required an offsetting empathetic response, a thank you, an expression of appreciation or respect.

In any family or close group, even now, this dynamic flows constantly, even in the smallest activities. In the small group, the rewards, the reciprocations, are mostly not quantified, but are diffuse. They become obligations—bonds—that hold the group together for protection or mutual survival. Nevertheless, they must reach some approximation of balance or the unresolved tension will build within the group and become disruptive.

Thank You and You're Welcome Courtesy Mitigates Behavioral Tension

Expressions for *thank you* and *you're welcome*, found in all known human languages, reflect this reciprocity and the behavior needed to sustain it. We call it courtesy. It greases the social skids. Without courtesy daily life would be almost unbearable. We would have to swallow all that tension or be at each other's throats.

The Gift

From these primitive, familial exchanges, emerged the gift: an empathetic act of providing or serving that followed the same algorithmic behavioral rules that governed provision for survival. It created tension in the giver—an expectation of reciprocity—and tension in the receiver, who was bound to reciprocate.

The rewards associated with the gift were at first diffuse, unspecified, unquantified—except by some subjective measure of feeling, emotion, or behavioral tension. A gift to a warrior or chief might vaguely obligate his protection. A gift to a prospective mate might vaguely obligate his or her attentions.

Path-breaking Study of Marcel Mauss Pervasive Reciprocity Expresses Neural Dynamic

In 1950 the Presses Universitaires de France published anthropologist Marcel Mauss's path-breaking earlier study about exchange practices in primitive and ancient societies called *Essai sur le Don*. It was most recently translated into English by W. D. Halls (1990) and given the title, *The Gift*.

Mauss was the nephew of Emile Durkheim, an influential figure in establishing the academic discipline of sociology. Mauss was not a neuroscientist, and from all indications had no interest in brain function. And considering the state of neuroscience at the time of his study nearly a century ago, knowledge of the discipline would probably have been of little or no help.

Mauss's findings of pervasive reciprocity in gift-giving in all of its varied forms throughout these seemingly primitive societies powerfully confirm the algorithmic dynamic tug-and-pull of Ego and Empathy of our neural architecture.

The Compelling Force as Our Neural Dynamic

In his introduction, Mauss tells us clearly of his intent. He sets himself the task of discovering of what rule, legal or informal, compels members of ancient or pre-market societies to reciprocate gifts received (1990: 3).

He seeks to identify the power resident in the object given that causes its beneficiary to pay it back. This binding power, Mauss finds expressed in powerful feelings and emotions, sanctified by ritual and even having religious overtones (cf. Godelier 1999). Gift exchange, then, is the essence of social life itself. It is no mere formality of practice.

At one point he identifies the compelling "force" as both mystical and practical (1990: 73). The "power" or the "force" Mauss seeks, but which he cannot identify in terms of neural science, is, of course, the reciprocal dynamic of our neural architecture.

The compelling power or force is no less than the homeostatically-driven behavioral tension that mandates the give and take of interpersonal reciprocity.

Economic and Political Consequences of Gift-Giving

There were serious social, economic, and political consequences attending the exchange of gifts. Generous giving brought honor and prestige. Failure to return an approximately equal gift brought a loss of status. Among the peoples he studied, the failure or refusal to engage in exchange of gifts was tantamount to a declaration of war (1990: 13).

Further Confirmation: Exchange Central to All Known Human Societies

To further confirm his findings among living tribes, Mauss searched the literature of ancient peoples—Romans, Germans, even the Hindu Vedic literature of ancient India. Through their legal codes, customs, practices, and myths he found the give and take of exchange central to the lives of all known human societies.

Such universality of practice and custom—worldwide—in all known peoples cannot be explained away by cultural contact or dispersion. Reciprocity in all its forms is driven by neural algorithms etched into the amino acid sequences built by our genes early in human prehistory.

Expanded Literature on Gift-Giving

The anthropological literature on gift-giving has expanded greatly since Mauss's work. It continues to the present day. Such literature overlaps with the literature on reciprocity. Although the total volume of work is too extensive to deal with here, I will point out some more recent works that show the continuing interest in this fundamental social phenomenon. For example:

Titmuss (1972) examined the commercial blood acquisition system of the U.S. with the voluntary one in Great Britain with the finding that the latter system was less contaminated, less wasteful, and less costly that the U.S. system.

French scholars have continued their interest in reciprocity and giving following the work of Levi-Strauss, Malinowski, and Mauss. Rather than the positivist, self-interest approach of Mauss, recent scholars have taken the perspective of altruism (e.g., see Gérard-Varet, et al. 2000). Davis (2000) reports on the altruism in gift-giving in sixteenth-century France.

Fennell (2002), an American scholar, is of special interest to the presentation here because she reports that empathetic, nurturing dialogue characterizes the gift even in modern society. On the other hand, Pyyhtinen (2014), a Finnish scholar, illuminates some of the paradoxes in the literature on gift-giving.

Derrida: The Impossibility of the Pure Gift Confirms Essence of Our Social Brain

Jacques Derrida (1992), the French philosopher of deconstruction, tries to separate the gift from reciprocity to examine its pure form. He concludes the pure gift is not only impossible but is *the impossible*, because any acknowledgment or even knowledge of it—even subjectively—by giver or receiver, constitutes a reciprocal that annuls the gift by his own definition by revealing it as a matter of reciprocal economic exchange.

Derrida, without apparent knowledge of evolutionary neuroscience, has, in pursuit of deconstructive logic, run up against the homeostatic algorithms of behavior. There is no separating Ego and Empathy, as they are bound together in our homeostatic neural architecture. There is no such thing as a pure gift without reciprocal.

Said another way: *there is no free gift*. Such is the essence of our social brain, now so widely recognized in psychology and psychiatry.

From Gift to Transaction

From the gift in all its varied expressions evolved the transaction—namely, the gift with the reciprocal specified or quantified.

The evolution of the transaction from the gift is widely supported by the anthropological literature (e.g., Polanyi 1957; Gregory 1982; Mauss 1990).

Defining the Contrast Between Gift and Transaction

The *Dictionary of Anthropology* in distinguishing the commodity from gift states that a commodity exchange creates a relationship between things (that is, it is impersonal) as opposed to gift exchange which creates a relationship between people (Seymour-Smith 1986: 44).

Gregory (1982) holds that commodity exchange is an exchange of alienable objects between persons who are in a state of reciprocal independence which establishes a quantitative (i.e., specified) relationship. Gift exchange, on the other hand, is an exchange of inalienable objects between persons who are in a state of reciprocal dependence that establishes a qualitative relationship between the persons involved in the exchange (see also Barfield, 1997: 73: Osteen 2002: 229–247).

Bohannan defines market exchange or the market transaction as the exchange of goods at prices governed by Supply and Demand under a free and casual contract. On the other hand, reciprocity or gift exchange is seen most clearly in kinship relations (1963: 231–232). Since kinship reciprocity precedes market transactional relations in human affairs, the latter clearly evolved from the former.

Hunt (2002) discusses human mammalian sharing in child-rearing, as well as sharing in small unit situations even in modern contexts, and other forms of exchanges or transfers. His approach has a quasi-evolutionary framework and may be compared with the approach I have chosen in this chapter. Appadurai (1986), in line with my presentation, has shifted from the standard anthropological focus on objects to the nature of the transaction itself.

Universalization of the Scale of Inclusiveness and Moral Ambivalence: Gifts that Corrupt

Because of its bonding function at the familial or small community level—its contribution to social solidarity (see esp. Komter 2005)—the gift has become somewhat idealized in comparison with impersonal, non-binding market or commodity exchange. In our larger mass societies of today, in which the scale of inclusiveness has become universalized or extended to include all, the one-to-one bonding effect of the gift can produce morally ambivalent if not downright pernicious or illegal effects.

Gift as Bribes

That is, individual gifts may become bribes to be reciprocated on a one to-one basis when given to political leaders, CEOs of large corporations, public servants, and others whose obligations of equal treatment extend to a large number of stakeholders or even to an entire nation (universalized) rather than to an individual gift-giver. That is why such gift-giving is often prohibited by law.

Hastings and Others of Bribes and Scandal

The trial in late 18th-century Britain of Warren Hastings, former colonial governor-general of Bengal, who was tried and acquitted over the problem of gift-giving versus bribery during the British rule in India, presents an interesting historical perspective (see Liebersohn 2011, esp. pp. 9–26). More recent and relevant cases include the Lockheed bribery scandal that brought down the Prime Minister of Japan (Clinard 1990: 122–123), and the Keating Five scandal that tarnished the reputations of five U.S. senators (Thompson 1993).

Corruption: A Concern of All Nations

Every nation is confronted with such immoral or illegal "gift-giving" under the rubric of corruption. At the time of this writing (2016) China is launching a national campaign against such corruption. Also at the time of this writing the woman president of South Korea faced impeachment charges on the same basis. Under the term "pay for play" it was an issue of considerable concern in our most recent national election.

Back to the Gift and Transaction

A large body of evidence, then, clearly establishes the case that the transaction evolved from the gift. The transaction probably evolved in groups larger than family or extended kinship units. It is here that we begin to deal with strangers. The transaction is the beginning of the contract, perhaps of the commercial market itself.

The Transaction Avoids the Behavioral Tension of Obligation

The transaction operates, however, by the same algorithms of behavior as the gift—except that it attempts to head off the residual, unresolved behavioral tension that creates a condition of obligation or bonding.

After all, in the commercial market, we may be dealing with complete strangers. We may wish to avoid any future obligation to them from our exchanges. We have not seen these strangers before and we may never see them again.

Further, we are naturally suspicious of them. They are not family or close neighbors. We feel it wise to avoid the left over tension that might oblige us to invite them home for dinner—to share the feast as our ancestors did.

Reciprocal Specified/Quantified in the Transaction

In such market transactions, then, both the gift object transferred and the reciprocal are specified to the satisfaction of giver and receiver. The exchange deal is done in equal or balanced return. There is no behavioral tension binding us socially and economically in a cycle of mutual obligation.

Nevertheless, despite these considerations, the transaction itself retains its essential mammalian characteristics. It is an act of Empathy, of nurturing, which requires a balancing reciprocal act in payment to Ego.

When we encounter its equivalent in the seemingly impersonalized and universalized market economy of today, how often do we feel the subjective experience of the transaction? We take our sick child to the physician, who with Empathy and care applies the knowledge it took ten years and a fortune to gain.

We pay the bill—that is, we make a return gift with money that represents a portion of our accumulated education and labor. The scenario is repeated in transactions with the plumber, the carpenter, the computer maker. The behavioral algorithms still apply, but the feeling, the subjective experience has to a large degree been lost.

Behavioral Tension Yet Drives the Transaction

But wait! Let the transaction go wrong—the expected reciprocal not be forthcoming—and the behavioral tension becomes immediately and personally felt. The reality of the transaction—the market—reveals itself with clarity and intensity.

Ask yourself, for instance, the following. If you responded to an ad from a local electronics store for a top-of-the-line TV set with all the bells and whistles—at the unbelievable bargain price of $99.00. You rushed down, ad in hand, before supplies were sold out and paid your money. You received your unopened box and hurried proudly home with it.

Pulling your prized purchase eagerly from the box in front of the waiting family, you discover that it is a cheap model with only channel and volume buttons and a set of squatty rabbit ears.

Would you feel behavioral tension at the unexpectedly unbalanced reciprocal? What would you do? Would you laugh it off? Or would you pack it back up and return it with a set of choice comments reflecting your behavioral tension in unmistakable terms? Likely, you would do the latter.

No one likes to be cheated or short-changed. And most of us will be motivated to take some action to correct the imbalance.

The small claims courts of the nation have their dockets crammed full, primarily with issues of unbalanced reciprocity in the marketplace. If we don't get satisfaction in expected reciprocity, we may very humanly harbor the behavioral tension indefinitely, hoping to get even in the future.

Our neural architecture assures this reaction.

9 Adam Smith and the Market

In the previous chapter I presented the evolution of the market in terms of the tug-and-pull of Ego and Empathy. The market was created by the human social brain—by like brains interacting with like brains. There is simply no other possible source.

No Market Based on Laws of Physics

If markets were established and run on the basis of Newtonian mechanics or nineteenth-century physics, as once thought by most economists in the nineteenth century and some in the twentieth century, we should expect to find them ready and waiting for us on the moon and Mars. After all, such principles apply there also. All we would have to do is move in and start using them.

The thought is, of course, absurd. Markets are the expression of human social exchange activity. And they don't exist independently of that activity.

For the last two hundred plus years the orthodox theory of free enterprise and economics has similarly inaccurately claimed that self-interest is the *sole primary motive* of the market.

How did we get it so wrong?

We Falsely Blamed Adam Smith

Open almost any basic economic textbook and you will find that we blame Adam Smith (1723–1790). Smith was a moral philosopher. He taught at the University of Glasgow, Scotland back in the eighteenth century.

Smith earned the reputation as founder of economics and the capitalist free enterprise system by publishing the *Wealth of Nations* in 1776—the same year the American colonies declared independence from Britain over economic issues.

The Misinterpretation of Smith's Motives

The source for the venerated self-interest motive was a quote from Book I, Chapter 2 of that volume. It goes as follows:

DOI: 10.4324/9781003303190-11

> It is not from the benevolence of the butcher, the brewer, or the baker, that we expect our dinner, but from their care for their own interest. We appeal not to their humanity but to their self-interest, and never talk to them of our own necessities, but of their advantages.

This often-cited quote, however, is taken completely out of context. On the same page and on either side of the famous quote, yet never included, are two clear references to the importance of benevolence or Empathy. Just two short paragraphs above the famed quote Smith reminds us that "man has almost *constant need* for the *help* of his brethren" (italics added, Smith 1937 [1776]). And, immediately following the famous quote he tells us: "Thus nobody but a beggar chooses to *depend chiefly* upon the *benevolence* of his fellow-citizens" (italics added, Smith 1937 [1776]).

When properly understood, then, Smith, in the celebrated quote, is not saying that there is only self-interest, but that there is both self-interest and Empathy and that we should show an empathetic concern for the self-interest of the butcher, the baker, and the brewer, in requesting their products and services—inducing them to engage in a transaction.

That is, being competent players in the market, we should not seize their products and services unjustly, or do so beggarly. Rather we should expect to compensate their labors.

With Smith Everyone Wins

In fact Smith makes the above absolutely clear—again on the same page—when he says in the line directly above the celebrated quote "Give me what I want, and you shall have what you want, is the meaning of every such offer" (Smith 1937 [1776] Book 1 Chapter 2).

In the above phrasing, Adam Smith has virtually stated the algorithms of reciprocity, the dynamic tug-and-pull of Ego and Empathy, self- and other-interest. Both you and I get what we need from the exchange. Nobody gets ripped off. In everyday parlance in our modern times, we call this intuitively—*win-win*. All parties get what they want and everyone is satisfied.

The exchange process, as Smith saw it, then, was more accurately aimed at a balance of self- and other-interest. And Smith didn't know anything about brain science or neural architecture. He was operating intuitively from common sense. After all he had the same neural architecture we have—although he had no concept of it as such.

The Further Evidence: The Theory of Moral Sentiments

The evidence goes even further. Smith wrote another book—a magnum opus called *The Theory of Moral Sentiments*, which he first published in 1759, well before the *Wealth of Nations*.

The second book, almost entirely ignored for two centuries, was for Smith the more important of the two. It emphasized morality, sympathy, and fellow-feeling. By the term *sympathy* Smith meant essentially what we define as Empathy in present day usage.

He wrote that sympathy "arises from bringing your case home to myself, from putting myself in your situation" (Smith 1790, part VII, sec. iii, ch. I, 317).

We might note that *putting oneself in another's situation*—or *walking in their moccasins*—is the very definition of Empathy.

Smith considered this book so important he revised it six times—the last time shortly before his death in 1790.

Smith's two volumes capture the tug-and-pull of Ego and Empathy, the algorithms of reciprocity. Their titles, in all their glory, may accurately be placed above the graph of the major ranges of the CSN model (Figure 9.1).

The Roots of Misinterpretation

How did such an historical oversight or misinterpretation occur?

I think there is a reasonable explanation. It goes, in part, along the following lines. The businessmen and entrepreneurs of that day were chafing under the excessive and invasive restrictions of the British mercantile system. The crown's bureaucracy was micro-managing everything, stifling especially free flowing international trade.

The businessmen saw what they needed to break the restrictive bonds of mercantilism in the self-interest motive and in the hands-off (laissez-faire) approach advocated by Smith. They pounced on the two like a fumbled football and off they went. After all, they were practical men interested in making money, not in theory. The Empathy—the moral concerns—of Smith got lost in the shuffle. The welcoming enthusiasm from the business perspective was abetted by intellectual trends of the time to be discussed in later chapters.

Negative Side Effects

The misinterpretation of Smith's motives and the overemphasis on self-interest that followed, however, had its negative side effects. It skewed business behavior toward egoism by its denial of Empathy. It often led to excess and greed—as in the 1890s, 1920s, the 1980s, and the greed epidemic of the late 1990s, the early 2000s, and most recently the sub-prime economic crisis brought on in large measure by flagrant greed.

The excesses periodically give the free enterprise system a bad press and lead to public reaction and regulation in the public interest to counter the negative tendencies.

Adam Smith, when properly understood, got it right. The free market, as an expression of our neural architecture, depends upon the interplay of Ego and Empathy, self- and other-interest. Not just self-interest alone. A look at the everyday presentation of the business marketplace bears this out further.

Empathy in the Marketplace

The overemphasis on self-interest and the lack of an adequate behavioral model have prevented us from seeing how the marketplace derives from brain structure, and how Empathy or altruism play an equal role with Ego or self-preservation. But the role of Empathy is clearly present in the language, if not the practice, of the marketplace.

The everyday language of marketing *is* the language of Empathy. Let's take a look.

Emphasis on Customer Service

Advertisements, almost without fail, emphasize service or benefit to the customer. Customer service is, in fact, the keynote of most businesses. Every retail store of any size has a customer "service" department in a prominent location. Never once have I seen a company "self-interest" department so proudly and prominently displayed.

Almost nowhere else are we treated with more exaggerated Empathy, even obsequiousness, than in some retail businesses. In marketing, as any good salesperson can tell you, Empathy works. People respond to it.

Features vs. Benefits Empathy and the Art of Selling

The features-and-benefits approach to selling is built almost entirely on Empathy. I was told long ago when I worked as a salesperson: "When you talk features, you're bragging; when you talk benefits to the customer, you're selling." Empathy rules. Depending on the skill and sincerity of the salesperson, the genuine feeling may or may not be convincingly displayed, but the basic empathetic behavior is there.

For another example, turn on the TV set at any time of day and count the appeals to Empathy—what great benefit of health, wealth, joy, and entertainment the products and services huckstered will bring you. In the Fall of 2002, with corporate greed and a losing stock market, I listened especially to the ads of the brokerage companies. They were very revealing about the nature of their business. How they wished to have it perceived.

A leading discount broker openly stated you must get the self-interest out of the transaction in order to properly advise the customer. A prominent non-discount broker claimed to identify with your dreams—to make your dreams their own.

The list of companies appealing to Empathy and other-interest as their primary purpose in the market goes on and on. Even if we choose to view such ads cynically, they nevertheless indicate the crucial importance of Empathy and other-interest in the exchange process.

The act of selling, therefore, clearly demonstrates not only the role of Empathy, but also the reciprocal algorithms of behavior. The salesperson's serving behavior toward the customer creates tension in the salesperson, who, acting empathetically, denies his or her own Ego to some degree, thereby producing the expectation of reciprocity, a reward.

The salesperson's empathetic behavior also creates tension in the customer—a sense of obligation to buy. The sales process not only demonstrates these algorithms of behavior, but it depends upon them.

We, thus, see clearly the contending forces of our neural architecture at work in the daily activity of selling and buying. Anyone who focuses only on self-interest sees only one side of this socio-economic equation. The dynamic of economic exchange, when properly understood, is an expression of the dynamic of our neural architecture—the equation of our social brain.

Rational Fools the Trick or Deception of Self-interest

The trick or deception of assigning a self-interest motive to everything—even to the most empathetic or altruistic acts—is made plausible by the fact that the reciprocal is always there. There is always an egoistic reciprocal to any empathetic act; and, likewise, there is always an empathetic reciprocal to any egoistic act.

The dynamic of our social brain supports the protesting observation by nobelist Amartyr Sen in his well-known article "Rational Fools." Sen writes that one can "define a person's interests in such a way that no matter what he does he can be seen to be furthering his own interests in every isolated act of choice" (1979).

I might reiterate with confidence, then, that reciprocity, proceeding from the evolved structure of our human brain, is the basic structuring dynamic of our social lives.

Anthropological and social research has convincingly shown that reciprocity underpins our most primitive and basic social relations, from family interactions, to gift exchange, to the foundations of more complex economic life. It continues to do so in a less obvious, but no less pervasive manner, in our modern systems of exchange.

10 The Invisible Hand as a Neural Algorithm

This chapter takes on that icon of economic lore—the Invisible Hand. As a staple of economic theory, the Invisible Hand appears in every economics textbook.

The Ubiquitous Hand

The fabled Hand also appears in many books on free enterprise and business. Television talk shows even take note of it. Libertarians, conservative Republicans, and even Democrats invoke it—sometimes reverently and mysteriously. It is generally traced to Adam Smith.

Fable of the Bees and Unintended Consequences

Actually it goes back a little further. No one knows exactly who first thought it up, but the principle is probably first clearly anticipated by the Englishman, Bernard de Mandeville (1670–1733).

In 1714 Mandeville published the *Fable of the Bees* in which he argued that individuals in pursuit of their own purely selfish goals, nevertheless, unintentionally produced benefits for society. This is known as the doctrine of "unintended consequences." It is the forerunner of the Invisible Hand.

Smith Follows Locke Seeking a Better Balance

Seemingly repelled by Mandeville's excessive emphasis on human selfishness in the already famous *Fable*, Adam Smith sought a more balanced interpretation.

Smith's teacher and predecessor at the University of Glasgow, Scotland, Francis Hutcheson, as well as his friend, the famed British philosopher David Hume and others of his circle, followed more in the footsteps of philosopher John Locke (1632–1704). They believed that mankind had an innate concern or sympathy for others—a concern that led to a moral sense. Smith states his position in the ongoing debate in his *Theory of Moral Sentiments* (1759).

Section 1 Chapter 1 of his moral masterwork, opens with the following paragraph:

DOI: 10.4324/9781003303190-12

> How selfish soever, man may be supposed, there are evidently some principles in his nature, which interest him in the fortune of others, and render their happiness necessary to him, though he derives nothing from it, except the pleasure of seeing it … like all the other original passions of human nature, [it] is by no means confined to the virtuous and humane, though they perhaps may feel it with the most exquisite sensibility. The greatest ruffian, the most hardened violator of the laws of society, is not altogether without it.

Thus, Smith described fellow-feeling or sympathy as he called it. And such is Empathy as I call it.

From Whither the Hand Human Nature by the Hand of the Deity

As noted in the previous chapter, Smith, our economic forefather, then, saw not one but two great natural motives somehow rooted in human nature—self-interest, the desire to accumulate wealth and better one's personal circumstances, and sympathy or fellow-feeling, the source of benevolence and morality.

Smith, we know, had no access to the findings of modern neuroscience. He knew nothing about brains or neural architecture. He sensed these two motives as somehow built into the nature of human beings by the Invisible Hand of Deity.

Smith's Dual-Motive Hand Greater Wealth and a Better Distribution

Smith felt that given freedom from government restriction, which was very extensive and invasive at that time, the dynamics of human nature in pursuit of wealth would produce more wealth and a better distribution of it than any deliberate system statesmen could devise. But unlike Mandeville, he saw the benefits proceeding from both self-interest and sympathy.

In *Moral Sentiments* he writes further on:

> [the rich] are led by an *Invisible Hand* (emphasis added) to make nearly the same distribution of the necessaries of life, which would have been made, had the earth been divided into equal portions among all its inhabitants, and thus without knowing it, advance the interests of society.

Here we have the idea of *unintended consequences* clearly expressed by Smith as the *Invisible Hand*. In other words, left to operate freely, the dynamics of human nature, driven by the principle motives of self-interest and fellow-feeling, will somehow work to create an approximate equality of distribution, at least at the level of the necessities of life.

Smith could see how fellow-feeling may work effectively to provide moral stability and provisioning among neighbors, but he was troubled when he tried to visualize its working at the higher level of nations and among nations.

To fill this gap, then, and following the thinking of some of his predecessors and contemporaries, he drew further upon the aforementioned *deus ex machina*, or miracle machine, of the Invisible Hand.

It was essentially an undefined, semi-mystical concept taken more on intuition or faith than any empirical evidence or observation. Among nations as among individuals, Smith saw it as a Deity-given natural law like the celestial mechanics of Newton.

A Handy Dynamic Demand and Provisioning

Smith went on from there to develop his famous economic principles of supply (or provisioning) and demand as the dynamic forces that drive the marketplace. These principles, now inappropriately elevated to the status of laws, have served as the foundation of economics up to the present day.

In fact, the Invisible Hand is even now taken to be the natural outcome of the workings of the so-called laws of Supply and Demand. Even Alan Greenspan, former head of the Fed, and longtime economic psychologist in residence for the nation, can be heard to invoke the laws of Supply and Demand and by implication, the Invisible Hand.

Demand and Supply: Expressions of the Social Brain

Let's go back for a moment. From the evolution of the market traced in Chapter 8, we can easily see that Demand and Supply are expressions of our dynamic neural architecture. Ego demands. Empathy provides or supplies.

Without Empathy there could be no market. We wouldn't know what to offer or how to offer it to respond to the demands or needs of others. We probably wouldn't even care to be bothered.

When Ego and Empathy meet in dynamic balance, fairness and cooperation tend to emerge in exchange activity. When Ego (demand) and Empathy (supply) intersect freely in the marketplace, we tend to have equitable exchange. Since the evolved algorithmic dynamic works imperfectly, I use the word *tend*.

Figure 10.1 sums up the discussion of the evolution of the market I began in Chapter 8. The figure also illustrates the emergence of the economic concepts of Demand and Supply as an expression of our neural architecture. Demand expresses our egoistic, survival-centered needs. Supply or providing proceeds from Empathy and is fundamentally an act of mammalian nurturing. Let's go over it in more detail.

In the sharing, egalitarian culture of early kinship hunting and gathering bands, the reciprocal obligation, mandated by our neural architecture, was—like in the smaller family unit—not specified, but diffuse. That is, the obligation was not clearly quantified, but had a general, somewhat formless effect of social bonding and obligation.

The emotions of gratitude, affection, respect, esteem, and prestige evoked or expressed in the exchange were the biological glue that held such units together for survival. Such emotions, of course, are expressions of our Ego/Empathy neural dynamic.

As I proceed to the level of social organization that we call a tribe, the mandatory exchange of gifts takes on a qualitative change. The reciprocal is no longer diffuse but becomes anticipated.

A roughly equal return gift kept the balance of prestige and obligation roughly equal. Behavioral tension was minimized. An unequal exchange, however, left a residual of unsatisfied obligation or behavioral tension. Unequal exchange led to contests of status and power always underpinned by the dynamic corrective tendency of behavioral tension.

The Gift Economy vs the Market Economy

It is perhaps at the tribal level that we find what anthropologists describe as the gift economy.

The Gift Economy as a Total Social System

The gift economy was a total social system of gift exchange in which the distribution of goods and services was open to public scrutiny. Judgments of fairness and equity were community-shared—there for all to see. Gift exchanges, and their balance or imbalance, defined the essential structure of the society. Gifts were the source of prestige, honor, and came to be backed up even by social sanctions of ceremony and religion.

The Gift Economy as Based on a Feminine Perspective

Canadian researcher David Cheal sees that the gift economy of today is based mainly upon a feminine perspective of relationships and love (1988: 183). This may very well hold true for early societies. Cheal's point is reinforced from an extreme feminist viewpoint by Genevieve Vaughan (1997, 2007).

Whatever the faults of Vaughan's one-sided emphasis, she accurately sees giving as based on mammalian mothering. The mammalian affectional architecture from which Empathy arises is, of course, shared by men as well as women.

This finding of giving as based upon mammalian affection goes against the widespread image of the bullying, overpowering alpha males who ruled by sheer physical power. Physical power may have given an edge, but prestige, status, and leadership in the gift economy were based upon the capacity to give away more than other contenders.

The gift economy is the forerunner of the commercial or transaction economy.

The exchange market, in keeping with the scale of inclusiveness, evolves as social distance from the family and its sharing relationships increases and the relationship factors become rarefied or depersonalized.

The Evolutionary Sequence from Gift to Exchange

The evolutionary sequence summarized here roughly conforms to the standard anthropological literature and follows the previous presentation in Chapter 8. Economic historian Karl Polanyi in his landmark work, *The Great Transformation* (1944), advanced the argument of a transformation from a gift economy to a market economy. Noted French historian, Fernand Braudel, in his sweeping three-volume work *Civilization and Capitalism* (1982), can be thought of as picking up where Mauss and others concerned with the gift economy left off.

Braudel's bottom-up approach to the development of the market beginning with the exigencies of material existence and the need for exchange evolving ultimately into capitalism built upon what Adam Smith saw as the natural or inborn propensity of humans to truck, barter, and exchange (Braudel 1982,V.2, pp. 71, 73; also Smith 1986: 117).

While focusing primarily on the development of capitalism in the West from the fifteenth through eighteenth century, Braudel presents historical examples of market exchange activity from societies in many centuries and differing cultures across the globe. Although he does not deal with gift economies, he seems to equate civilization—the appearance of towns and cities—with the beginning of transactional markets.

From Gift to Exchange as a Continuum

Anthropologist Marshall Sahlins most fully developed this theory in his *Stone Age Economics* (1972). Sahlins made the important point that the difference between gift exchange and commodity exchange should be viewed as a continuum not as a bipolar opposition. As Parry and Bloch note "one may evolve rather easily into the other" (1989: 8).

Gift exchange, as indicated in Figure 10.1 and the supporting presentation, tends to be between people who are kin. As the kinship or social distance lengthens—in keeping with the scale of inclusiveness— into towns and cities the transactors become strangers, and commodity exchange emerges (see Sahlins 1972: 185–276). Commodity exchange is characterized by impersonal relationships, no desire for social bonding characteristic of kinship exchange, and specified or quantified reciprocals. For a critique of several theoretical treatments of the gift/commodity distinction see Osteen (2002: 229–247).

From Gift Economy to Transaction Economy Changes in the Manner of Social Exchange

Notable changes in the manner of social exchange mark this transition and justify our calling them differently. But what are some differences that distinguish the two?

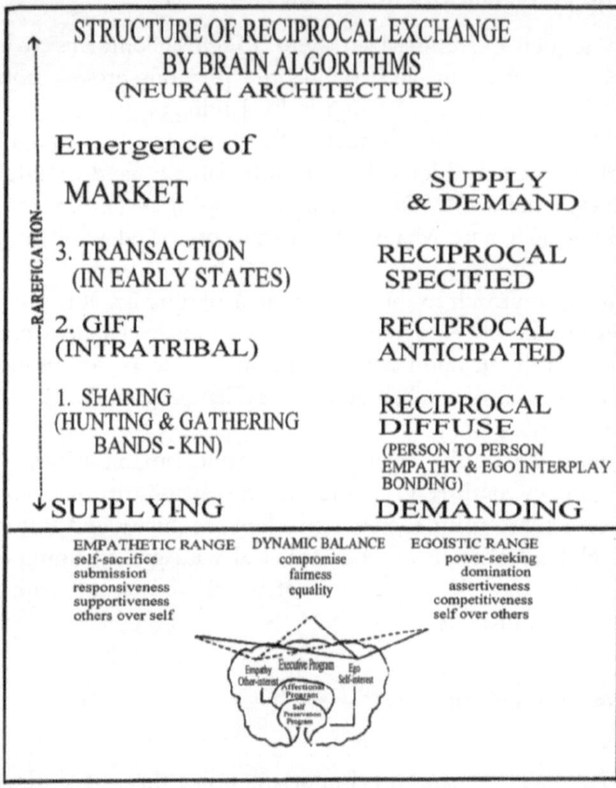

Figure 10.1 Evolution of the Market Shaped by Neural Architecture.

There are at least three.

First, in the gift economy you get the gift whether or not you can reciprocate equally. The relationship is much more personal, bonded, and inclusive. You are not left to starve or die of exposure because you cannot return an equal amount of valued goods.

Of course, you make payback in loss of status and residual obligation to your benefactor. There is no free gift.

As we move to the transaction, however, the relationships become more impersonal, probably deliberately so.

This brings us to the second difference. In the transaction economy the reciprocal is specified or quantified. You don't get the gift or object of exchange in the first place, if you can't produce the specified reciprocal. The exchange just doesn't take place. If you can meet the specified reciprocal, of course, then well and good. The exchange does take place.

The third difference follows from the second. That is, the transaction involves no gain or loss of social prestige. It carries no residual obligation or behavioral tension. It's a clean deal with minimal social effects.

Gift economies and market economies to a great extent existed side by side over much of human history.

The patron-client relations of the great feudal systems were primarily an extension of a gift-exchange economy. They were bound by residual obligations between patrons and clients underpinned by the behavioral tension of unequal exchange.

In such a system when the patron could no longer provide, he/she lost the support and loyalty of the clients. Sometimes the breakdown of the social exchange relationship was marked by violence and bloodshed.

In the Middle Ages the emergence of the towns, merchant class, and the transactional market economy challenged the feudal patron-client power structure. And there were considerable tensions between the two.

By the modern age the transactional, market economy had prevailed. Of course, the gift economy never went away. It still functions on a less visible scale among isolated social groupings, as well as among families and groups even in the most highly developed commercial economies.

The Invisible Hand in the Structure and Behavior of the Marketplace

As Figure 10.1 illustrates, in the transactional or commercial market, the dynamic tug-and-pull of Ego and Empathy becomes expressed as Demand and Supply. The behavioral tension driving toward a proper reciprocal balance between Demand and Supply in the marketplace accounts for the basic motive force for the Invisible Hand.

Scholars have previously accounted for the Hand's illusive dynamic in various ways. Early thinkers, beginning with Smith, saw in it the prescriptions of Deity or natural law. Later scholars, with somewhat more sophistication, appealed to Newtonian mechanics or other inappropriate physical processes. Some just gave up on the question, but still quoted it on faith.

Such variables as history, culture, and institutions, of course, play their part. And they do so importantly. They give the market its unique expression in any social context. The Hand can't do it all by itself.

To grasp the functioning of the Invisible Hand in the marketplace, it helps to keep a clear distinction between structure and behavior.

Structure

The Invisible Hand, as driven by our neural algorithms, tends to work despite the one-dimensional overemphasis on self-interest in classical economics. This is because the *very structure* of the market itself is the *institutionalized product* of the Ego/Empathy dynamic of our evolved brain structure.

Our basic self-survival Ego demands are rooted ultimately in our ancestral amniote neural complexes.

Contrastingly, the act of providing or supplying, is fundamentally an act of mammalian nurturing.

The market exchange system originated from this dynamic. The market could never have evolved or been maintained on the basis of Ego or self-interest alone. Without Empathy we would not know how or what to do to respond to the needs of others.

Behavior

Behavior, in individual choices and transactions within the above institutionalized structure, may vary considerably in the mix of Ego and Empathy motives on both the Demand and Supply sides.

Nevertheless, even in the most Ego-skewed (or self-interested) market behavior the overall tendency of the market will be toward a dynamic balance of Ego and Empathy. Individual and collective actors, whether seemingly motivated primarily by self-interest or not, will be compelled by the very market structure itself—to survive in the market—to perform the *structural equivalent* of *Empathy*.

That is, they will be required to provide (supply) a proper service or product to fill the needs (demand) of others or be driven out of business by competitors willing and able to do so. This is the source of the unintended consequences aspect of the Invisible Hand—referred to by Adam Smith himself as well as modern economists.

Nobelist Milton Friedman, without knowledge of our mammalian neural architecture, makes essentially the same point in different terms:

> So long as effective freedom of exchange is maintained, the central feature of the market organization of economic activity is that it prevents one person from interfering with another in respect of most of his activities. The consumer is protected from coercion by the seller because of the presence of other sellers with whom he can deal.
>
> (1962: 14)

Friedman also equates the voluntary cooperation of individuals in the free market as the source of the Invisible Hand (1962: 14 & 200).

On a level playing field, then, left to its own dynamic, the Invisible Hand, stripped of its ghostly demeanor, will tend to come forth. The architecture of our social brain drives it. The dynamic equation of our social brain represents it.

From Egalitarian Gift to Hierarchical Exchange

The Invisible Hand largely expressed itself more fully in the small social units of primitive humankind. The interplay of Ego and Empathy in face-to-face groups led to a generally egalitarian sharing of resources and power.

Primatologist Christopher Boehm in his study of the origins of egalitarian behavior notes that all known foraging societies were egalitarian. He comments that one of the great mysteries of social evolution is the change from egalitarian to hierarchical society (1999: 88).

Anthropologist, Mary Douglas (1990), writing in the foreword to Marcel Mauss's *The Gift*, makes the same point. She observes that the mandatory reciprocal nature of giving, present in pre-market societies, functioned as the equivalent to an Invisible Hand.

As the size of social units expanded, however, and the division of labor grew increasingly defined, the natural tendency could be obstructed in many ways. The very complexity and distances of the emerging market could block the natural tendency at many points. Such obstructions permit inequalities that would be unheard of in the small, largely kinship group environment of our evolutionary adaptation.

The Extension of the Scale of Inclusiveness and the Universalization of Dual-Motive Values

The evolution of the market economy over the centuries of human politico-economic history has been shaped by the motivating dynamic of our dual-motive neural architecture. This evolution has led progressively in modern times to the gradual extension of the scale of inclusiveness to all and the ultimate universalization of the values inherent in the dynamic-balancing of our homeostatic neural architecture.

This dynamic is expressed in the seemingly conflicting values of freedom (Ego) and caring for others or equality for all (Empathy). With universalization, of course, the caring that bound the small kinship group has been emotionally thinned out and depersonalized. The Empathy that motivated fair play and rough equality in kinship groups had been codified into laws and principles of equity in market and social behavior. It has now become *structured Empathy*.

The universalization of the scale of inclusiveness driven by our evolved neural architecture underpins the concept of unintended consequences or the action of the Invisible Hand in early social exchange and in the evolved structure of the modern market. The idea comes to us intuitively and naturally based on the dynamic of our social brain—the Ego/Empathy dynamic playing out within each of our skulls as well as between us in social interaction.

The intuitive doctrine of unintended consequences or the Invisible Hand launched a determined research program to *scientize* it. This program, called general equilibrium theory, has been the core of modern economic theorizing from Adam Smith to the present day. The next chapter will take a closer look at the evolution and status of general equilibrium theory.

11 General Equilibrium Theory

From Newtonian Physics to Organic Dynamics

The publication of Adam Smith's *Wealth of Nations* (1776) spurred a movement to further refine his concepts. Additionally, scholars sought to move economics from the status of a moral science to that of a positive or objective science.

The Unsuccessful Effort to Find Physical Laws

The effort to find the universal physical laws driving the market to equilibrium occupied economists and mathematicians over the next 200 years. Almost every conceivable approach was tried without producing satisfactory results. The efforts continue to this date with, at best, some limited success but with mostly discouraging outcomes.

The model initially chosen was, of course, physics. The monumental work of Isaac Newton (1642–1727), with his laws of gravity and the motion of heavenly bodies, was the natural inspiration. Economists sought to discover the natural clock-like laws of the universe that drove the market to equilibrium—like the forces of physical nature and the dramatically precise mathematical calculus that had been developed to describe them.

The main challenge, then, was to account for the anticipated market equilibrium in terms of the equilibrium of natural force vectors. The Invisible Hand was, ambitiously, to be moved from the vague status of a divine intervention or intuited but ill-defined force of human nature or natural law into the status of a mathematically definable set of natural force vectors comparable to those of physics.

During the proximal decades before and after the pivotal decade of 1870s, the so-called "neoclassical" economics—still dominant today—emerged. The emergence marked greatly increased synergy between physics and economics. In tracing the historical relationships, Mirowski wrote:

> Once one starts down that road, one rapidly discovers that the resemblances of the theories are uncanny, and one reason they are uncanny is because the progenitors of neoclassical economic theory boldly copied the reigning physical theories in the 1870s. The further one digs, the greater the realization that those neoclassicals did not imitate physics in a desultory or

DOI: 10.4324/9781003303190-13

> superficial manner; no, they copied their models mostly term for term and symbol for symbol, and said so.
>
> (1989: 3; for a detailed presentation and discussion of this copying see chapter 5 of the cited work)

The "borrowing" from physics in the search for the underlying regularities of the Invisible Hand became known as general equilibrium theory (or GET). For the most comprehensive historical analysis of the invisible hand and general equilibrium theory consult Ingrao and Israel (1990).

GET: Off on the Wrong Foot

Thus, GET got off on the wrong foot. Neuroscience was not yet developed at this time. Therefore, the appropriated models of physics seemed the only way forward from the prevailing philosophical speculation about human nature, natural law, or the mystical attributes of the Deity.

Furthermore the Newtonian system and methodology of physics were overwhelmingly venerated as the standard of true science in the intellectual circles of the day. This veneration held in England and also on the continent of Europe.

It was impossible to know at that time that the foundation of the market was in the organic algorithms of our social brain—like brains interacting with like brains—not in the mechanical laws of physics.

GET, thus, took the wrong path to a long and tortuous history. But perhaps it couldn't be helped. There was no equivalent or acceptable alternative available.

The largely vain search has led some theorists to suggest that a new approach or paradigm may be needed. The proper model, the CSN model, based in neural architecture did not become available until the full emergence of evolutionary neuroscience in the closing years of the twentieth century.

I will briefly trace the main developmental features of GET up to the present. In doing so I will omit much historical detail but hopefully still provide an appreciation of where GET came from and where it stands today.

Léon Walras and the Full Establishment of GET

Equilibrium thinking had long occupied the minds of many European scholars. The effort to Newtonize the concept of the invisible hand, therefore, shortly shifted from Adam Smith's Scotland to continental France.

Montesquieu (1689–1755), historically associated with the doctrine of the separation of powers so fully expressed in the American constitution, was early concerned with exploring the equilibrium of social forces in analogical keeping with the Newtonian paradigm.

The French economist Léon Walras (1834–1910), however, is the one credited with putting GET effectively on the economic landscape. Drawing upon the partial work of a number of important predecessors and more recent developments in nineteenth-century physics, he put together a set of equations for all the markets of an economy. These equations were to be solved simultaneously to achieve an economy-wide equilibrium.

Distortions of Physics and Plato

It was an ambitious project motivated by the belief that there were God-given or natural laws of economics, like the laws of physics, and that these laws could discovered and expressed precisely in mathematical form.

Walras not only followed the model of physics, but also Plato's concept of universals. Citing Plato, Walras held that the purpose of science is the study of universals; the only difference among the sciences is with the facts their practitioners select for their study (Walras 1954: 61).

The Platonic approach created a further distortion. Universals, of course, do not hold in evolved systems, because of their inherent variability I discussed in Chapter 7. Walras, as well as his followers in GET, was putting too great a demand for precision upon a variable organic dynamic that they imagined to be not only a Platonic universal of the cosmos but analogous to the laws of physics.

Utility Theory of Value

Especially important in Walras's system was his development of the utility theory of value. Previous scholars like Ricardo and Karl Marx believed that the amount of labor put into a product determined the value. Walras held that not the labor but the utility or satisfaction that the product yielded to buyers in the market was the proper measure of value.

The prices, then, that people were willing to pay, marked the level of utility for buyers and these prices changed continuously as they groped for a stable equilibrium between sellers and buyers in the market guided by natural underlying law-like market forces. A stable equilibrium of price vectors became the aim of GET.

Axiomatization and the Top-Down Formalization of GET

The bottom-up approach of Walras and his followers, attempting to match the success of physics, failed to produce the desired results.

The mechanical model, then, later gave way to the top-down modeling of mathematician John von Neumann and mathematical economist Oskar Morgenstern. In 1944, they published their jointly authored *Theory of Games and Economic Behavior.*

This work launched a new impulse toward axiomatization. This was matched by a somewhat parallel effort by economist Paul Samuelson of Harvard in his *Foundations of* Economic Analysis (1947).

Axiomatization involved the building up of a system or model economy by proposing, without necessity of proof, a set of principles that dictated the direction of movement within the model system. Such a system, then, may or may not have any connection with reality. It was primarily an effort to determine under what conditions a system *could* work.

Quantum Uncertainty Becomes Economic Uncertainty

The new approach was inspired in large part by developments of uncertainty in modern quantum physics. The uncertainty principle, articulated by German physicist Werner Heisenberg, revealed at the quantum level the particle-wave duality plus the fact that both the momentum and the position of a particle could not be determined simultaneously.

The precise measurement of momentum and position was a process fundamental to the Newtonian system. The findings of quantum physics shook the previously unshakable foundations of straightforward Newtonian mechanics.

With uncertainty produced at the foundations of physical science, it was plausible and justifiable to move to a top-down posture of formal modeling in economics. Formal modeling was an attempt to impose some certainty on what had now become an uncertain reality.

Debreu and Arrow Existence, But No Uniqueness or Stability

The new approach, in turn, led to the top-down axiomatic approach of French economist Gerard Debreu and American economist Kenneth Arrow. What the bottom-up approach failed to achieve, the top-down approach tried anew.

The modeling and axiomatic approaches made little attempt to connect with real economic systems. Their purpose was to try to capture the illusive pattern of the intuited law-like market forces from the top-down by rigorously structured highly simplified models of possible economies.

The pursuit of the question of a market equilibrium produced by the intuited invisible hand became formally divided into the three categories of *existence, uniqueness*, and *stability*.

Existence required a general equilibrium of sorts. *Uniqueness* required that the equilibrium settle at one overall set of prices. *Stability* required that the market forces themselves drive inevitably toward equilibrium—and not away from it into disequilibrium.

All three aspects were considered to be essential to the proof of GET.

The axiomatic formalization of Arrow and Debreu, published jointly in the journal *Econometrica* in 1954, applied the new methodology to the earlier but recently updated GET theory of John Hicks. Hicks, who spent time at both the London School of Economics and Cambridge, published his *Value and Capital* in 1939.

These efforts, and some follow-on ones using the same approach, did achieve demonstration of the *existence* of GET under very general assumptions inherently fundamental to the basic Walrasian theory.

On the additional problems of *uniqueness* and *stability*, however, the results have been disappointingly unsuccessful. Nevertheless, failure did not deter the committed.

Formalization continued apace. In the continuing formalization process, however, form has taken precedent over content. Models have become more and more divorced from reality and equally from empirical verification.

GET to the Future: The Assisted Free Enterprise

The over-formalization of GET and the limited success at the end of the past century led Michio Morishima, a theorist at the London School of Economics, to judge the world of GET to be in fact a dream world not workable in the context of actual society (1992: 70–71).

Of Dreams, Faith, Utopia, and Alice in Wonderland

I should note that previous scholars had also noted the "dreaminess" of GET. For example, George Stigler, near the end of his clearly stated and popular work on the basics of price theory, made the following statement about GET:

Perhaps this brief and highly incomplete sketch is sufficient to illustrate the basis for the economist's *faith, for such it is*, in the general interdependence of economic phenomena (italics are mine) (1952: 289).

Morishima went on to say that GET economists, including specialists in von Neumann mathematical modeling, had sunk into excessive mental estheticism. He predicted a poor future for GET in the twenty-first century unless economists could forgo the delights of mathematical display and proceed to build models based on reality.

The disillusionment with GET has continued. Frank Ackerman, of Tufts University has bluntly declared it dead (1999). He sees "the roots of the problem in the early history of general equilibrium theory: a mathematical framework transplanted from nineteenth-century physics was far less fruitful in economics, due to fundamental differences between the two fields" (1999: 2).

Alan Kirman, University of Aix-Marseille III, France, in his pessimistic report on GET writes: "The extent to which the analogy between physics and economics has ensnared economics in a position that could have been avoided had it found its source of inspiration elsewhere—for example in biology, as Marshall suggested—is well documented" (2006: 254; also see Marshall 1920, xiv, also bk I, ch. IV).

Jonathan Schlefer, a former editor of MIT's *Technology Review* and author of *The Assumptions Economists Make* (2012) reports that Thomas Palley, a *Financial Times* contributor and liberal economist, has called GET a paradigm "drawn from Alice in Wonderland" (Schlefer 2012: 97). Schlefer himself, has called it "utopian" because of its lack of connection to reality (2012: 72–92).

The Absentee God's Model vs. Intelligent Design

Nobelist Thomas Sargent, of New York University and Hoover Institution at Stanford has referred to the assumed but yet to be discovered "correct" underlying model of GET as "God's model" (reported in an interview by George Evans and Seppo Honkapohja 2005, esp., pp. 566, 570, 575).

Of course, there is none—that is, there is no correct or God's model. As previously noted, the vain search for such a model was first motivated by mystical intuition and then by the desire to ape the success of Newtonian and later nineteenth-century physics. When the latter effort failed, economists shifted to the top-down modeling of von Neumann mathematics. That, too, has now come to a dead end.

I repeat: there is no underlying God's model to be found. The neural architecture of our mammalian ancestry, with its dual motives of Ego and Empathy, self-and other-interest, is the foundation of all social exchange. It motivates us to look for balance, fairness, or equilibrium in personal relationships, gift-giving, and market exchange.

Owing to the constraints and complexities of social organization it has never historically been generalizable or aggregate-able on its own at the society level. Thus, any model developed at the macro level will necessarily be situational: as Sargent suggests—intelligently designed —to achieve the desired equilibrium under existing situational constraints (2008).

In the Final Analysis: Pragmaticism and Intelligent Assist

The so-called God model or natural law model analogous to physics does not exist in economics. It is a chimera chased in vain for some two centuries by some of the best minds in economic theory.

My own evaluation, based on the recent findings of the foundation of the market in the dynamics of evolved brain structure, is that the further pursuit of *uniqueness* and *stability* are exercises in futility. They were parts of the God model.

The neural algorithms, although likely providing an intuitive motivational basis for the search for laws and patterns, are too weak and variable—too subject to blockage and frustration in the complexities and distances of the greater market—to ever assure us of getting to an unassisted equilibrium that is unique or stable.

Our challenge is, therefore, to pragmatically assist the market to reach these goals of meeting the needs of society with a minimum of inequalities and the accompanying social (behavioral) tensions. Of course, the motivation to do so is likewise an expression of the Ego/Empathy dynamic represented by the equation of our social brain.

We will achieve the sought-after dynamic equilibrium in the society-wide market of the future only by an Empathy/Ego-motivated intentional, pragmatic (in Sargent's words "intelligently designed") assist to the market forces which themselves emerge from our neural architecture. Such assistance to the market will surely require wisely limited regulation to avoid stifling the incentives that challenge us to produce the societal wealth for the benefit of us all.

The *assisted* free enterprise market can lead us into the future and serve the purpose of a global democratic society.

From Nearly Full Circle: The Return to Morality

When the study of economics eventually shifts to its proper organic foundation in the dynamic of our neural architecture, it will have come nearly full circle from the days of Adam Smith.

From its origins as a moral or normative science, through its failed transition to a purely positive science, the new economics will emerge as a mixed positive-normative science that may serve us properly into the globalized future.

When that happens, the dynamic architecture of our social brain will provide the guiding framework.

12 The Social Brain and the Idealized Version of Price Theory

From here I take the analysis to greater depths. I've shown that the neural dynamic of the social brain drives the dynamic of market evolution, the idealized theoretical interplay of Supply and Demand, and provides the motive power behind the semi-mystical concept of the Invisible Hand and general equilibrium theory.

So far this is pretty impressive.

But these are large-scale generalities. How does the social brain dynamic stack up when we get down to the nitty-gritty of microanalysis? Let's take a look at price theory—a likewise idealized derivative of GET and one of the most well-worked and established branches of theoretical economics. I will look at how well the dynamic of our mammalian neural architecture can account for and further illuminate the essentials of price theory.

The Neoclassical Approach: The Schizophrenic Duality of the Market

The foundational premise of traditional price theory is that self-interest is the only primary motive of economic exchange. Theorists present and interpret theoretical demand curves, supply curves, and the combined form illustrating their intersection at the equilibrium price, from a self-interested viewpoint.

Two functions: Demand and Supply. One motive: self-interest.

The presentation seems superficially ok. The interpretation, however, is schizophrenic.

The two functions, Demand and Supply, are themselves the motives of our social brain, Ego and Empathy, given new names from an economic vocabulary. In reality we have two primary motives disguised as functions—with one disguised to the point of denial.

The disconnect from reality in economics, like the disconnect from reality in the mental condition, is not harmless. It creates problems.

The denied motive of Empathy asserts itself from under the covers as an amorphous irritant.

DOI: 10.4324/9781003303190-14

Economists have to deal with its effects while denying its existence. I will return to this later on in the chapter. Right now let's take a look at the various single motive curves and see if the duality shines through.

The Demand Curve

The demand curve claims to represent one economic function. With a little effort, however, two motives can be clearly distinguished. The declining curve represents the quantity of something that will be demanded or purchased at different prices. At high prices a smaller amount will be demanded. As prices go down, the amount demanded will go up. We see two elements, then, quantity on the x-axis, price on the y-axis.

When we look closely, we can easily see that this represents a give and take relationship. For instance, if the figure below is taken as my demand curve (as a single buyer), it tells the world that if I must *give* \$5 for a unit of a product, I will *take* only one. However, if I only have to *give* \$1 for a unit, I will *take* five of them. Clearly, I both take and give in the possible transactions this curve represents.

Take and give are just different words expressing the motives of Ego and Empathy, self-interest and other-interest. If I take something, I expect to reciprocate out of respect or Empathy for the other person's interest. That is, I am not going to steal it. If I were to cheat or steal—show no Empathy for the other's interest—the demand curve would be meaningless.

The demand curve, then, clearly shows the dual motives assumed in the transaction but denied in the theory and interpretation. There is not self-interest only, but also Empathy or other-interest.

So much for the demand curve. But does the dual motive show up in the other economic curves? Let's take a look at the supply curve.

Price	Quantity
	Demand
\$5	1 unit
\$3	3 units
\$1	5 units

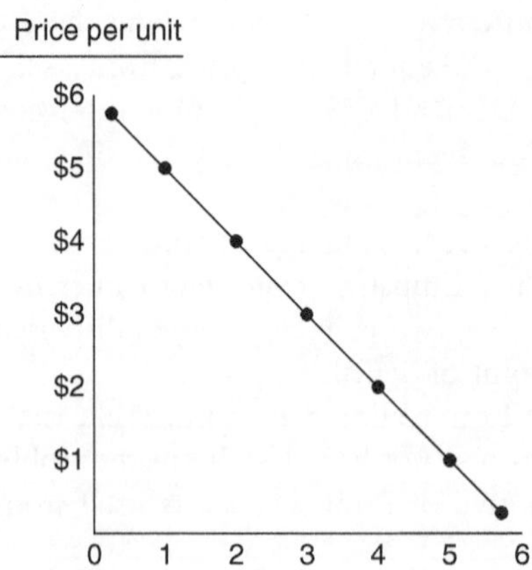

Figure 12.1 Demand Curve.

The Supply Curve

The supply curve represents the giver, provider, or supplier's viewpoint. I put all three words in—*giver, provider, supplier*—to show the continuity of meaning.

Sometimes we lose this continuity when we shift words around. We get the impression we're talking about something new when we're really saying the same thing. This shifting and loss of continuity happens all the time when we cross the boundaries of academic disciplines.

I can also add another word to the list—*seller*. Of the now four-word list, *seller* maintains the continuity but adds the special meaning of the transition in market evolution from the gift to the transaction. When we use the word *seller*, we clearly know for the first time that we have a transaction—an exchange with the reciprocal *specified*.

We know that the giver, provider, or supplier—as a seller—expects to be paid a price for the product provided. The reciprocal is not diffuse but is now specified. The shift in market evolution, as discussed in earlier chapters, is clearly marked historically by the shift in words. History repeats itself every time we subliminally make this word choice.

The supply curve represents how much this giver or provider, now become seller (we know the historical shift has taken place because we see the prices on the y-axis), will provide at the prices indicated.

The supply curve goes up because the seller is willing to provide or sell more as the price gets higher. That is, at $5 per unit, the supplier would be willing to provide five units. On the other hand, if the price were $1 per unit, the supplier would be willing to supply only one unit.

As in the demand curve the dual motives come through clearly on close inspection. The provider-seller performs the empathetic structural role, the role of mammalian nurturing. His/her Ego is reaffirmed by an expression of

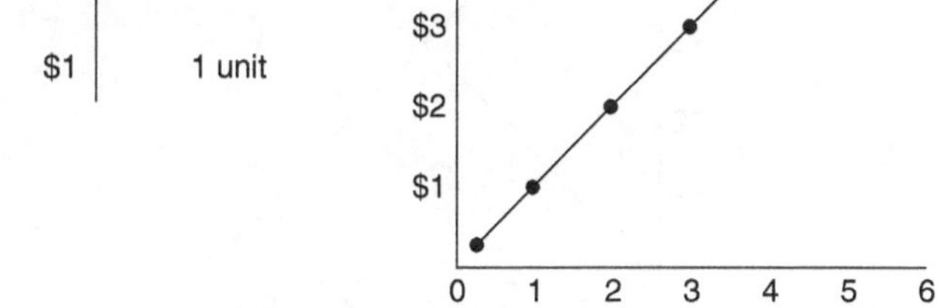

Figure 12.2 Supply Curve.

gratitude, a thank you, in the form of a payment specified by the price. Good job. Well done.

The give and take, Ego and Empathy, of the supply curve are there for all to see. Not one primary motive of self-interest, but two primary motives working together.

Both the demand and supply curves, then, when we properly interpret them, confirm the hidden duality of the transaction. But what about the combined curve—that great artifice of price theory that brings Supply and Demand together? What does it say about duality?

Market Equilibrium

Nowhere to hide! Piece of cake. Of the three, the combined curves show most clearly the duality of the market.

Both supplier and demander, giver and taker, are overtly represented. True, they were always there in the demand and supply curves, but now they're out in the open.

The driving motives of Ego and Empathy are revealed in all their splendid duality. To claim that self-interest is the only primary motive, as mainstream economic theory does, is clearly a flat denial of reality.

In standard price theory, the intersection of the two curves is said to represent the equilibrium price. Demand and Supply equal each other and the market is said to clear.

Dynamic Balance: Pinned and Pegged

On close inspection, however, the illustration says more. It represents the function of our dynamic neural architecture, the tug-and-pull of Ego and Empathy, in balance.

Price	Quantity	
	Supply	Demand
$5	5 units	1 unit
$3	3 units	3 units
$1	1 unit	5 units

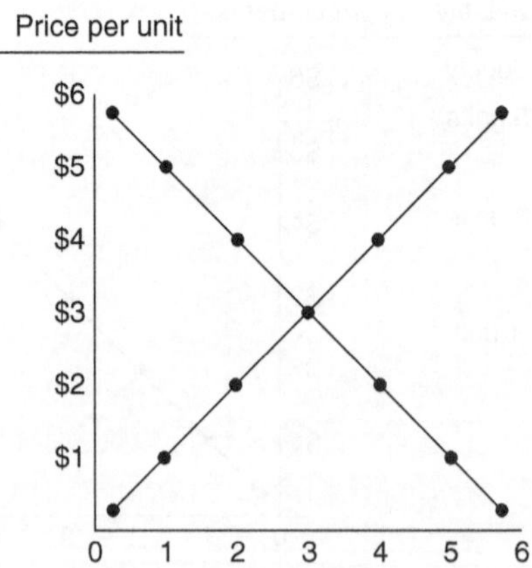

Figure 12.3 Equilibrium Curves.

The dynamic tug-and-pull has been pinned down, fixed artificially at a moment in time by price—the specified, impersonal reciprocal.

On the grand scale of the market as a whole, the illustration can be said to represent the Invisible Hand as attested by such economist luminaries as Walras and Alfred Marshall, among many others.

The Expanded Social Equation

The entire process, then, at a microlevel of analysis, clearly shows the shaping power of our dynamic neural architecture. Let's crank in the expanded social equation to cover the dynamics of Supply and Demand as they reach equilibrium in price theory:

$$\begin{aligned} \text{BT} &= \text{EP}\left(\text{equilibrium price}\right) = \frac{\text{Demand}}{\text{Supply}} \text{ or } \frac{\text{Supply}}{\text{Demand}} \\ &= \pm 1\left(\text{approx. equilibrium, unity, or dynamic balance}\right) \end{aligned}$$

The Homeostatic Equation and the "Haggle" Range

Behavioral tension (BT) as it approaches dynamic balance is the same as or equal to equilibrium price (EP). That is, as Demand and Supply reach equilibrium demanders and suppliers are experiencing minimal behavioral tension or, in other words, they are willing to deal—to complete the transaction at a common price.

The plus or minus (±)1 in this application of the equation not only represents the homeostatic, never stationary, tug-and-pull of the Ego/Empathy dynamic, it also captures the negotiating approach to equilibrium price traditionally seen in small markets, such as flea markets or bazaars.

In such markets buyers and sellers almost always haggle over prices and eventually narrow the range from which both may be satisfied and agree to consummate the transaction.

Of course, in the larger markets prices are often artificially fixed within the normally anticipated "haggle" range of Demand and Supply. But even here, adjustments are often made by the devices of sales and clearances.

The Homeostatic, Self-Correcting Market Dynamic

Another interesting point is that the homeostatic dynamic allows for the reversibility of numerator and denominator. This reversibility represents the self-correcting tendency of the two interacting forces, Ego and Empathy, Demand and Supply toward a homeostatic equilibrium.

It is not a Newtonian but an organic process.

As in other homeostatically regulated physiological processes such as temperature, blood pressure, and others, this reversibility is made possible because the convergence or divergence from unity is what is of interest. With reversibility the ratio between Supply and Demand can reveal in a single equation relationships of disequilibrium in prices as well as magnitudes of excess demand or excess supply.

Price Theory: An Expression of the Social Brain

Price theory is a motivated expression of the social brain. The social equation mathematically represents not only the dynamic of our neural architecture, of Supply and Demand, as well as the Invisible Hand—it is the foundational calculus for price theory.

Further, it cures the schizophrenic condition produced by the faulty interpretation of self-interest as the sole primary motive. The social equation allows us to see clearly the duality of the market. It heals the split between motives and functions in price and market theory.

A Bonus: Price Becomes an Endogenous Variable

As if the healing of schizophrenia were not enough, we get a bonus effect from the foregoing analysis.

In conventional economics, especially as presented in basic textbooks, price is treated as a given—essentially as an exogenous variable. Given or exogenous means that price itself is outside the frame of analysis. In so-called Walrasian equilibria economists don't know where price comes from or why it changes. They just take it for granted—as given (see Landsburg 2002, esp. p 651).

That means that in standard economic theory, demand and supply curves are related *only* at the equilibrium price. Price, as a given or exogenous variable, draws them together, but remains unaccounted for.

Tâtonnement, *Groping, and the Auctioneer*

This lack of explanation is troubling to economic theorists and they often introduce an artificial device to make things sound sensible. Some use the French concept of *tâtonnement* or "groping" to characterize the indeterminate sourcing of price. For example, Walras used the *tâtonnement* or groping process to explain the upward and downward movement of prices which solved his set of equations bringing Demand and Supply into equilibrium (Walras, 1954: 170).

Others introduce the fiction of an auctioneer that calls the various prices across the span of the market and notifies both the suppliers and demanders when equilibrium is reached so that they can take advantage of it.

Needless to say, it's a rather awkward, if not humorous, set of devices—not designed to inspire confidence except, perhaps, in the minds of the most committed devotee or true believer.

Enter the Social Equation

The social equation, however, changes price from a given to an endogenous variable. It connects the dynamic of neural architecture with price theory and demonstrates the continuing relationship between Demand and Supply that exists at all other points on the demand, supply, and combined curves.

Behavioral Tension: Motivating Price Change

We can now identify behavioral tension as the source of motivation for change that brings Demand and Supply into price equilibrium.

At all points outside the equilibrium point, demanders and suppliers are unable to get the reciprocity they expect and want.

Result? In keeping with our reciprocal neural algorithms, these market participants experience behavioral tension. This behavioral tension is what motivates buyers and sellers to change their behavior to bring price into equilibrium.

Therefore, all points on the demand and supply curves that do *not* match the equilibrium point are clear indicators of behavioral tension. This, again, effectively confirms the dynamic unity of neural architecture with economics.

Nobelist Paul Krugman and coauthor Robin Wells in their well-known microeconomics textbook use the term "frustration" to explain why buyers and sellers move price from disequilibrium to equilibrium (2013: 85–86). "Frustration" is, of course, an expression of behavioral tension. However, they leave "frustration" unexplained—they do not tie it to our archetypal mammalian neural architecture since they have no concept of it.

Of course, this change brought about by the social equation only explains the motivational source for price changes. The problem of communicating the changes to buyers and sellers across the greater market remains.

Additionally, we should keep in mind that the curves of price theory are a highly simplified idealization of market function. They rarely if ever come close to matching the complex reality of the aggregated market. Nevertheless, the application of the social brain dynamic clarifies both the foundational premises as well as the internal logic of the neoclassical idealized market function.

13 Calculus and Neural Algorithms in Price Theory

Continuing the analysis, I take up in this chapter some simple applications of calculus used in price theory. Calculus is loved by some, scary to many. I may be going back on my promise to keep the math simple. So I don't blame you if you choose to skip this chapter.

If you hang in there, however, I think you'll find it worth doing. I will demonstrate further the important linkage between our dynamic neural architecture and the theory of the market. I will also show you how clarifying that linkage brings new insights. Together we can see relationships that were invisible before—hiding there in the shadows—like the duality of the market theory that was obscured from view by the faulty assumption of the sole self-interest motive.

With a little background in basic algebra I think you can follow the math. I will assume you are staying with me and plow right ahead.

Some Calculus in Price Theory

Standard texts on price theory tell us that Demand and Supply are represented as *functions* that convert prices to quantities. So what are these things called functions?

Functions are mathematical devices that are defined by what they do. In this case, functions take numbers in one group and assign them to numbers in another group. Economists use the mathematical notation of functions to *represent* the relationship which they *perceive* to exist between Demand and Supply. For example:

D(P) = Quantity demanded at price P

S(P) = Quantity supplied at price P

The notation D(P), when used to indicate a function, does *not* have the usual algebraic meaning of multiply D by P.

And it is not read that way. As a function, it is read D of P or D at P. And D at P assigns a specific number demanded at P which amounts to a specific price. The number assigned is the quantity demanded at that price.

DOI: 10.4324/9781003303190-15

S(P) is read and treated the same way. S at P assigns a specific quantity supplied at a specific price.

From functions we can move to *derivatives*.

Simply put, derivatives are rates of change. They are indicated by placing a prime marker at the upper right of the symbol for function.

The derivative, or rate of change, for the demand function D then is indicated by D'. It is read D prime. The same holds for the supply function. S' is read S prime. When expressed with the parenthetical P for price, they are read as follows: D'(P) reads D prime of P. S'(P) is read S prime of P.

Derivatives as used in price theory are expressed as follows:

The fact that the demand curve slopes downward is expressed by the inequality

$$D'(P) < 0$$

The above is read D prime of P is less than zero. A rate of change (derivative) less than zero means that the value of the rate of change is negative.

Therefore price is declining (as reflected on the y-axis) and so the curve slopes downward. The curve also moves forward along the quantity demanded line (x-axis), marking the increase. The net effect is to illustrate or *represent* the standard relation believed ideally to exist between price and quantity demanded—as price declines the quantity demanded increases.

The fact that the supply curve slopes upward is expressed by the inequality

$$S'(P) > 0$$

The above is read S prime of P is greater than zero. A rate of change (derivative) greater than zero means that the value of the rate of change is positive.

Therefore price is rising (as reflected on the y-axis) and so the curve slopes upward. The curve also moves forward along the quantity supplied line (x-axis). The net effect is to illustrate or *represent* the standard relation believed ideally to exist between price and the quantity supplied—as price increases the quantity supplied increases.

Equilibrium price is the price at which the functions D of P and S of P are equal to each other. This is *represented* by the notation

$$D(P) = S(P)$$

Equilibrium quantity is the common value that must be identified as the quantity both demanded and supplied at the equilibrium price or point on the graph. On the graph presented in Chapter 12, the common value is about 3 units at the equilibrium price of $3.

When treated in the standard manner outlined above, Demand and Supply are related *only* at the point of equilibrium—the equilibrium price. As in Chapter 12 when analyzing the demand, supply, and equilibrium curves, price is a given or exogenous (originating outside) variable that brings Demand and Supply together but remains essentially unexplained. As apparent, in the calculus used above, Demand and Supply are treated separately prior to their intersection at the equilibrium point.

The calculus model used in standard price theory, then, fails to represent the relationship that we discovered earlier in Chapter 12—that behavioral tension *exists at all other points.*

We must, therefore, return to the equation of our social brain as expressed in Chapter 12 to include this obscured but very important relationship. I repeat for effect:

$$\begin{aligned} BT &= EP(\text{equilibrium price}) = \frac{\text{Demand}}{\text{Supply}} \text{ or } \frac{\text{Supply}}{\text{Demand}} \\ &= \pm 1(\text{approx. equilibrium, unity, or dynamic balance}) \end{aligned}$$

To recap, this extension of the neural social equation, applied in Chapter 12, means, of course, that all other points (prices) on the demand and supply curves are indicators of behavioral tension. Behavioral tension, then, equates to price differentials; or, said another way, price differentials are an indicator or measure of behavioral tension.

Price or behavioral tension *not* in equilibrium is what motivates demanders and suppliers to alter prices in the direction of equilibrium. Price at equilibrium indicates minimal behavioral tension and so is acceptable to both demanders and suppliers.

The plus or minus (±)1 indicating approximate or approaching equilibrium maintains the representation of the tug-and-pull homeostatic dynamic of the neural architecture. At the same time it represents the possible range of acceptable prices as buyer and seller haggle to reach agreement.

In this case the equilibrium price can be the single price arrived at out of an equilibrating range of prices. Such is the essence of any negotiating process in the market, no matter how formalized. The give and take negotiating that leads to an acceptable price is seen clearly in domestic flea markets and in many similar institutions (e.g., bazaars) around the world. In our larger, impersonal markets, of course, the price may be arbitrarily fixed. But here, too, the price is often effectively negotiated within a range by such devices as sales or clearances.

Price, therefore, by linking with the dynamic of neural architecture, now becomes an endogenous rather than given variable. That is, it becomes a variable that we can explain or account for within the now extended frame of analysis.

Added to the analysis of demand, supply, and equilibrium of Chapter 12, this brief excursion into calculus as used in price theory sets the groundwork for the further application of the homeostatic social equation to economics.

14 Further Application of the Basic Homeostatic Equation to Economics

In the previous two chapters I analyzed the standard curves of economics as well as some simple calculus of price theory in terms of our neural dynamic. This prior analysis has laid the groundwork for going further. This chapter, then, will further demonstrate the application of the basic organic, homeostatic equation to economics.

Demonstration: Unit Change Above/Below Equilibrium Price

In Figure 14.1 below, I have arbitrarily assumed an equilibrium price and units of price, Supply, and Demand.

In applying the organic equation, units of change or the first order derivative per calculus must be used, rather than the actual numerical value. Solving for EP $\pm$ 1 we go above or below the EP by a unit increment of 1. Demand and Supply as used in this demonstration, of course, refer to quantities demanded and supplied. Thus

$$\text{BT}@\text{EP}+1=\$40.\ \text{At P}\ \$40\frac{\text{Supply}}{\text{Demand}}=\frac{4}{2}\ \text{numerically or}\ \frac{2}{1}\ \text{units of magnitude}$$

$$\text{BT}@\text{EP}-1=\$20.\ \text{At P}\ \$20\frac{\text{Demand}}{\text{Supply}}=\frac{4}{2}\ \text{numerically or}\ \frac{2}{1}\ \text{units of magnitude}$$

Since we are representing an organic homeostatic algorithm (in contrast to a point reduction force vector of Newtonian mechanics) in which the opposing forces (circuits) constantly tug and pull against each other in countering deviations from homeostatic equilibrium, a decrement in one is counterbalanced by an increment in the other.

Therefore, there is no change in magnitude of divergence or behavioral tension at equal increments above or below EP.

DOI: 10.4324/9781003303190-16

Price	Quantity	
	Supply	Demand
$50	5 units	1 unit
$30	3 units	3 units
$10	1 unit	5 units

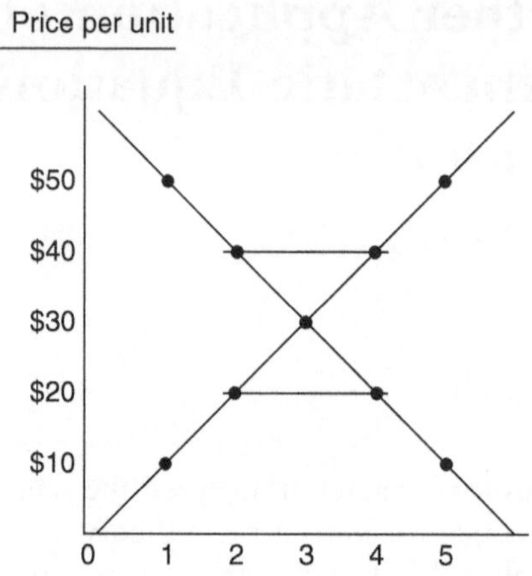

Figure 14.1 Equilibrium Curves with first order derivatives.

The Constant Case

The previous example represents a special case chosen to demonstrate the application of the equation in easily understandable fashion. In this simple case both the unit magnitude and numerical value have the same ratio. More complex applications require additional recourse to calculus and rely upon the unit magnitudes of divergence.

For example, in all cases where price and quantity increments or units are constant, the rate of change is constant as represented by straight line curves of demand and supply, the unit change between demand and supply will likewise remain constant.

For each unit price change above or below EP, the unit change between demand and supply will be two.

Like two cars driving away from the same place in opposite directions at the same speed bound by an elastic counterforce, for each unit of time the distance increases by two units of distance.

The Elaborated Equation

This can be represented by the following elaboration of the basic equation to calculate divergence from balance and to derive values to be substituted into the original equation:

$$BT = \frac{d(D \leftrightarrow S)@EP \pm X}{r(D \leftrightarrow S)@EP} = ?$$

The letter d refers to the difference, differential, unit difference, or rate of change.

The double arrows indicate that Demand and Supply are interconnected and the magnitude of their divergence is a fundamental measure of the homeostatic, self-correcting function of BT (behavioral tension) as one circuit acts to counter the other in deviations from homeostatic equilibrium.

Thus, a value decrement in one is countered by a value increment in the other. No loss in magnitude of BT occurs. The unit magnitude of divergence between them is what is of interest as a measure of BT.

The letter X represents the specific value of increment or decrement to EP.

The letter r denotes the ratio between Demand and Supply at EP which by definition is unity or 1.

In simple terms, then, BT equals the unit differential between Demand and Supply or vice versa at values of EP plus or minus 1 or more, divided by the ratio between Demand and Supply, or vice versa at EP, which is, by definition of equilibrium, unity or 1.

As a Function

The constant rate of change can be expressed as a function.

That is, BT = f(x) @ EP ±?; f(x) is the unit differential between D & S, or S & D, or f(x) is d (D↔**S**), which represents an increment of 2 at every unit of price above or below EP as D & S increasingly diverge.

The following table results as divergence begins:

f(x) at EP ± 1 = 2

f(x) at EP ± 2 = 4

f(x) at EP ± 3 = 6

f(x) at EP ± 4 = 8

f(x) at EP ± 5 = 10

Substituting the values of the table into the elaborated equation:

$$BT@EP = \frac{1}{1} = 1$$

$$BT@EP \pm \frac{1}{1} = 2 = 2$$

$$BT@EP \pm \frac{2}{1} = 4 = 4$$

$$BT@EP \pm \frac{3}{1} = 6 = 6$$

$$\text{BT@EP} \pm \frac{4}{1} = 8 = 8$$

$$\text{BT@EP} \pm \frac{5}{1} = 10 = 10$$

Inserting values into the original basic equation approaching equilibrium:

$$\text{BT} = \frac{\text{Demand}}{\text{Supply}} \text{ or } \frac{\text{Supply}}{\text{Demand}} \text{ at EP} \pm 1 =$$

At equilibrium with no divergence

$$\text{BT@ EP} = \frac{\text{D}}{\text{S}} \text{ or } \frac{\text{S}}{\text{D}} = \frac{1}{1} = 1$$

For positive values of EP above equilibrium, supply is the numerator.

To adequately represent the ratio, Demand, then, is held constant at 1 as the units diverge between demand and supply:

$$\text{BT@EP} + 1 = \frac{\text{S}}{\text{D}} = \frac{2}{1} = 2$$

$$\text{BT@EP} + 2 = \frac{\text{S}}{\text{D}} = \frac{4}{1} = 4$$

$$\text{BT@EP} + 3 = \frac{\text{S}}{\text{D}} = \frac{6}{1} = 6$$

$$\text{BT@EP} + 4 = \frac{\text{S}}{\text{D}} = \frac{8}{1} = 8$$

$$\text{BT@EP} + 5 = \frac{\text{S}}{\text{D}} = \frac{10}{1} = 10$$

For negative values of EP below equilibrium demand is the numerator.

To adequately rep resent the ratio, in the negative case, supply, then, is held constant at 1 as the units diverge between Supply and Demand:

$$\text{BT@EP} - 1 = \frac{\text{D}}{\text{S}} = \frac{2}{1} = 2$$

$$\text{BT@EP} - 2 = \frac{\text{D}}{\text{S}} = \frac{4}{1} = 4$$

$$\text{BT@EP} - 3 = \frac{\text{D}}{\text{S}} = \frac{6}{1} = 6$$

$$BT@EP-4=\frac{D}{S}=\frac{8}{1}=8$$

$$BT@EP-5=\frac{D}{S}=\frac{10}{1}=10$$

The Nonconstant Case

When the conditions of constancy do not hold—rates of change are not constant—the determination of BT and the unit differences of Demand and Supply will require more complex mathematical operations, to include averaging processes. This, however, does not affect the validity of the organic equation's application to economics.

Interim Summary

Based upon the integration of the neural dynamic with Demand and Supply, we can again conclude:

All points on the Demand and Supply curves not at equilibrium represent points of behavioral tension. And it is this behavioral tension that motivates demanders and suppliers to change their behavior toward the equilibrium price.

> Without such an organic motivating, self-correcting force the market could never come to equilibrium on its own except by accident or randomly.

At all prices, as long as the first order derivative, or rate of change is constant, or the slope is a straight line, and the units are of equal increments, the ratio between the unit differentials or Demand and Supply at EP $\pm$ 1 will be 2:1 or a magnitude of divergence of 2.

The ratio of divergence from EP will increase by an increment of 2 for each unit change of price.

At EP $\pm$ 5, for example, the unit differential between Supply and Demand, or vice versa, will be a magnitude of 10. This is the fundamental measure of behavioral tension.

When the rate of change is not constant, the determination of differential magnitudes will become more complex and will require an averaging process.

Differences in Representing the Organic, Homeostatic Equation

Representing an organic, homeostatic algorithm, such as that of our social neural architecture, with a constant counterbalancing tug-and-pull of two forces or circuits, requires some modification in mathematical representation.

The magnitude of convergence or divergence from equilibrium is what is of interest, not the numerical value.

Equal increments above or below the equilibrium point represent the same magnitude of behavioral tension because one force makes up for the other. That is why Demand and Supply may be inverted in the equation to represent the magnitude of divergence more accurately.

This magnitude is the fundamental calculus of behavioral tension, which may be amplified or diminished further by price as an indicator of significance of the transaction.

Extended Application of the Organic Equation

Up to this point economics has lacked the conceptual apparatus to meaningfully and mathematically ask the question of socio-behavioral tension in the market.

The very question of motivation for change toward equilibrium has been largely begged, brushed over simplistically, or left as an implicit assumption.

Importance of a Metric for Socio-behavioral Tension/Stress

The degree of socio-behavioral tension or stress in the market is, of course, of great importance to behavioral and socio-economics as well as to sociology and political science in general. The organic social exchange equation provides a framework for addressing this important issue.

Summary

Confirmation that Social Neural Dynamic Shapes the Exchange Process

I have now completed the excursion into mathematical analysis.

The outcome of this excursion provides confirmation that the dynamic of our neural architecture shapes the exchange process. And the application of the social equation, expressing that dynamic, clarifies much that has previously been obscure in the analysis of Demand and Supply in standard price theory or microeconomics.

15 Self-Interest and the Fallacy of Self-Reference

After completing the microanalysis started in Chapter 12, I want to sum up the case against self-interest as sole primary motive in economics.

First Principle or Faulty Ideology

In the preceding chapters, I have repeatedly made the case against self-interest as the sole primary motive driving social exchange as represented in economic theory. Self-interest has long been viewed as a first principle or the foundation of economic theory (e.g., see Force 2003: 7–47). It is very much a matter of ideology for the faithful rather than science.

Granite Is Not a Jewel a Foundation of Clay?

Distinguished nobelist, George Stigler (1911–1991), once stated that Adam Smith in *The Wealth of Nations* built a great palace of economics on the *granite* of self-interest (1971: 265). Such a statement makes me wonder if Stigler ever read *The Theory of Moral Sentiments*. Or understood what Smith was really saying in the *Wealth*. In either case he got Adam Smith wrong.

But Stigler was wrong on another point. A sole motive of Self-interest is not a foundation of granite, but of some softer, mushier substance, perhaps rather of clay.

Stigler was, however, historically in good company. Many others have expressed similar devotion. For example, Francis Y. Edgeworth, wrote that "the first principle of Economics is that every agent is actuated only by self-interest" (1881: 16). William S. Jevons, considered the father of "scientific" utilitarian economics made the conscious choice to ignore moral aspects and base his scientific economics on the baser motive of self-interest (1888).

The Enshrinement of Ideology

By the mid-twentieth century, self-interest as the basis of economics had become so enshrined that it was no longer seen to be paradoxical (Arrow & Hahn 1971: vii). More recently another nobelist, Paul Krugman in a coauthored

DOI: 10.4324/9781003303190-17

textbook (2012: 2–3) as well as Timothy Taylor, former editor of the *Journal of Economic Perspectives* in a more popular introductory work (2013: 4–5), still hold to the icon of self-interest. They say that self-interest is what economics is all about.

The granite seems apparently to be in the heads of the true believers, rather than in the foundation of social exchange. After all, economics is *social* exchange. And sociality requires Empathy. You cannot be socially engaged without the capacity to put yourself in the others' moccasins—see things from their viewpoint. Self- and other-interest, Ego and Empathy, the archetypal circuits of our mammalian brain, are the very essence of social exchange. Without the dual motives there would be no exchange.

Defense in the Face of the Challenge of Change

At this point I want to acknowledge the well-known animal behavior or ethological phenomenon of defense of territory in the face of the challenge of change. Both aspects—resistance to change and defense of territory—are common among academicians as well as other higher primates. And economists are no exception.

When I examined the fundamentals of price theory—to which Stigler made significant contributions—I exposed an unacknowledged schizophrenic duality lurking in the shadows. The schizophrenic condition was resolved by linkage with the dynamic of our social brain. The expansion of the social equation represented mathematically the linked relationship between the neural and market dynamics.

$$\begin{aligned} BT &= EP\left(\text{equilibrium price}\right) = \frac{\text{Demand}}{\text{Supply}} \text{ or } \frac{\text{Supply}}{\text{Demand}} \\ &= \pm 1\left(\text{approx. equilibrium, unity, or dynamic balance}\right) \end{aligned}$$

In spite of the convincing demonstration, most economists will likely be reluctant to accept it. I know. I have presented the material at numerous economic conferences. Economists, like other creatures, don't like change and they defend their territory. And, in this case, they have marked their territory meticulously—that is, they have pee-marked the sidewalk fireplug of self-interest.

In some cases they even defend it by naïve and native skepticism.

Naïve and Native Skepticism: I See It but It's Impossible!

Returning by air from one such academic conference, a fellow economist who had attended my presentation was seated a couple of rows ahead. He looked back, saw me, and asked to look at my paper again.

Obligingly, I produced it.

He studied it intently during a thirty-minute leg of the flight. Finally, he handed it back to me saying, "I think it's accurate as far as the psychology or neuroscience, but it's not possible to apply it to economics."

Déjà vu. The response reminded me of when my mother and father took us kids to visit New York for the first time back in 1946. At that time the Empire State Building was famously the tallest building in the city if not the world. My 11-year-old younger brother, who was always the skeptic, stood with the family on the sidewalk in front of the building and gazed up at the towering structure almost disappearing into the low clouds.

After a few studied moments, he muttered profoundly: "That's impossible!" Here was my first experience with the naïve skeptic's denial of barefaced reality.

Territorial Defense and Homo Economicus

As noted above, economists, of course, are very human in their skepticism, dislike of change, and their defense of territory. Their pet concept *homo economicus*, or economic man, has been a proud icon of the discipline—of their territory. They rush to defend it when it appears threatened. The core of *homo economicus* is rational, self-interested man.

From Defense to Academic Imperialism

Economists take considerable pride in the explanatory power of this venerable concept. Like true believers they, missionary-like, try to extend its reach beyond economics into other social science disciplines. They even take pride in turning such venerated human institutions as marriage and child-rearing into the self-interest calculus of *homo economicus*. Gary Becker is a good example.

One colleague of mine, a supporter of dual motive theory, sees the dual motives as the foundation for a "meta" economics. His meta version of economics seems umbrella-like to incorporate not only evolutionary brain science, but pretty much all the other social sciences. Needless to say this is a rather ethnocentric projection—a touch of academic imperialism. Perhaps we should have more multi-disciplinary or, at least, interdisciplinary programs in our universities, rather than the silo-ed structure we currently have. Ethnocentricity of disciplines should have no place in a "university."

In Face of the Evidence

Nevertheless, in recent years the evidence for Empathy and cooperation among humans has accumulated dramatically. This has caused some embarrassment for economists subscribing faithfully to *homo economicus*. Reacting to criticism of the exclusive emphasis on self-interest in the face of evidence for Empathy, cooperation, and even altruism, economists have compromised.

The Grudging Acknowledgment

They grudgingly acknowledge the interlopers, but don't give them full status. Self-interest remains the only primary motive. The "softer" human qualities—soft-headed some might say—are called preferences or tastes.

Let's take a look at the problems this half-hearted compromise creates.

By Slight-of-Hand Self-Interest Via Self-Reference

It's an old magicians' trick! Economists maintain the primacy of self-interest while accommodating other motives by a *slight-of-hand* shift in perspective.

They do this by shifting from *self-interest* to *self-reference*. Unlike the magician whose job it is to deceive us, this is probably an unconscious defensive stratagem on the part of economists.

Nevertheless, it amounts to a logical fallacy.

The Fundamental Fallacy

The confounding of *self-reference* with *self-interest* is, in fact, a fundamental fallacy of the entire traditional economic approach. The fallacy allows the subsuming of all motives under the rubric of self-interest and obscures the roughly equal role of Empathy.

Taking the individual as the starting point, microeconomic theory mistakenly *transforms* this individual or self-referential *perspective* into an all-inclusive *motive* of self-interest. From this logically unwarranted transformation any other motive is, thus, obscured or swallowed up in self-interest.

Accordingly, Empathy—and its derivatives of cooperation and altruism, even love—cannot be considered true motives. They must, therefore, be trivialized as tastes or preferences—indistinguishable in significance from such banalities as coffee, tea, or milk.

Fallacy Revealed

But as revealed in Chapters 12 through 14, under the sweeping searchlight of the social brain dynamic, the hidden duality of Ego and Empathy is clearly exposed in every demand curve and every supply curve, especially when both are combined to show price equilibrium. The dual roles, then, are always present implicitly if not explicitly.

The demander performs the egoistic role. The supplier performs the empathetic role.

Empathy as a Preference or Taste: The Distortions That Follow

Economic theory has not yet come to terms with the new findings from evolved brain structure that I have been presenting so far. It's new stuff and many economists are probably still totally unaware of its existence.

So mainstream economics currently proceeds happily on its way from the self-reference perspective to treat self-interest as the only primary motive. Empathy is treated as a taste or preference.

The distortions accompanying such treatment are numerous. I have summarized the most important ones below:

1. Empathy becomes optional. One may have such a taste or preference, or not. This is distorting because Empathy is *not* optional. Empathy is a fundamental motive of our neural architecture roughly equal with self-interest or Ego. It proceeds from the very large, very visible, and very identifiable mammalian neural structures.
2. Empathy is trivialized. Empathy, as a preference or taste, is indistinguishable from a taste or preference for Hummers or Hondas or for slippers or sandals.
3. It distortingly forces a rational self-interested perspective.
4. It misconstrues the real nature of the market.
5. It obscures the dynamic shaping effect of the Ego/Empathy interplay in all social exchange.
6. It is not consilient with evolutionary neuroscience—a more fundamental science.

All together, the above six shortfalls add up to serious error.

A discipline, claiming devotion to the scientific method, should display some uneasiness about such a gap between theory and fact. Economists should, perhaps, wake up to the new reality—forego their defensiveness and inertia to change, and meet the new challenges presented head-on.

I think the changes will do little damage to the discipline as a whole and will equip it to move more hopefully into the twenty-first century.

Escaping the morally-challenged straitjacket of sole self-interest should be refreshing to economists as well as the rest of the world.

A Personal Anecdote

As a final comment on the implicit but unrecognized pervasiveness of Empathy in our economic thinking, I will relate a personal experience. In conversation with an unnamed, unconvinced professorial colleague who stood emphatically by self-interest as the sole primary motive in economic exchange, I asked:

"Do you believe that you are motivated solely by self-interest in your exchange behavior?"

He responded: "Absolutely."

Then, do you also believe that others are so motivated?

He again responded in the affirmative.

I immediately followed up with: "Then, do you also equally believe in and respect the self-interest of others?"

He quickly responded, "Yes", like the question was obvious, if not stupid.

Seeking further clarification, I continued: "Then, you are telling me that when you seek your self-interest in an exchange you also equally respect the self-interest of the other?"

He replied impatiently and emphatically, "Of course!"

I quickly closed the trap. "If in pursuing your self-interest you also acknowledge and respect the self-interest of others—that *is* the definition of Empathy."

In the Face of Economic Crises: Some Questions

In the face of recent economic crises we have an obligation to confront some pressing questions. Examples of such questions may be:

Should we continue educating our budding economists and business leaders in the fundamentals of self-interest?

Should we cling to a flawed theory that provides subtle justification for corporate greed?

Should we continue to promote a theory that mistakenly presents our very valuable free enterprise system to the developing world, in the throes of globalization, as a heartless, materialistic expression of human selfishness?

Especially, do we really need to hang on to a theory when that theory is no longer scientifically justifiable?

16 Hayek

Wishful Thinking and a Not So Spontaneous Order

Recently, I walked into the office of the Department of Economics of a major state university.

In the course of conversation the chairperson informed me that her department was Austrian. I asked what she meant by that, having in mind the old institutional theorists of Austria. She replied: Hayekian.

I was a bit taken aback. I had always thought that academic departments should be diversified. Nevertheless, the point as made was understandable. At the beginning of the twenty-first century the thought of Austrian born Friedrich Hayek (1899–1992) is most influential among theoretical economists in the Western world. He represents the standard model of economics, par excellence.

In keeping with the new findings linking neural architecture with economics that were explored in the previous chapters, it is relevant to take a close look at Hayek's influential thinking.

A Man of His Time

Hayek was a man of his time. *The Road to Serfdom*, his 1944 classic, made the case against socialist command economies. He argued that socialism, as collective or government ownership of the means of production, is not only unproductive, but also intrinsically not free.

Hayek felt that individual freedom could not exist under central planning and that private property is essential for both economic productivity and political freedom.

Later works essentially expanded on Hayek's original line of thought. *Law, Legislation, and Liberty*, published in three volumes by the University of Chicago Press (1973, 1976, & 1979), developed his concept of the spontaneous order of the free market. In *The Fatal Conceit* (1988), he attacked the assumption of socialism that the spontaneous institutions and practices of the market can be done away with in creating a command economy.

DOI: 10.4324/9781003303190-18

In the years following the collapse of the Soviet Union, Hayek's position has become, in large part, conventional wisdom.

Hayek spent many of his years in the United States, principally at the University of Chicago where he interacted with numerous prominent economic thinkers. He received the Nobel Prize for economics in 1974.

Spontaneous Order vs. the Invisible Hand

Of special interest here is Hayek's concept of spontaneous order. On the face of it, the concept sounds similar to Adam Smith's Invisible Hand. Hayek saw this similarity and acknowledged it.

The two concepts, however, are significantly different. Hayek's spontaneous order was an order based on the rule of law. Individuals could exchange and interact with each other freely, limited only by the rules of civil society.

There was no place in his spontaneous order for the role of sympathy, fellow-feeling, or benevolence as Adam Smith saw it. In fact, Hayek saw such moral feeling as injurious to the production of wealth and its equitable distribution. Hayek's spontaneous order was the Invisible Hand without the reciprocal of Empathy.

Or was it? Let's take a closer look at Hayek's thinking, especially since it is so widely accepted today.

Moral Instincts: Impediments to the Market System

Unlike Thomas Hobbes, Hayek acknowledges that we are not just self-interested but also have moral instincts. He sees these moral instincts, however, as unhelpful in the spontaneous order.

In fact, he insists that the moral instincts that we inherited from the face-to-face societies of our primitive ancestors are the chief obstacle to the moral approval of the market system that creates our wealth. This somewhat counter-intuitive contention by Hayek deserves some inspection.

Moral Instincts: As Primitive Necessity

According to Hayek, these moral instincts, driving concern for the visible needs of others, were necessary to the survival of the group in primitive times. Such moral instincts required that we consciously try to benefit others.

Self-interest as Market Rule of Conduct

The market system, on the other hand required that we concentrate on our own self-interested gain in order to achieve, unknowingly and unintentionally, the best outcome for others. This market rule of conduct conflicts with our inherited moral instincts because we cannot see the benefit to others of our own self-interested efforts in the impersonal market.

Conscious Pursuit of Social Justice: As Destructive Mirage

The moral discomfort we feel, then, leads to the idea that we must consciously act to bring about social justice. This idea, in turn, interferes with the proper functioning of the market and is conversely destructive of the wealth necessary to provide benefits to all.

From this Hayek concludes that the conscious pursuit of social justice is a mirage and destructive of the spontaneous order under which the unrestricted free market will take care of social justice automatically.

Implicit Empathy: Law and the Rules of Civil Society

Hayek denies a role for Empathy—or, as he sees it from his mid-twentieth-century perspective, moral instincts—in the free enterprise market.

But does his system, in fact, omit Empathy as a necessary component of the market?

To answer this question, we need to get past the rhetoric— past the obvious— to the basic reality. When we do this, we see that Hayek builds Empathy implicitly into his system.

As a constitutional theoretical lawyer, Hayek lays the requirement for the free enterprise market in the rule of law combined with the rules of civil society. Both are implicit expressions of Empathy. Both mandate concern for the interest of others or all.

Law, of course, empathetically enforces and guarantees protection of everyone's private property, requires people to keep their word in the form of their contractual agreements, and demands they avoid cheating, committing fraud, and other criminal behavior inherently harmful to others.

The rules of civil society empathetically require courtesy, consideration of others, and playing by the established fair play rules of the game.

Hayek, then, implicitly and apparently unknowingly, sets, by law and civil behavior, the essential empathetic framework within which the supposedly unrestricted free market must work. Indeed, owing to the scale of inclusiveness, no vast market system could work without them.

Hayek, thus, sets fair rules and assumes fair outcomes. Given this setup, Hayek clearly feels we should not waste our energies worrying individually about social justice. The system, as defined, will take care of that by itself—if we just go for it, egoistically.

In other words, given the right framework, we can proceed to behave like sociopaths in the market, with the assurance that all will work out well for the good of us all.

A *Not So Spontaneous* Order

From within the framework of the rule of law and the requirements of civility, Hayek assumes a spontaneous order will proceed. Actually, within the framework so defined, it would be stretching the point to call any emergent order *spontaneous*. At best it would be a guided, channeled, or facilitated order.

Hopefulness and Wishful Thinking

Hayek's case is, therefore, a hopeful one based, in part, upon implicit, unclarified assumptions and wishful thinking. We can understand and appreciate his motivation as a reaction to the abuses if not horrors of National Socialism in Germany and the failure of command, centrally planned economies under communism.

Nevertheless, his position is, at best, a theoretical, if not an ideological one. There is very little evidence to support the positive and relatively balanced outcomes that he anticipates from an unrestricted market, bound only by the minimal rule of law and civility. And because of the harshness involved in establishing such a market, no government has yet been able politically to implement such a system.

Although the evidence is clear that a relatively free market (there has never been a completely free market) does produce more wealth than centrally planned or centrally controlled ones, there is no evidence to show that the unfettered market achieves, on its own, anywhere near an equitable distribution or even the elimination of poverty.

There are just too many obstructions—among them the very scale of inclusiveness itself—that prevent the natural tendency from achieving its ideal equilibrium state.

Resolving the Hayekian Conflict

However, the conflict Hayek sees between the market and our inherited moral instincts can be resolved with a proper understanding of his own implicit assumptions coupled with a grasp of the evolutionary structure of the market as the institutionalized expression of our neural architecture.

Just knowing that the productive, supplying side of the equation is fundamentally an expression of mammalian nurturing should relieve the moral discomfort somewhat.

Moreover, paying close attention to one's productive enterprise—that is, insuring quality of product and service, being trustworthy and honest in business relationships, having concern for consumer safety and welfare—is not simply and solely self-interest.

It is, rather, the combined expression of self-interest and Empathy that is necessary to a proper working of the free enterprise market system. The essential Empathy component may be implicit and obscured as in Hayek's system; or it may be explicit as in the acknowledged dynamic of our social exchange neural architecture.

Market Structure and Market Competition

It is, also, important at this point to keep in mind the real nature of market competition. Competition can be properly understood by holding in memory the distinction made in Chapter 10 between market structure and market behavior.

In the institutionalized market structure—especially in the ideal of the perfectly competitive market (PCM)—expressing the dynamic of our neural architecture, behavior is different toward competitors than toward customers. This critical distinction is often forgotten or not grasped in the first place.

In the mammalian structure of the market, suppliers and producers *compete*—not with customers or buyers—but with each other to *serve* or *provide* for the needs of the *customers or buyers*. The very structure of the PCM requires or forces this as a fundamental posture.

Providers or sellers don't *compete* with the customers to see if they can delude, outfox, or rip them off. Although this is a flawed posture that some seem to fall into. They compete with other providers.

To repeat—market competition, then, is not between providers and customers. It is between sellers and providers, to better serve the demands of customers—and, of course, to receive in reciprocity the reward or profit they well deserve for so doing.

Structural Empathy and Behavioral Empathy

Empathy always plays its reciprocal role in the market. That role may be structural, behavioral, or both.

In the PCM, confronting the relentless fact of market competition, suppliers—to survive in the market—*must* perform the *structural* equivalent of Empathy.

They *must* do so even if they do not feel Empathy as a personal motivation. That is, in the face of competition from other suppliers, they must provide the best possible product or service at the lowest possible price to meet the needs of the customers. If they fail to do either, they will eventually be driven out of business by competitors who do both.

Here, again, I might repeat the quote from nobelist Milton Friedman cited previously in Chapter 10. Without knowledge of our mammalian neural architecture, he makes essentially the same point in different terms:

> So long as effective freedom of exchange is maintained, the central feature of the market organization of economic activity is that it prevents one person from interfering with another in respect of most of his activities. The consumer is protected from coercion by the seller because of the presence of other sellers with whom he can deal.
>
> (1962: 14)

On the other hand, however, if suppliers perform their services with concern for quality, care for the well-being of the customer, with a sense of social responsibility, and with a commitment to fair play, they express Empathy in behavior. Empathy in market behavior builds trust and in the long run reduces the costs of market transactions.

Empathy in behavior may also act as a limiting influence on the runaway corporate greed we see so flagrantly practiced in the market.

At least the acknowledgment of Empathy's primary motive status would undercut the moral rationale for greed implicitly provided by the emphasis on self-interest as a sole primary motive.

This faulty overemphasis on self-interest characterizes Hayek's so-called spontaneous order as pervasively as it does mainstream economics.

The free enterprise market, when properly understood, then, does *not* conflict with what Hayek calls our inherited moral instincts (Empathy), but provides the opportunity to consciously and intentionally satisfy them.

Creativity, Innovation, and the Free Enterprise Market

A proper grasp of the dynamic nature of the competitive free enterprise market leads to a better understanding of one of its most important features—its remarkable creativity.

Creativity

As providers or suppliers seek, under terms of full and relatively free competition, to better respond empathetically to the needs, wants, and desires of the buyers, they each seek differential advantage in so doing. The natural outcome is a process of continuous innovation and creativity.

The very institutionalized Ego/Empathy dynamic structure of the ideal market not only forces but also incents this posture. In a dynamic, competitive market, those providers who fail to innovate, fail to survive. Competition among suppliers and providers is essential to the innovative, creative process.

Creative Destruction and Innovation: Whither Go'ist?

Economist Joseph Schumpeter coined the term *creative destruction* to characterize this constantly innovative aspect of the economy of capitalism (Schumpeter 1942). Creative destruction and creative innovation are but two sides of the same coin.

Lacking an understanding of the true nature of the market as the expression of our neural dynamic, Hayek, however, was unable to grasp the essential structural role of Empathy in the creativity of the competitive market.

Schumpeter, writing in 1942, saw the capitalist entrepreneur always seeking new commodities, new technologies, new sources of supply, and new organizational forms. This process brought large-scale change if not upheaval. The great advances brought by computer and information technology seem to bear out Schumpeter's vision.

Additionally, Schumpeter saw an inevitable tendency toward socialism propelled by this dynamic innovative, destructive aspect of capitalism. It remains to be seen if he eventually proves right on that score.

Creativity and innovation continue to be at a premium in the competitive high tech environment.

Creative Destruction, Sustainability, and Inequality

Of course, as Schumpeter recognized, there are dangerous side effects to this unrestrained innovation and creativity. We face the rapid depletion of resources, the pollution of the environment, global climate change—even international conflict.

There is also the problem of inequalities. Such effects might provoke political intervention that stifles the productivity of the system. How to cope adequately with such side effects constitutes one of the greatest challenges facing the free enterprise system in the new century.

This takes us back to the problem of Hayek's spontaneous order.

Pragmatism vs. Ideology: Responding to Market Failure

Despite the wishful thinking of Hayek's poorly comprehended *not so spontaneous order*, the market fails. And in recent decades, it does so dramatically.

With the variability of the tug-and-pull of Ego and Empathy within the market structure, the scale of inclusiveness, and other blocking factors, the market notably falls short of achieving its anticipated or predicted equilibrium states.

In the vast markets of today, there is more than ample room for market failure and the creation of undue suffering and inequality—even the persistent poverty we see existing among riches.

Such market failure permits the creation and accumulation of undesirable and destructive levels of socio-behavioral tension. To cope with this I believe we must take a pragmatic approach, not an ideological one.

In any countermeasures, however, we must keep the market sufficiently free to incent for production and the creative growth of wealth. At the same time we must assist the market where it fails to provide adequately or achieve an acceptable level of equitable distribution. Our responses to market failure should be pragmatic and situational, not ideological, or based upon wishful thinking with little evidence to back it.

Hayek's naïve concept of spontaneous order, which excludes, presumptively if not actually, both the structural and behavioral role of Empathy, fails before the new evidence from evolutionary neuroscience.

The structure of the market, as the expression of the interplay between self-preservation and mammalian nurturing, provides the basic dynamic for the intuited Invisible Hand. The neural dynamic is the causal underpinning for the emergence of any spontaneous order. Empathy, or our moral instinct, properly understood, constitutes the necessary reciprocal for any market to exist.

Hayek's concept of spontaneous order is, in the final analysis, no improvement on Adam Smith's intuitive concept of the Invisible Hand. It is, in effect, a step backward, modified somewhat by law and civility, to the earlier position of Mandeville in his *Fable of the Bees.* (See Bianchi [1992] for an interpretation of Hayek's debt to Mandeville.)

17 Nash

Modeling Equilibrium with Beautiful Minds, Beautiful Equations

This chapter applies the social brain dynamic to economics with a look at a more popular theme. We were captivated by the story of Nobel recipient John Nash. Our fascination derived more, perhaps, from the human-interest story than the mathematical achievements themselves.

A Dose of Mystique and Weirdness

The book and the movie *A Beautiful Mind* played upon the mystique of mathematics as well as the popular fantasy that insanity and genius are closely related. We like to believe in the mysterious. And we also like to think that those who are different from us are a bit weird. Both mystique and weirdness played together to capture the popular imagination.

But mystique and weirdness contribute nothing to understanding. They, in fact, get in the way. Mystique emerges from superstition; weirdness from ignorance. Neither have a legitimate place in science.

And neither help to clarify the nature of the so-called Nash equilibrium. Nash himself did not grasp the underlying dynamic necessary to such equilibria. In fact, the fundamental nature of the Nash equilibrium remains unclarified to this date.

Dangling in Space

As it stands the Nash equilibrium is simply a concocted mathematical structure without inherent roots. It dangles unanchored out in mathematical space tethered only tenuously to reality by the statement of arbitrary and not justified conditions, assumptions, and axioms, accepted as given and not subject to challenge—constraints called forth from the depths of a source unknown.

Why then has it drawn so much attention in the social sciences?

The Mystique of Mathematics

The answer is: Partly because of the mystique about mathematics. Partly because of its perceived utility.

DOI: 10.4324/9781003303190-19

Representation vs. Reality

Math has been exceptionally useful in physics. What we require in physics is a good mathematical *representation* of a physical reality so that we can manipulate it and perhaps eventually control it. The key word here is *representation.*

Mathematics *represents* the reality. It is not the reality itself. And it does not have the same authority.

Anything that can be systematically discriminated—time, space, speed, or change can be disassembled and reassembled tautologically, following the patterns of our neural network architecture, by clarifying, refining, and re-invoking the same relationships that held in the initial discriminations.

In such cases math can be made to have application to the real world.

But then the mystique makers take it further. Captivated by the seeming ethereal uniformity of brain-discriminated and created units of representation—their so-called symbolic beauty—many have seen math as existing independently of the human brain that creates it.

The Platonic Romance

Such persons see the elements of math as platonic universals having an existence in the universe independent of humans or anything else. Perfect forms in themselves. Forms themselves existing without substance but strangely applicable to all substance.

It is quite a romance, this platonic math—this math of pure forms. But pure forms are one thing, utility in reality another. The success of math in representing, describing, and quantifying the forces and processes of real-life physics is quite impressive. It is also understandable.

Dancing Among Arbitrary Discriminations

There is, thus, an inherent duality in our perception of math.

On the one hand, in applying math to physics as well as our daily lives, we are playing back and forth across the patterns of our neural architecture upon our own arbitrary units of discrimination. The fact that the units seem inherent in our neural architecture leads easily to the platonic illusion.

On the other hand, math has proven of great heuristic tool for clarification of the relationships among matter-energy, time-space. This is an accomplishment of substance—not the speculative and highly dubious platonic math of pure and empty form.

Math need not dangle, disembodied and unanchored, devoid of meaning but esthetically beautiful, in empty space. Math can lead us to something of value, some dynamic reality.

But the mystique of math combines the two, the empty speculation as well as the discovery and description of substance. The success of math in quantifying the discriminations of physics has inspired envy and mimicry by the social sciences.

And the social sciences have imported not one but both aspects of the mystique indiscriminately.

Mathematical Mystique and the Social Sciences

The social sciences have thus become pervaded with mathematics.

Not necessarily meaningful mathematics. But math for the sake of math. Entire journals are dedicated to such exercises. Almost all journals are infected by them. No matter how insignificant the research questions, if the math is presented in good form, the article is almost always judged on just that alone.

The result is an outpouring, an overwhelming cascade of the trivial, transient, and ephemeral. Snapshots in time of shifting, moving, amorphous and dubious variables with no long term or generalizable significance. Mathematical manipulation of trivia almost totally lacking in social, economic, or political utility. Form without substance.

Appeal of the Nash Equilibrium

Why then has the Nash equilibrium captured the imagination of so many and been so widely called upon?

Because it is expressed in terms of formal math, thus indulging our fascination with mystique? Probably.

But also equally probably because it is innately, subjectively appealing. Why the subjective appeal? What social reality, if any, does the Nash equilibrium connect with that makes it intuitively appealing to us?

If it does connect, we should be able to see its outcomes, its applications. We should also be able to discover the dynamic upon which it turns gropingly in the yet unpenetrated shadows of causality.

Pre-gravity and the Nash Equilibrium

Consider this: we know the cause of the force of gravity. Before we knew the cause and properly described it, we just knew that things fell off other things in an earthward direction. They always fell down. They never fell up, except temporarily when impelled by an identifiable force.

We are still in the pre-causal-gravity-stage of understanding the Nash equilibrium. Nash's formalized artifice seemingly grasps at a social phenomenon—not as clearcut as gravity—but we think we see something like it occurring out there.

We follow Nash through elaborate formal symbolism to try to frame the elusive dynamic—to prove our subjective intuition of its importance and reality. Yet we haven't the foggiest idea of why it does what it does. We have no grasp of the causal dynamic.

Where should we look?

The Clues in the Conditions, Assumptions, and Axioms

Perhaps we should look first at the triad upon which Nash's formalization is based: the conditions, assumptions, and axioms.

These are the givens. They are not to be questioned. They are asserted—the framework that the dynamic must work within to achieve the equilibrium.

But where do they come from?

Anybody's guess. The mathematician doesn't justify them or explain them. Like the first premises of the French renaissance philosopher, Rene Descartes, they come from intuition or common sense without having to be established or justified.

By postulating the triad, the mathematician gropingly attempts to see if she or he can corral the intuitive, vaguely apprehended causal dynamics. This approach has heuristic or exploratory value. It can lead to eventual discovery and definition of the causal dynamics. But it is not a very scientific or objectively empirical beginning.

Rather, it is a highly subjective one. Nevertheless, in the conditions, assumptions, and axioms may lay clues to the unarticulated, indeed not understood, dynamic. What are they saying or suggesting about the dynamic? Which amorphous unspecified force are they trying to corral?

The Social Equation as the Causal Dynamic

The Nash equilibrium as conceived by John Nash applies to human behavioral interactions.

And Nash's modeling proceeds like standard economic theory on the explicit assumption of rational self-interest as the primary motive.

Some game theorists have applied Nash's methodology to nonbehavioral situations in such areas as ecology, gene theory, and population biology. Such efforts draw on Nash's formalism, but they tap a different fundamental dynamic. They are at best analogous in form only. They are not and should not be called Nash equilibria.

The Nash equilibrium is always social and the social equation is the dynamic underlying the Nash equilibrium. Without the social dynamic the equilibrium—even the assumption of the equilibrium—would be impossible.

Although entirely dependent on the social dynamic, the Nash equilibrium is not based on a conscious grasp or clearly stated articulation of that dynamic.

Empathy as Implicit in the Nash Equilibrium

The *essential* condition of a Nash equilibrium is a social exchange relationship—or a social game as implied and treated by the terminology of formal and mathematical game theory.

And there could be no social exchange without Empathy. Social exchange requires the ability to put oneself in the other's shoes, otherwise one would not be able to appreciate or evaluate the preferences of another.

The understanding and evaluation of other's preferences are essential to a Nash equilibrium. The understanding and evaluation of other's preferences are also fundamental to any concept of Empathy. Empathy, then, is foundational to any concept of a Nash equilibrium.

It appears not to be only because it is obscured by the formal methodology. We should not be fooled by this.

Empathy: A Foundational, but Unclarified Assumption

Empathy, then, is a foundational, but unclarified assumption of any Nash equilibrium.

But does it sometimes appear explicitly? Yes, it does.

To see this we must go to the original statements by Nash himself, avoiding some later extensions of his work which in some cases have become so overly formalized as to be totally vacuous abstract exercises.

Noncooperative vs. Cooperative Games: Implicit vs. Explicit Empathy

First we have to look at Nash's distinction between noncooperative and cooperative games.

In both games players reach an equilibrium in which no player may improve his/her position as long as other players maintain theirs.

Noncooperative Games

In noncooperative games, no prior negotiation or agreement is assumed. Individual players just act on their own independently.

But don't be fooled. The action inevitably takes place within a *social context*. Without the social context, there is no game. The social context, then, is crucial. Preferences of others must be understood and evaluated.

And besides, Nash lays on the requirement of "accepted ethics of fair play" (1951: 294). Fair play means we play by the rules and respect the rights of others. Such is the essence of Empathy. Empathy is implicit but nevertheless clearly required.

Cooperative Games

In cooperative games, prior negotiation and agreement take place. This is the only distinction between cooperative and noncooperative games.

In the negotiation and agreement of cooperative games, the role of Empathy becomes more obvious. To bargain and reach agreement *explicitly* requires the ability to understand, evaluate, and respect other's preferences, strengths, and so on.

Even when the additional condition of enforcement by a referee is added (1951: 295), this represents in itself just another agreement requiring Empathy.

Without the agreements and ethics of fair play—the implicit and necessary Empathy—the structure of both noncooperative and cooperative games, as conceived by Nash, simply collapses.

The games become impossible, except perhaps in the most trivial, inconsequential form. Solutions become random.

The Name of the Game: Accommodating Self-interest and Empathy

Both noncooperative and cooperative games then involve the estimation and accommodation of self- and other-interest (Empathy).

In fact that's what the game is all about.

Further Examples

Let's take some further examples from Nash's own words.

In an early paper (1950), titled *The Bargaining Problem*, Nash opens with the following statement: "A two person bargaining situation involves two individuals who have the opportunity to collaborate for mutual benefit" (1950: 155).

"Mutual benefit" engages Ego and Empathy. It implies a chance to balance self- and other-interest.

The game further requires equal bargaining skill, full knowledge of each other's preferences, the agreement of the two parties on what is a fair bargain, and both a give (Empathy) and take (Ego) between the two (1950: 159, 161). Empathy is, thus, clearly fundamental in this paper.

In a later paper (1953) called the *Two-Person Cooperative Game*, Nash expands on the bargaining problem. He writes:

> The theory presented here was developed to treat economic (or other) situations involving two individuals whose interests are neither completely opposed nor completely coincident. The word cooperative is used because the two individuals are supposed to be able to discuss the situation and agree on a rational joint plan of action.

This statement clearly requires consideration of self- and other-interest and a consent to give and take within agreed rules.

The concept of a Nash equilibrium, as conceived by Nash, thus, rests clearly on the causal dynamic of the reciprocal algorithms of our evolved neural architecture.

In terms of the social equation, a Nash equilibrium is an equilibrium that approaches dynamic balance as well as optimizing utilities.

The Shortfalls of the Game Model: Inherent Blindness to Social Dangers

There are several shortfalls of the game model set out by Nash. Most of these Nash himself acknowledged. Some of them characterize almost all mathematical and economic modeling. De ja vu. Some, if not all, of these shortfalls also apply to the formalized modeling of GET discussed in Chapter 11.

Shortfalls or Limitations

Some, but not all, of these shortfalls or limitations are:

1. The modeling is highly idealized. This is openly stated by Nash and is necessary to get where he wants to go with his modeling. Highly idealized means the formalized modeling is divorced from the messy details of reality as we saw in the formalized modeling of GET. It has none of the rich texture of real-life situations.
2. It is totally dependent on the stated conditions, assumptions, and axioms. These are not justified but are asserted subjectively from intuition. They are all dubious in reality.
3. It doesn't deal with ongoing change. It fixes a transaction or situation artificially at a moment in time. It can't deal with change except at another artificially fixed moment in time. It can't and doesn't deal with shifting reality.
4. It draws on the causal social dynamic, but doesn't identify it. Further, it falls short of grasping the fullness or significance of the dynamic. Like most transactional analysis in economics, it is incomplete. It misses reality in truly important ways. Listed below are a few of these ways.
    a. It assumes the game is complete at the chosen moment in time. It allows for no after effects.
    b. It doesn't tell whether the players like their best solutions. The solutions are the best under the extensively stipulated conditions, assumptions, and axioms.
    c. It obscures the effects of behavioral tension. If players are dissatisfied, feel cheated, have ambition to do better, and are motivated to change their outcomes, this means that, in reality, the game is not over! The game solution, then, just represents a snapshot in time of an ongoing process (e.g., see d'Autume 1997: 241).
    d. It obscures the cumulative effects of transactions. Given the human capacity for memory and the dynamic of behavioral tension, these cumulative effects are, in reality, potentially very significant.

Blindness to Dangers

The modeling lacks any predictability for cumulative behavioral tension that might motivate change or even revolution to redress the progressive, less than equal or less than dynamically-balanced, so-called equilibrium solutions.

The obscuring of the behavioral tension inherent to the dynamic of social neural architecture is the most serious reality flaw in the modeling. The game of the moment is only over for the mathematician or economist who is doing the modeling.

In reality—for the rest of us—the game goes on with cumulative, potentially momentous and dangerous effects. It may even blow up in our faces. The modeling blinds us to the cumulative dangers that may confront us, economically and politically.

Practical Wisdom vs. Obfuscation

In sum, Nash's modeling intuits and rides upon the causal dynamic of the social architecture. It rests implicitly upon the social equation.

Subjectivity in the Guise of Formality

Nash, however, has no consciously articulated concept of such a dynamic. He tries gropingly to corral the intuited but undefined dynamic by a formal framework of conditions, assumptions, and axioms mediated by symbols—all largely subjectively based.

As constructed, the entire edifice rests not upon empirical reality, but upon intuition and subjectivity. Only the mathematical formality gives it unjustifiably the aura of objectivity. It is not objective, but only formal.

By the time all the conditions, assumptions, and axioms are added in to force the solutions, the connection with reality is often very tenuous indeed.

The Utility of Modeling

There is, nevertheless, some real utility in such modeling.

It is useful to the extent that it helps us to focus attention, identify alternatives, and to facilitate systematic thinking. In other words, it can be a helpful tool as long as we don't take it too seriously, or endow it and its practitioners with an unwarranted mystique of infallibility.

Of course, the mystique is facilitated and played upon for effect by the entertainment industry which regularly shows actors, representing geniuses, in front of chalkboards full of esoteric mathematical symbols designed to befuddle and awe-inspire the unsophisticated viewer.

Part III
The Wider Context

18 The Emergence and Promise of Neuroeconomics

Neuroeconomics is a new discipline that emerged upon the field in the late 1990s. It aims essentially at bringing together the imaging methodology of medical neuroscience with the questions of economics.

Paul Glimcher, one of the pioneers of neuroeconomics, puts it somewhat more ambitiously:

> The ultimate goal of any neuroeconomic approach must be to provide an overarching theory of how the computations that underlie behavior are organized and produced by the brain.
>
> (2003: 322)

Neuroeconomics and Consilience

Neuroeconomics, as an interdisciplinary effort, has potential to advance my favorite direction in science—*consilience*, as Ed Wilson of Harvard dubbed it (1998)—the unification of the natural and the social sciences. I have, therefore, high hopes for neuroeconomics.

My own first effort at unification of the natural with the social sciences was my doctoral dissertation done at Stanford in the early 1970s under Air Force sponsorship. Since, at that time I was a somewhat senior regular Air Force officer with successful hands-on experience in the intricacies of sensitive international activities in East Asia, I was enrolled in the political science department.

My dissertation was titled *The Biopsychological Basis of Political Socialization and Political Culture* (1974). The term *biopsychological* was used because *neuroscience* was not a well-known term in those days. Also, despite the necessary emphasis on political science terminology—which I was being paid to study—I was fascinated by the implications for the whole range of social sciences, especially economics, sociology, and anthropology.

Since then, and wishing to advance the cause of consilience, I believe I have written more books bearing *consilience* in the title than any other academic author. They are: *Toward Consilience: The Bioneurological Basis of Thought, Behavior, Language, and Experience* (KluwerAcademic/Plenum) (2000); *The Consilient Brain: the Bioneurological Basis of Economics, Society, and Politics* (Kluwer

DOI: 10.4324/9781003303190-21

Academic /Plenum)(2004); *Consilience and Spirituality: the Scientific Foundations for the Choice to Believe or Not to Believe* (2009); *Consilience, Brains, and Markets: Saving the Free Enterprise Market for a Global Society* (2010); and *Consilience, Brains, and Leadership: The Emergence of Human Alliance* (2012).

The latter two were published in Chinese translation by Fudan University, Shanghai in 2011 and 2013 respectively. I was honored to be Fudan University Press's celebrated author in the Shanghai Book Fair 2013. The last three books were published by the press of International Technological University, a high tech graduate university located in Silicon Valley where, in the most recent decade, I had been a teaching professor as well as executive academic vice-president.

The Challenge and Promise of Neuroeconomics

Back to neuroeconomics. The emergent discipline has been motivated largely by the new imaging techniques of medical neuroscience. In truth, it seems governed principally by the well-known law of instrument—that is, "give a kid a hammer and he will find something to nail." It has been criticized for its fascination with and overuse of *f*mri (functional magnetic resonance imaging) and other issues (Ross, forthcoming).

For me, the disconcerting feature of *f*mri neuroeconomics is that it shows no connection with or knowledge of evolutionary neuroscience, which has been around considerably longer and has long been influential in medicine. Perhaps this is owing to the somewhat taboo status of evolutionary studies in the United States.

Or perhaps the neglect is due to the highly inaccurate, prejudicial, and unscholarly reviews of Paul MacLean's masterwork, *The Triune Brain in Evolution: Role in Paleocerebral Functions* (1990) in the leading journals *Science* (1990) and *American Scientist* (1992). Hopefully Ann Butler's very helpful article discussed in Chapter 2 will facilitate moving forward in the consilience efforts.

Steven Pinker was a victim of the *Science* review and his own lack of scholarly due diligence in his virtual caricature of MacLean's work (Pinker 1997: 370, 580). Paul MacLean was the leading scholar in evolutionary neuroscience of the second half of the twentieth century. Or perhaps the neglect is just a result of the isolated, departmented (silo-ed) character of the sciences in American universities. They simply don't talk to each other enough, if at all.

The theory (and the CSN model) presented in the first chapters of this book and applied throughout is a highly integrated, overarching theory based on updated evolutionary and medical neuroscience. Its relevance and applications to economics are sweeping and have been demonstrated in previous chapters of this book as well as my earlier works.

It is my conviction that the current research program of neuroeconomics, if done with care, can help to fill out the detail of the neural circuitry relevant to economics. I have cited some of its contributions in earlier chapters. I believe, however, that it will not change substantially the utility or accuracy of the highly integrated theory built upon the evolutionary perspective. The evolutionary fact that we humans are mammals is hardly arguable.

The transition from the ancestral amniote line to the synapsid line that evolved into mammals was a landmark evolutionary event leading to us humans. That evolutionary process produced the neural architecture or social brain that we share. That social brain is characterized by self-preservation and caring for others expressed at a high level of integration as Ego and Empathy. The main elements of the circuitry have been known for some time but the circuitry is very complex and much more research is needed on fully defining the details.

A Noteworthy Exception

Neuroeconomist Paul Zak is an exception to the above cited law of instrument. Instead of relying on *f*mri, he uses blood drawing and analysis for his study of oxytocin, a mammalian neurotransmitter and hormone. A cautionary tale is represented in Zak's emphasis on some effects of oxytocin. His singling it out as the "moral molecule" may be a bit of marketing overstatement. Oxytocin has its effects acting within and upon a complex network of interacting hormones, neurotransmitters, and neural circuitry. Several criticisms have called it an oversimplification.

For example, Ulrich J. Pfeiffer, of the Neuroimaging Group, Department of Psychiatry, University Hospital Cologne, Cologne, Germany has criticized Zak's oversimplification and concluded with the following:

> recent results demonstrate that the oversimplified view of the "moral molecule" is misleading and treacherous. Although further research is needed, it is conceivable that depending on the interaction partner and the context of an interaction, oxytocin might exert as many antisocial (or negative approach-related) as prosocial effects.
>
> (2013: 10)

There is also experimental evidence that culture affects the expression of oxytocin (e.g., Sherman, et al. 2009). For a more complete understanding we must also examine further the epigenetic effects of environmental experience and prior learning on higher and lower doses of oxytocin.

In the closing chapter of *The Moral Molecule* (2012) Zak sets up what could be seen as a war between testosterone and oxytocin. I feel a bit uncomfortable about so bald an adversarial posturing over hormones that have proved vital to our survival in the past. We should remember that the various hormones and neurotransmitters need to operate in relative balance or homeostasis to guide our behavior. Disturbing that balance by sniffing or other methodology is an interesting experiment that helps to confirm one if not all the functions of oxytocin—but we should be cautious.

Mostly, in real life, hormones are stimulated by environmental events and are designed to preserve us by motivating appropriate behavioral responses for survival and other good things. I spent over 20 years as a military officer during the turbulent decades of the 1950s, 1960s, and 1970s—Yes, I am old! Since a positive imbalance of oxytocin often makes people more trusting, I can think of many instances in which an overdose of oxytocin could be harmful or even fatal. In our ongoing nuclear negotiations with North Korea and Iran, should we have our team use oxytocin nose spray to increase their trust of the North Korean and Iranian negotiators?

The second to last paragraph of Zak's interesting book raises some other concerns for me. He writes:

> My mother's faith also held that "the kingdom of God is within you," which is, at its root, a very bottom-up kind of idea. God is love. God is within you. Oxytocin is love. Oxytocin is within you.

Such statements are reminiscent of the flower child days of the 1960s and the Beatles' famous song "All You Need is Love." The song was first broadcast to millions of viewers in 1967 at the height of the Vietnam War. Perhaps it could be viewed over simplistically as an oxytocin-driven response to the testosterone-driven dynamics of the unpopular war.

One molecule a panacea for all that ails! I am always a little suspicious of true believers. The statement also makes me wonder why the book wasn't titled instead—*The God Molecule*. The precedent has been set. Other authors, who searched for the most basic particle of physics, called their book *The God Particle* (Lederman & Terisi 1993).

I guess, then, I would caution modesty. I am personally more comfortable with a dynamic balance of our evolved archetypal neural circuitries. Being out-of-balance seems to be the source of most social tensions. Scholars, to include myself, should perhaps be cautious and moderate the enthusiasm over our findings and publications. In short, avoid the temptation of marketing overhype.

At any rate, neuroeconomics is an exciting new approach, so even if we stumble a bit in our enthusiasm, it will go on. Especially as the grant money keeps pouring in. The further detailing of the relevant circuitry of our mammalian neural architecture unquestionably is an important scientific quest and may prove to be the lasting contribution of the neuroeconomic approach.

19 The Larger Context

The Stiff Upper Lip, Original Sin, and Western Science

In this chapter I shift from a primary focus on the market and economics to the larger context of Western science within which economics exists and from which it draws perspective if not inspiration.

The "Silo" Effect of Departmented Academia

There is, of course, no real separating of the subject matter across the social sciences. Our academic disciplines, our departmented university systems, force artificial divides upon the seamless texture of society as well as their consilient unity with the natural sciences (e.g., Cory 2000b: 15; Margulis 1998: 26; Dyson 1999: 2).

These artificial divides produce a "silo" effect, similar to that of the financial sector that so disastrously impacted the subprime economic crisis of 2008 and 2009 (see Tett 2009).

Often this "silo"-ed effect introduces confusion and distortion into an otherwise seamless fabric—splitting it by alternative language, definitions, and concepts that in many cases only say the same things in different ways.

So I will almost inevitably continue to draw upon the themes of economics as I make the transition into the issues of the wider context.

The Wider Context

In Chapter 9, I blamed the misrepresentation of Adam Smith on merchants eager to escape the intrusive micromanagement of the mercantilistic bureaucracy. Like all one-dimensional explanations, this was a partial explanation of a more complicated subject.

For a more complete understanding we must look to the larger social and intellectual context. This context was colored by centuries of the Judeo-Christian tradition with its emphasis on the struggle between good and evil.

DOI: 10.4324/9781003303190-22

The Judeo-Christian Tradition: Cosmic Good and Evil Plus Original Sin

In the Judeo-Christian tradition, which dominated the Western world across the centuries from the fall of the Roman Empire to the Renaissance, good and evil were seen as cosmic forces personified as the Deity versus Satan. Central to this dichotomous tradition was the doctrine of original sin. Humans fell to the temptations of evil Satan to be ultimately redeemed by the Deity of goodness.

The Enlightenment: Is Human Nature Good or Evil?

As England and other parts of Europe emerged from the tradition-bound Middle Ages into the Enlightenment, the religious dichotomy took on a secular form. The struggle between good and evil was shifted into human nature itself. The big question became: Was human nature good or evil? As is customary in human affairs scholars split on this issue.

Human Nature as Evil

One stream of thought, in keeping with the Judeo-Christian tradition and the doctrine of original sin, saw humans as evil.

This group was represented in part by the English philosopher Thomas Hobbes (1588–1679) who held forth in his *Leviathan* that men must submit to an absolute ruler in order to control their conflicting, self-interested motives and assure their safety in an orderly society.

Hobbes saw humans as motivated by two forces: self-preservation and the desire for conquest. On this belief, in the absence of an absolute sovereign, Hobbes saw the natural state of humans as a war of all against all.

Human Nature with Good Moral Sense

An alternative group centering around the thought of John Locke (1632–1704) saw humans as having a strong sense of moral obligation as well as self-interest. Based upon his perception of human nature, Locke argued for a limited rather than absolute form of government. Adam Smith, with his dual concept of self-interest and fellow-feeling, fell closer to the position of Locke.

But the essential dichotomy prevailed in discussion. Evil was replaced with selfishness; good with morality and altruism.

Into the midst of this controversy was injected the momentous advent of Darwinian theory.

Charles Darwin: Survival, Self-Interest, and Altruism

With the publication of Charles Darwin's *The Origin of Species* (1859) seventy years after Adam Smith's death, the one-sided emphasis on self-interest, already running strong, was powerfully reinforced as the dominant view of humankind in the world of capitalism and capitalist economic thought.

Darwin's classic work created an intellectual revolution with its demonstration of evolution based on natural selection—with natural selection interpreted as the bloody struggle of the fittest to survive. His theory influenced almost every area of serious thought and stirred controversy throughout society.

The Misinterpretation of Darwin

Like Adam Smith, Darwin suffered from misinterpretation. "Fittest to survive," in Darwin's view, referred to reproductive success or fitness—the capacity to produce more descendants (see David Loye, 2007 for a comprehensive analysis of the misrepresentation of Darwin).

However, the more dramatic connotations of terms like "struggle" and "fittest" were seized upon by some zealous enthusiasts to evoke, in the words of the poet Alfred Lord Tennyson, "nature red with tooth and claw"—the personal struggle to the death for survival among nature's creatures.

This was, original sin—selfishness and self-interest—to the extreme.

Reinforcing Hobbes: The Rise of Social Darwinism

The bloody tooth and claw interpretation of Darwin's work certainly reinforced the already prevalent Hobbesian position.

It led to a philosophy called Social Darwinism, which excused all forms of economic exploitation and inequality as the natural and inevitable expression of the law of evolution—"the fittest to survive."

The wealthy were judged as more biologically fit than the poorer classes. Social Darwinism thrived in the latter part of the nineteenth century as a justification for such excesses of industrial capitalism as sweat shops, slums, and child labor. It was abandoned as an overtly influential school of thought because of its conspicuously negative social effects.

The Making of "Scientific" Economics

Parallel to the rise of the tooth and claw interpretation of Darwin, the nineteenth century launched the movement to a "scientific" economics.

The Moral Beginning

The academic or intellectual study of economics had previously been a moral enterprise. It was pursued primarily by moral philosophers like Frances Hutcheson, the mentor of Adam Smith, David Hume, Lord Shaftesbury, and Smith himself.

The Move to Newton: Economics and the Emergence of "Physics Envy"

Economic thinkers, however, who were inclined toward science, had always taken as ideal the model of Isaac Newton's physics and mathematics. Newton represented the epitome of science with his model of a clockwork universe working on immutable laws of physics. The well-known "physics envy" of the social sciences which prevails even today began here.

The Emergence of "Scientific" Amoral Economics

To model their scientific version of economics on physics and math, the "scientific" economists sought to be objective in the manner of physics and quantitative in the manner of math. The normative issue of morals had no place in an objective, positivistic economics bent on aping the prestige and success of physics.

Science was considered to be value-free or value neutral. Morals, underpinned by the motives of Adam Smith and other's fellow-feeling and sympathy, were declared unscientific and eliminated from the newly evolving economic calculus.

The Marriage of Induction and Deduction in Economics

The effort to move to a positivist economics involved the marriage of both inductive and deductive approaches. The inductive component required the collection and analysis of sufficient economic data. The deductive component required identifying the mathematical equations that represented the law-like relations of economic behavior.

Induction and Statistics

On the inductive side the emerging discipline of statistics provided the main empirical thrust. Acting in the path of notable predecessors—John Graunt (1620–74), Sir William Petty (1623–1687, Richard Cantillon (1680–1734?) and others—British scholars Thomas Tooke (1774–1858) and William Newmarch (1820–1882) set statistics firmly on course by publishing a six-volume work titled *History of Prices and the State of the Circulation from 1792 to 1856*.

This work constituted an extensive compilation and systematic ordering of empirical data for the period covered. In 1861, Newmarch commented in an address to the British Association for the Advancement of Science that economics, by drawing upon empirical, statistical data, had ceased to be an abstract science.

Newmarch further noted that the only safe basis on which we could establish economic laws was not hypothetical deduction but careful collection and analysis of empirical facts. From the standpoint of statistics, however, Newmarch was aware of the difference between the inductive approach and the deductive one of mathematics.

He stated that in statistics there was no body of general laws such as those found in the mathematical and physical sciences. Nevertheless, he viewed statistics as a useful tool for investigating recurring phenomena (1861: 457). This view suggested, of course, that *some* deductive methodology must be applied to make sense of the inductively acquired data.

Deduction: The Jevonsian Utilitarian Approach vs. the Cartesian/Walrasian Approach of GET

On the deductive side William Stanley Jevons (1835–1892) stands out. He is, in fact, considered the father of "scientific" utilitarian economics. The utilitarian approach of the Britisher Jevons is to be distinguished from the French grand Cartesian deductive approach of GET (general equilibrium theory). GET, as represented by Walras, was discussed earlier in Chapter 11.

Jevons, as appropriate to his utilitarian perspective, focused not on the grand design of GET but rather on the troublesome, yet fundamental issue of defining the concept of utility. He was drawn to new developments in physics. He openly copied the newly derived formulas of contemporary nineteenth-century physics on energy, changed the names of the variables, and applied them to the economic concept of utility.

Also, as an accomplished mathematician, Jevons sought to develop the deductive framework that could handle the statistical data produced by the likes of Newmarch.

Jevons: The Conscious Choice to Ignore Morals in Favor of Baser Self-interest

In developing this mathematical framework, borrowed from physics, Jevons made a conscious decision to ignore moral values in his economic analysis. It is important to note that Jevons did *not* deny the existence of caring, moral motives. He simply chose to eliminate them from consideration.

Jevons admittedly felt that the calculus of economics could best be built on the baser or self-interested motives of humans. He chose to give the fellow-feeling and sympathy of earlier thinkers no role in his calculus and focused on self-interest as the sole primary motive.

Jevons' deductive value choice, combined with the inductive emphasis on empirical data, resonated well with others who wished to model economics after mathematics and physics.

Effects and Aftereffects: A Historical Observation

Jevons stated his position in at least two of his publications. In the introduction to his *The Theory of Political Economy* (1888) he provided justification for his decision to exclude the higher moral motives of humanity and to concentrate on the lower self-interested ones in economics. In the same introduction he presented his case for economics as a mathematical science.

In the introduction to his *Essays on Economics* (1905), Jevons drew upon Jeremy Bentham's utilitarian philosophy (see Bentham 1789: Ch I, p. 1). He included all subjective economic forces under the utilitarian doctrine of maximizing pleasure and minimizing pain. This was matched by Freud's roughly contemporary co-opting of the same Benthamite proposition into the pleasure principle of psychoanalytic theory (Freud 1915–1917; 1920).

The All-Inclusive, Hedonic Approach: Obstructing the Interplay of Ego and Empathy

Thinking based on this principle is called the *hedonic approach*. This approach has recently been carried forward and developed by economic Nobelist Daniel Kahneman and associates in their edited volume on hedonic psychology (1999).

The very high level of generalization or integration of the hedonic approach is defensible and virtually inarguable at that particular high level. It has, however, the unfortunate effect of obscuring the dynamic tug-and-pull of Ego and Empathy since both motives can be subsumed under maximizing pleasure. After all, we are wired for both Ego and Empathy and it can, therefore, be considered pleasurable to express or satisfy either or both.

We must, however, drop to a lower level of analysis or integration than the sweeping, all-inclusive pleasure principle to appreciate the interplay of Ego and Empathy and the dynamic shaping effects of that interplay. This provides a striking illustration of a major and well-known problem inherent in the levels of analysis (reduction and integration) issue in the sciences. In this case, where the level is too high, it loses power to discriminate adequately.

In the case of economics, the effect has been profound. The hedonic level of integration (accompanied, also by the fallacious transition from a self-interest motive to an all-inclusive self-reference perspective as discussed in Chapter 15) does not permit a proper understanding of the dynamic of social exchange or the evolution of the market.

The Hobbesian Victory over Smithian Morality a Subjective, Nonscientific Choice

With Jevons' deliberate value choice to exclude moral motives from consideration, "scientific" economics, thus, moved away from the position held by Adam Smith and adopted, for such "scientific" purposes, a position more consistent with Hobbes. It was, of course, not a truly scientific choice but a subjective value choice of convenience.

The development of the "scientific" school of economics, then, contrary to economic lore still passed on in the standard texts, was based on Hobbes view of human nature, not the view of Adam Smith.

In sum, it was clearly a choice made, not on the basis of science, but on the basis of values, convenience, and the desire to look like physics—to capture part of the reflected glory of that esteemed science.

The Ultimate Denial: Fallacy in the Making

As frequently happens in the social sciences, what is deliberately excluded from examination comes eventually to be denied in reality.

"Scientific" economists, who followed in the 19th and 20th centuries, seemingly forgot that Jevons did *not* deny the existence of Empathy or higher motives, but rather specifically chose to exclude them to concentrate on what he personally acknowledged to be the baser motive of self-interest.

This post-Jevons transition constitutes, in effect, an instance of the naturalistic fallacy by economists. That is, they made the forbidden leap from value to fact. Jevons had made a value choice to ignore Empathy and morals in "scientific" economics. His followers moved from that value choice to a denial-in-fact of the existence of Empathy as a primary motive in the exchange process.

The effects of Jevon's choice and the associated "forgetting" were to be profound.

The Choice to Ignore Half of Human Nature: Cracks in the Foundation

So-called scientific economics chose to ignore half of human nature in building the foundations of its edifice. The inadequate foundations were, thus, faulty and unstable.

As the discipline moved into the twentieth century, it began showing cracks in the faulty foundations. These cracks had to be pasted over—much like the epicycles created to explain "deviant" planetary motions by the Ptolemaic geocentric theorists prior to being swept away by the Copernican Revolution in the early Renaissance.

The Epicyclic Patchwork

There are two conspicuous examples of epicyclic patchwork work of the faulty foundations of modern economics.

The first includes the treatment of fundamental empathic motives such as altruism, love, and caring as tastes or preferences, not as the true human motives that they are.

The second egregious epicycle is the extended conceptual fabrication called *enlightened self-interest*. This fabrication was an attempt to justify embarrassingly observable cooperation and other expressions of Empathy in terms of long-term self-interest.

Such examples were created in a vain attempt to hang on to the erroneous sole self-interest motive. The epicycles conceal only poorly the flaws in the self-interest centric perspective of economics.

The Negative Social Side Effects

The negative social side effects of the mistaken perspective are, of course, considerable. They include the encouragement of greed and the promotion of cynicism in society.

When everything is at bottom self-interest, such primary empathetic motives as caring, love, and altruism—the precious co-foundational motives of the family, the gift, and the market itself—cannot be admitted to be the genuine motives that they are.

They are dehumanized. Such motives must then be the result of fakery, or otherwise trivialized and turned to self-interested purposes. On the other hand, when the duality of the market, the tug-and-pull of self-interested and other-interested (empathetic) circuitry is recognized, the flaws in the foundation disappear taking the bad side effects and the epicycles with them.

Logical Positivism and Radical Behaviorism

The focus on self-interest gained additional allies from two related perspectives that emerged in the early twentieth century—logical positivism in philosophy and radical behaviorism in psychology.

Both denied consciousness and subjectivity as valid for investigation by science. The entire focus was to be on externals—primarily on experimental methods applied to such externals that could be repeated in the laboratory.

Although good as far as it went, this focus became much more than just a useful methodology. Again, as in the case of "scientific" economics, researchers came to deny the very existence of what they declined to study.

Stiff Upper Lips and Original Sin

The externalized objective perspective fed into the original sin, tough-minded, stiff-upper-lipped mainstream of Anglo-American thinking. Science bought it hook, line, and sinker.

Behavioristic psychology, which denied the existence of consciousness or inner mental states, went in lockstep with "scientific" economics, logical positivism, and original sin. The result was an externalized, so-called objective concept of science that denied and tried to divest itself of all things subjective and seemingly softheaded.

Being hardheaded, tough-minded, and stiff-upper-lipped meant one must focus on such human attributes as selfishness, fear, aggression, and nastiness in general. And nineteenth- and twentieth-century science did just that—with a vengeance. Altruism, cooperation, affection, and love were softheaded and few stiff-upper-lippers would dare consider them seriously.

The Selfish Gene: Original Sin in Biology

All the foregoing contributed mightily to a parallel trend in biological approaches, particularly the Anglo-American approach, toward a form of objective negativism. The approach has a detached, self-deprecating, long-suffering quality about it.

Stiff-Upper-Lippers or Autistic Savants?

As previously in this chapter, I have chosen to call this mindset the stiff upper lip approach in acknowledgment of its characteristic Anglo-Saxon ambience. It bespeaks the "too painful to be endured, but I will do so nevertheless." It carries the "I can stoutly confront the difficult truth with head painfully, but resolutely unbowed" demeanor.

The practitioners of this approach were largely attracted to the cold disciplines of mathematics and game theory. They seem to utterly lack warmth in their presentations. They suggest autistic-like savants unable to connect with any emotion except the negatives of fear and aggression. Their pessimistic calculus sees little good in human nature.

Selfish Genes and Bloody Teeth

An example? Without necessarily ascribing all the above attributes to him, British nonmathematical—but mathematically-inspired—ethologist Richard Dawkins comes readily to mind. In his negatively titled *The Selfish Gene*, widely read and admired by the hardnosed mathematical game theory community, Dawkins identifies himself enthusiastically with the bloody tooth and claw perspective on evolution (1976: 2).

Early on in *The Selfish Gene*, he writes with true stiff upper lippedness:

> Be warned that if you wish as I do, to build a society in which individuals cooperate generously and unselfishly toward the common good, you can expect little help from biological nature. Let us try to teach generosity and altruism, because we are born selfish.
>
> (1976: 3)

Original Sin! The biology version. We are born sinners, worms. Shades of medieval monastic spiritual masochism! But don't despair totally. As Dawkins notes, we are redeemable, at least in theory, by training and education.

Redeemability and Dilemma

But by whom are we redeemable? And where do their credentials and expertise come from? Following Dawkins' logic, certainly not from the detached-from-human-warmth physico-mathematical scientific community. After all, according to them, we lack the emotional neural substrate from which a sense of morality can be derived.

Who then is to save us? To be the teachers?—the fundamentalist religious zealots who easily reject the cold logic of the scientific community. Certainly they are eager candidates. Is Dawkins suggesting this indirectly? If so, surely, he can't be serious.

We have a dilemma. How can we achieve what "science" denies we have the capacity for by nature?

The Dawkinsian Fallacy

Fortunately, we can all relax. The dilemma is a false one. Dawkins is simply wrong. Whatever the marketing advantages of such dramatic, socially misleading titles as *selfish gene*, we will, hopefully, see less and less of such anti-social, fallacious, and inaccurate science in this new century.

Other than being simply wrong on his science, Dawkins commits a glaring fallacy of reasoning in the quoted passage. He reasons fallaciously from gene to gene-created mechanism.

The selfishness he attributes anthropomorphically to the gene, he totally inappropriately extends to the motivated behavior of the phenotype or the individual. There is no logical basis for making this jump. And the empirics contradict him.

At the end of *The Extended Phenotype* (1982), in which Dawkins extends the story of the selfish gene as the unit of selection for some 264 pages, he writes as follows:

> The integrated multicellular organism is a phenomenon which has emerged as a result of natural selection on primitively independent selfish replicators. It has paid replicators to behave gregariously. The phenotypic power by which they ensure their survival is in principle extended and unbounded. In practice the organism has arisen as a partially bounded local concentration, a shared knot of replicator power.
>
> (264)

In the case of humans, whom he seems to be writing for, if Dawkins had any knowledge of evolutionary neuroscience and truly understood the implications of his own words above, he would never have made his earlier statement in *The Selfish Gene*.

The contradictory findings come from evolutionary neuroscience, about which mathematical game theorists, and likely Dawkins himself, seem appallingly uninformed. The so-called "phenotypic power," that is produced by genes (which are neither selfish nor unselfish, but complex chemical interactions without choice) in the human phenotype has produced the neural circuitry of the mammalian architecture.

The Phenotypic Power of the Mammalian Architecture and Behavior

In the emerging discipline of evolutionary neuroscience, then, we go to the physiological or biological source—the evolved circuitry of our mammalian neural architecture. Here we look at what evolution *has* produced, not what we think it *should* have or *could* have produced.

We study the structure of the brain through actual physical examination. We code its responses through experiment and observation. The anatomical structure of the human brain can be and has been studied extensively and compared with the brain structures of other mammals and vertebrates.

We also explore further with the new imaging techniques the neural sources of Empathy, parental nurturing, social bonding and expressions of fairness and justice. And we affirm the conservation of ancestral vertebrate and warm-blooded mammalian circuitry through molecular genetic studies.

Evidence shows clearly that certain behaviors first appeared in fully-articulated, integrated form with mammals and still exist in the mammals we study today. These behaviors are nurturing: nursing, seeking contact comfort, clinging, using vocal and visual signals of attachment—a set of behaviors that have been called affectional.

Emergent brain structures—as well as more ancient ones—were significantly elaborated and interconnected with the full appearance of these behaviors and are experimentally as well as logically held to be responsible for them. We still have a lot to learn about the interactive detail of brain structure and behavior, but the general features of the wiring diagram are well-established and indisputable.

Brain circuitry and behavior show, above all, that mammals are social animals. Humans, as the most highly evolved mammals, are the most social—and the most dependent on social life.

We humans are born in social groups, live in society, and reproduce in society. And it is obvious that we must have the behavioral equipment to make this possible—that is, our contending behavioral circuits of self-preservation and affection, Ego and Empathy, along with the homeostatic rules that govern their operation. This is the dynamic expressed so elegantly by the equation of our social brain.

Therefore, if we wish, as Dawkins say he does, "to build a society in which individuals cooperate generously and unselfishly toward the common good" we can confidently look to our biological nature. We are not born solely selfish as Dawkins claims, but we are born with a mammalian neural architecture that includes parental care, extended social bonding, and empathy. Building on this "phenotypic power" we can create—through conscious neocortical effort devoted to better education and socialization—the cooperative, generous, and unselfish society we all want.

20 Evolutionary Neuroethology and Inclusive Fitness

A major shift of scientific interest in human behavior emerged in the last quarter of the twentieth century. The previously forbidden domain of human cognition and consciousness was opened up to scientific study.

The Cold World of Computer Mechanism: Humans as Information Processors

The intrepid few who breached the gates did so, at first, very cautiously. Emboldened by the newly spectacular success of computers, the new researchers adopted the model of information-processing. It was a timid first step, anchored in the safe haven of cold, nonhuman mechanical analogy.

In their view we humans would now become reducible to a mechanical information-processing device. From this perspective the brain was nothing but a computer, an information processor. And information-processing was all that was studied.

Emotions, human warmth and caring, were excluded from the researchable. It was an essentially barren effort that soon exhausted its useful research programs, but it did open the gates to the more adventurous.

Ethology: The Study of Animal Behavior

Parallel to the behavioristic tradition, popular principally in the U.S. and the former Soviet Union, the study of animal behavior, called ethology, had been progressing largely in continental Europe.

European ethologists Konrad Lorenz, Niko Tinbergen, and Karl von Frisch earned Nobel prizes in 1973 for their pioneering work in the new field. These ethologists did across-species comparisons and proceeded from an evolutionary perspective.

They observed and described behavior. They did not, however, look into the black box of the brain and attempt to speculate on neural mechanisms.

DOI: 10.4324/9781003303190-23

Evolutionary Biology to Evolutionary Psychology

At the same time evolutionary biology powered by the engine of Darwin's insights proceeded on a track largely isolated from mainstream psychology, whether behaviorism or the more recent cognitive information-processing endeavor.

Despite a few heroic efforts at integration of the biological with the psychological and social sciences, the isolation remained essentially intact.

In the last two decades of the century, the evolutionary perspective and psychology finally hesitatingly married up in what became known as evolutionary psychology.

Evolutionary Psychology, Behaviorism, and the Black Box of the Human Brain

Like the behavioristic psychology before it, evolutionary psychology viewed the black box of the human brain largely from the outside.

It began speculating upon what could be within—that is, what could be there that was passed on in the evolutionary process through our genes.

Evolutionary psychology paid little attention to actual brain structure, but sometimes made elaborate speculations about presumed isolated and dedicated processing modules that dealt with specific environmental challenges that had arisen.

Such modules were likened to a Swiss knife, each blade put neatly in place with imaginary precision in the manner of an equally imaginary professional engineer represented by the process of natural selection.

Such improbable speculation proceeded largely unchecked. It was, at times, reminiscent of the pseudoscientific phrenology of the previous century. Phrenology had notoriously sought to identify human characteristics through external examination of lumps on the cranium.

The unwritten command driving evolutionary psychology seemed to be "find a behavior, posit a dedicated brain module." The approach was considerably naïve and open to endless proliferation of imaginary neural components.

Evolutionary Neuroethology

In the broad panorama of science many tracks proceeded independently at varying levels of reduction and integration—and in isolation because of our siloed university system. One of these tracks that moved outside the mainstream of emerging research on neuroscience was the evolutionary neuroethology of Paul MacLean discussed in the opening chapters.

In a sheltered laboratory of the National Institutes of Health, MacLean, a medical doctor, began a research program in the 1950s aimed at understanding evolved behavior through a study of the substrate neural circuitry at various stages of evolution. His emphasis was on certain lizards and lower mammals.

MacLean chose lizards because they resembled most closely the ancestral bridge between ancient vertebrates and mammals. His research program focused upon the neural circuitry underlying behavior with emphasis on emotion—especially those nurturing emotions and motivations that lay at the foundation of mammalian family life and that were apparently lacking in ancestral vertebrates.

MacLean's emphasis on the evolution of emotion was ahead of its time and out of step with the mainstream research in the emergent area of behavioral neuroscience. In keeping with the superficial behavioristic tradition, mainstream neuroscience lacked an evolutionary perspective and focused only on the mechanics of information-processing.

It called itself cognitive or behavioral neuroscience, acknowledging, in its name, the exclusion of emotion.

When emotion was occasionally studied, it was under the limited, coldly formal information-processing aspect of "learning." When actual emotion was admitted into the chill halls of such science, it was the usual faire of fear, aggression, and human nastiness in general.

Original sin, in sublimated guise, still dominated the paradigm. Stiff-upper-lippers, real he-men, tough guys of science—with some very rare exceptions—didn't study love, nurturing, warmth, caring.

At the close of the twentieth century, the study of emotion, based in part on the long-neglected pioneering work of MacLean and his predecessors, combined with the dramatic efforts of a few dispersed, but bold researchers, seemed at last to gain attention.

The big challenge now seemed to be how the externalized, essentially cold-blooded, gene-centered perspective of evolutionary biology and evolutionary psychology could be reconciled with evolutionary neuroscience and the study of warm-blooded, nurturing side of humanity.

Inclusive Fitness: The Genetic Reconciliation

The conceptual bridge came principally from the work of British scholar W. D. Hamilton.

In his kin selection model, Hamilton (1964) formalized the issue of how genes for cooperation and altruism *could* evolve and be etched into the human ancestral genome.

The core of this inclusive fitness model is that it weighed the effect of genes not only on the individual that carried them but also on kin individuals who shared the same genes.

Hamilton's Rule

According to what has come to be called *Hamilton's rule*, genes coding for cooperation, reciprocity, or altruism could evolve if the costs of cooperative behavior to the individual were outweighed by the benefits to related individuals carrying the same genes.

Hamilton's rule is expressed varyingly as

$$rb - c > 0 \text{ or } c < rb$$

In this formula r is the coefficient or degree of relatedness or kin, b is the benefit of the cooperative or altruistic behavior to the kin, and c is the cost of the behavior to the individual.

The equation predicts that as r increases, benefits will exceed costs and cooperation, reciprocity, or altruism would be favored by natural selection.

Hamilton's rule gives the basic formula for inclusive fitness from the external gene's eye view. It shows mathematically how it is possible for such traits as altruism and reciprocity to get into the genome.

The Essential Mechanisms Unspecified

Neither the concept of inclusive fitness nor the formula, however, can predict the mechanisms created by the genes to sustain altruism and reciprocity. And, accordingly, Hamilton, displaying no knowledge of neural architecture, did not speculate on the actual nature of such neural mechanisms.

Empathy Improves Survival Odds of Self *Plus* Others Inclusively

According to the algorithms of our social neural architecture, *any* empathetic, cooperative, or altruistic behavior will serve to improve the odds of survival of self *plus* others *inclusively* over purely egoistic or self-interested behavior.

This is compatible with Hamilton's rule which says that as long as the benefit to related individuals exceeds the cost to the behaving individual, the genes supporting such behavior can be favored by natural selection.

From Inclusive Social Architecture to Love of All Via Education and Socialization

Of course, once the neural mechanisms, the social architecture, is in place, as it has been for tens of thousands of years, the empathetic or altruistic behavior may be extended to non-kin.

It may even be led epigenetically to embrace the universe itself—by extending the scale of inclusiveness through appropriate education and socialization. All this extension can be achieved through the cognitive and emotional media that draw upon, modify, and elaborate the existing neural substrate. Such a capacity has been acknowledged by other scholars (e.g., see Buss 1999).

The factor of inclusive fitness, combined with the findings of evolutionary neuroscience of the homeostatic circuitry of the social brain, constitutes the motivated foundations for society as an expression of social exchange.

This dynamic is, of course, represented by the equation of our social brain.

21 Social Exchange and the Structure of Society

From the give-and-take of the family to the give-and-take of one-to-one friendships, groups, communities, even up to nations and beyond—all societies are societies of social exchange.

Wherever and whenever individuals are in social contact there is give-and-take or social exchange. The neural substrate for such exchange is the mammalian Ego/Empathy dynamic expressed by the homeostatic equation of the social brain.

And to the extent that these exchanges are out of balance there is behavioral tension/social tension and inequality.

The Social Brain Equation as a Metric of Socio-Behavioral Tension and Inequality

To the extent Ego and Empathy approach dynamic balance behavioral tension is reduced and inequalities are likewise. The following form of the social equation mathematically represents such social exchange relationships as they approach dynamic balance:

$$BT = \frac{\text{Ego}}{\text{Empathy}} = \frac{\text{Dominance}}{\text{Submission}} = \pm 1$$

As the ratio diverges from ±1 or dynamic balance, the equation indexes the behavioral tension in the society. The equation also allows us to conceptualize mathematically the relationship between equality and inequality.

It gives us a framework for estimating the magnitude of inequality and ultimately to quantify it ever more precisely.

Social Stratification

Social stratification represents a major concern of sociologists. A truly vast literature expresses the extent of that concern.

DOI: 10.4324/9781003303190-24

Stratification as Structured Behavioral Tension

In terms of our social equation such institutionalized inequalities represent structured behavioral tension.

Most sociologists, apparently intuiting the tension through the dynamic of their own neural architecture, see the inequality of social stratification as a problem.

Some see it as an *un*necessary evil based on exploitation of one group by another. Others see it as a necessary evil proceeding from the inevitable division of labor in any society of any appreciable size. Such perceptions are not value neutral and they are emotionally charged.

For example: Radical institutionalist William Dugger exhibits a frank, emotionally charged, and clearly normative position on inequality, when he writes:

> We can pretend to be value neutral about inequality, but we never are.
>
> (1996: 21)

On the other hand, Friedrich Hayek worries normatively, and with evident emotion, about social or distributive justice when he writes:

> I am not sure that the concept has a definite meaning even in a centrally directed economy, or that in such a system people would ever agree on what distribution is just. I am certain, however, that nothing has done so much to destroy the juridical safeguards of individual freedom as the striving after the mirage of social justice.
>
> (1991: 388–389)

Such are the normative variants that our reciprocal brain structure pushes upon us, as Ego and Empathy, self- and other-interest, tug-and-pull against each other within our skulls and between us in society.

And such clearly normative, value-bound variants are not dispassionate, but are emotionally charged as is equally clearly displayed in the rhetoric of both Dugger and Hayek. The value as well as the emotional charge reflects the behavioral tension that drives the dynamic of the reciprocal brain.

Between Dugger and Hayek: Where Most of Us Belong

Between the extremes of Dugger and Hayek, almost all will agree that stratification, with its accompanying inequality, represents a source of tension even when it appears to contribute to stability.

Almost all will also agree that those on the lower levels tend to envy or resent those above and would change the situation given the chance. Likewise those above seemingly empathetically sense this tension and react to defend or rationalize their upper position in the inequalities.

What Any Fool Knows

On the one hand this is common sense. According to the algorithms of our neural architecture (discussed in Chapter 4) no one, given the choice, would *willingly* and *knowingly* choose to be on the short end of a significant or meaningful inequality. This is intuitive—any fool knows it.

Has Evaded Scientific Explanation

Nevertheless, we have never been able to explain such response to inequality coherently or scientifically by linking it to neural architecture. We have previously intuited or postulated a sense of justice in human nature without a grasp of the dynamic. And we have justified and qualified "what is just" almost beyond recognition based on accommodation to the existing social context.

Social Context vs. Ideal Definition

The CSN model and the social equation allow us to change that. We now have a dynamic framework that explains the fundamental tension behind the motivation, the associated dislike of inequality, and the desire for social justice.

That dynamic framework is our neural architecture driven by behavioral tension. The rest is *contextual* and *situational.*

When social justice is defined *contextually*, *situationally* it accepts, reinforces, and justifies the existing social system.

When social justice is defined *ideally* it foresees or calls for change in the existing system.

Self-Corrective Tendency vs. Social Stratification

Our neural architecture evolved in small family units where the interpersonal interactions resolved the tension of inequalities.

Evolution of the Fundamental Homeostatic Logic of Equality

The logic of the evolved neural architecture tells us that while most of us will willingly accept some inequality in favor of ourselves, none of us will willingly and knowingly accept less than a position of rough equality on all matters of true significance.

The interactive, negotiating exchange process that goes on in small face-to-face family groups driven by behavioral tension tends, homeostatically, to come to dynamic balance or rough equality. Even within the family, members will tend to ally with each other to overcome or moderate efforts at domination by one member.

For example, the average dad of today's democratic societies is no match for an alliance of mom and the kids. Lesser developed societies still, however, may block such natural corrective tendencies by restrictive tradition and institutions.

Larger Groups, the Division of Labor, and the Emergence of the Scale of Inclusiveness

In larger groups this self-corrective tendency, historically, became increasingly hampered by the lack of close interaction. Both the distance of interaction and the division of labor contributed to hobbling the self-correcting action demanded by the evolved neural architecture.

Thus was created the scale of inclusiveness or inclusive fitness.

The Necessity for Rationale: From Ideology to Coercion to Force

Frustration of the neural tendency built socio-behavioral tension in the societies. The resulting inequalities and behavioral tension, then, had to be rationalized or made minimally palatable by institutions or ideology—or, ultimately, maintained by coercion or force.

Socio-political Participation and the Pressures for Equality

The somewhat steady movement toward democracy in the overall social exchange system today is propelled by this homeo-statically-regulated self-correcting tendency of our neural architecture. In the United States, as well as other countries around the world, we have seen this tendency expressed in the movements toward equal socio-political participation.

In the United States, following WWII, we saw the emergence and successes of first the civil rights movement and, then, the women's movement. These have been followed by the call for equal rights by gays, lesbians, and other minorities.

Such minorities have been held in unequal states of behavioral tension by institutions, ideologies, or outright force. Their movements emerge, motivated by the pent-up tension, as change becomes possible—that is, as institutions, ideologies, and force become weakened, tolerant, or otherwise subject to challenge.

A recent social thinker, Francis Fukuyama, following the German philosopher Hegel, has even gone so far to say, rather prematurely, that with the failure of communism and the breakup of the Soviet Union, Western-style democracy has become the end system of human political history.

The barriers to the natural corrective tendency, reflected in the scale of inclusiveness and other factors, then, will tend to be overcome if the relations among the components of the total social exchange system are permitted to operate freely. For further insight into why this is so, we can look to the evolutionary process of species closely related to our own.

The Instability of Social Stratification Among Primates and Humans

The emergence of evolutionary neuroethology permits new insights into social stratification.

Evolutionary neuroethology combines the study of evolutionary neuroscience with the perspective of evolutionary ethology or the study of behavior across the range of animal species. Like others, it is a Darwinian perspective.

An emphasis on the pervasive presence of social hierarchy or dominance/submissive relationships is a hallmark of the ethological approach in animal studies. Paul MacLean building on the work of predecessors, pioneered the study of brain circuitry substrating such behaviors.

The term neuroethology, which encompasses the study of both brain and behavior from an evolutionary perspective, captures this combined focus well.

An important insight emerged from these conjoined efforts. The earlier vertebrate circuitry common to fishes, amniotes, and pre-mammals which scripted self-preserving, often life and death contests for dominance, became integrated with the attachment or affectional circuitry of mammals.

The Emergence of Social Competition, Alliances and Hierarchy

This combined circuitry permitted the emergence of social competition—the tug-and-pull of Ego and Empathy that is captured in the CSN model. Dominance modified by affection leading to cognitively emergent Empathy became possible among higher primates and humans.

Although dominance, without engagement of affectional circuitry, could still be a life and death, all or nothing contest, hierarchy could now be achieved through alliances, serving and preserving others by engaging affectional circuitry. Submission could be accepted and integrated into the social fabric.

Conflict Resolution and the Instability of Hierarchy

Conflict resolution, as we currently practice it in our behavioral, social, and management sciences, thus, became possible.

Of course, the behavioral tension, motivating the contests remained. The tug-and-pull of self-preservation and affection, Ego and Empathy, persisted latently or covertly to drive later changes in the hierarchy when the supporting contingencies and/or relative prowess of the contestants changed.

Thus, human hierarchies, like those of other mammals and primates, are inherently unstable because of the latent or potential behavioral tension. Depending on the degree of social, economic, or political inequalities, they must be held in place by institutions, ideologies, and/or police or military power.

In other words, social stratification is inherently unstable based upon the dynamic of our neural architecture.

Society as an Overarching Social Exchange System

Our neural architecture evolved in the extended nuclear family. For millions of years of hominid evolution before we reached our final species level of homo sapiens some 100,000 years ago, we survived and evolved as small, kinship, or family groups or bands.

The deeply binding interactive dynamic of self-preservation and affection, Ego and Empathy, preserved us from one precarious generation to the other. All aspects of our economic and political lives were bound into the family unit, driven and maintained by the social architecture.

Motivated by deeply felt and powerful affectional reward circuits, we shared with each other and cared for the young, the weak, the handicapped, and the aged. There is growing evidence that higher primates who trace back with us to a common ancestor do the same. The kinship groups were essentially egalitarian. All shared in the power and the economic necessities for survival.

Of Power and Economic Functions: From Primitive Family to Modern State

This leads us to a fundamental fact of social organization. In the larger units of modern social organization the power and economic functions of the primitive family have been split. All social units, from the modern family on up, are social exchange units.

Society, at the very top, then, can be viewed as an overarching social exchange system (see Figure 21.1). It occupies the place of the extended family and combines its functions.

A large-scale society like a nation-state has two essential societal-level components previously combined in the primitive family unit: an economic exchange system and a politico-legal exchange system.

Although the two systems have different jobs or functions, they work together to form the essential character of the society. Both are needed. One can't do the job of the other.

The equation of our social brain helps us to make the distinction as well as recognize the necessity for both. Let's look at the different jobs they do. The market exchange system first.

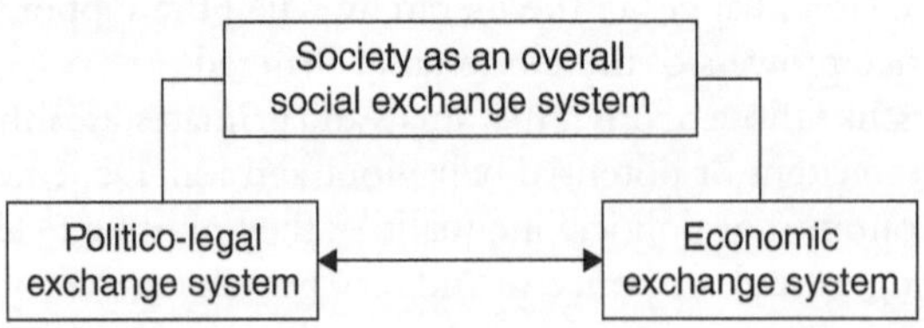

Figure 21.1 Social System with Subsystems.

The Market or Economic Exchange System

The free enterprise market exchange system operates according to the so-called laws of Supply and Demand. Supply and Demand, as we have seen repeatedly, are not really laws but are an expression of our neural dynamic.

In the market exchange system, however, the neural dynamic or equation is constrained by the definitions of economics.

In economics, demand consists of two elements: (1) taste and (2) ability to pay.

To be counted among demanders in the market exchange system, then, an individual must have a taste for a certain commodity and must also have enough money to pay for it. The economic definition, thus, excludes all those who may need commodities of necessity, like food, clothing, shelter or health care, but who lack the money to buy them.

The poor or needy, then, whether they desperately need essential commodities, or even clamor vociferously for them in street demonstrations, are excluded from the economic concept of demand. That is, economists simply don't count them anymore. They drop out of the traditional economic equation.

The concept of supply is similarly constrained in the market exchange system. Suppliers, likewise, must meet two requirements: (1) they must be able to sell and (2) they must be willing to sell.

The ability to sell means, of course, the suppliers must be able to cover their costs of production and supplying or else they would soon go out of business. They also must be willing to provide at the prices available. Sometimes they may be willing to sell at a loss for short periods to avoid further losses, but they can't go on doing so forever because they will be forced out of business by the very structure and definitions of the market system.

The constraints of the economic definitions of Demand and Supply place limits on what the free enterprise market exchange system can do. It may produce a vast number of commodities—more than not-free systems—but it may still fail to meet the actual needs of the society. By its very structure and definitions, then, the market intrinsically may fail to meet all the needs of the society.

In fact, historically speaking, there has never been a free market system that has, without assistance, met all the needs of society. Even the best free market system, operating on its own defined principles, has failed to eliminate poverty and social deprivation. This takes us to the role of the politico-legal exchange system.

The Politico-Legal Exchange System

The politico-legal exchange system (hereinafter often referred to simply as the political system) requires a different set of definitions. It must respond to the overall social exchange system.

Countering Market System Failures Balancing Out the Social Brain Equation

In response to behavioral or social tension, the political system must act to counter failures or limits of the market system. It must balance out the social brain equation over the entire overarching social exchange system like the primitive family did over evolutionary history.

Social Demand vs. Economic Demand

Demand in the political system may appropriately be called social demand as opposed to economic demand.

And the definition is different. Social demand contrasts with economic demand on the two elements of its definition. In social demand taste becomes need. The second element ability to pay is dropped. In a truly humanistic society it may be replaced simply by presence in the community. That is: as a society we must provide for the needs of children, the disabled, and the elderly.

Complementing and Balancing the Market Exchange System

The political system, then, complements the market exchange system and ideally balances out its failures.

The political system must readjust, by taxation, subsidy, or other method, the imbalance or failure that is an inevitable outcome of the market exchange system as defined.

Fulfilling the Charter of the Primitive Family

Ideally, the political system fulfills the charter of the primitive family in which the neural dynamic evolved.

It cares for the unemployed, the handicapped, the aged, and others who lack the ability to qualify in the demand definition of the market exchange system.

Civilized democracies, responding to the interactive dynamic of Ego and Empathy, cannot afford to allow their citizens to lack the necessities of life. The behavioral tension created by the market failures drives this corrective action.

With Caution

Of course, for its part the political system must exercise great caution and prudence to avoid stifling the creative energy of the market system while correcting the inevitable failures, distortions, or imbalances. It is a challenging and often precarious balancing act.

Price	Quantity	
	Supply	Demand
$5	5 units	1 unit
$3	3 units	3 units
$1	1 unit	5 units

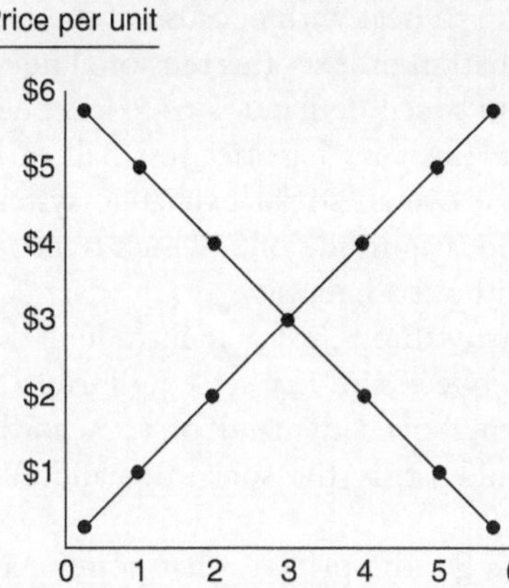

Figure 21.2 Equilibrium Curves.

Graphing and Grasping the Challenge

The equilibrium curve of Chapter 12 may be used to illustrate the essential challenge in easy to grasp terms (see Figure 21.2).

Assume the equilibrium graph to represent the total social demand for an item of necessity. This means, as a simple example, that there are six (six billion, if we include the world population) items of necessity and six (six billion, if world) persons comprising the society.

Under the concept of economic Supply and Demand the three items above the equilibrium point as well as the three items below the point are dropped out of the picture.

The market is said to clear. All those who have the taste and ability to buy have been supplied by those able and willing to supply. That is, we have a perfect market! It sounds great, but it is misleading.

Social Demand and Excess Price

Viewed from the perspective of social demand, things are not so good.

In fact, we have a serious problem.

Assuming the excess supply above the equilibrium point will go away or simply not be produced may get us out of difficulty on the supply side.

But what about the three (three billion?) items which represent items of necessity to three (three billion?) social demanders or citizens? Their essential needs go unmet. As a result we have substantial inequity in the market and substantial socio-behavioral tension.

Will these three, or say three billion, persons demonstrate in the streets, commit crimes, initiate an insurrection expressing this tension? Or will they instead appeal to the political system for redress to this imbalance in necessities of life? And will the political system respond? Whatever happens, we have socio-behavioral tension to deal with because of the market failure.

The social equation indexes this tension. The ratio between what is supplied in the market and social demand is 6/3 or a behavioral tension magnitude of 2. The market in this case has met just half of the social demand. From the perspective of the overall social exchange system, we have to deal with the behavioral tension magnitude of 2, which translates numerically into half of its citizens going without a necessity.

To further clarify things, we may introduce the term *excess price* to describe the difference between the market equilibrium price and the price we must reach to fulfill the social demand of 6. According to the graph, a price of about $0.25 would satisfy the social demand. Anything above that would be excess price.

So how do we get the price to that point? As a civilized society we cannot tolerate the socio-behavioral tension in the situation—that is, we cannot allow half or, for that matter, any of our citizens to go without necessities.

But we can't ask suppliers in the market system to lower the price below their ability to recover costs. The suppliers would go broke. In effect we would destroy the market.

So what do we ask of our political system?

Essentially we have two options. We may subsidize the supplier or give aid to the demander. That is, for example, we have the choice of industry subsidies or welfare payments and food stamps. Our political exchange system has been known to use both.

The equation of our social brain quickly reveals the problem as we shift from necessities to non-necessities under the contrasting definitions or constraints of the market and the overall social exchange system.

Market Standard for Non-Necessities? Social Standard for Necessities?

To satisfy the discrepancy or behavioral tension that exists between the market exchange system and the overall social exchange system, we must act politically.

We must, perhaps, apply the market standard or set of definitions to non-necessities and the social standard or set of definitions to necessities. We already do this in a fuzzy sort of way in the United States. Some of the European free enterprise democracies do it much more self-consciously.

The Predictions of the Social Dynamic

The dynamic of our neural architecture predicts that to the extent that the two subsystems—the market system and the political system—interact freely, behavioral tension and inequalities within the society will tend to dynamic balance.

Necessary Conditions

This condition of freely interacting can best be met in a democratic society with a free enterprise market exchange system.

In a freely functioning democratic society the limitations or failures of the market exchange system will tend to be corrected in the political system. That is: when the market fails to produce or distribute adequately or when businesses show excessive greed or corruption, citizens will demand counter-action through legal or political processes. We see this on almost a daily basis in developed democratic countries.

A Major Challenge of a Free Society: Preventing Undue Interference or Obstruction

A major challenge facing a free society is to keep the interactions between the two key systems free of undue interference or obstruction.

This is what intuitively drives most government regulation of business. It conspicuously drives such movements as campaign finance reform—which aim is to correct attempts to interfere with the normal self-corrective tendency via the political system by those holding greater power in the market system.

In sum, the inequalities generated in the market exchange system will tend, driven by behavioral tension, to be corrected in the political exchange system if allowed to work without interference. In the overarching social exchange system, then, driven by the behavioral tension of our neural architecture, things will tend to balance out.

Incentives, Productivity, and Behavioral Tension

If there is one thing we learned from the experiments in socialism in the twentieth century, it is that incentives are required for a highly productive economy.

The varying of incentives, of course, means the creating of inequalities. This exploits the fundamental expression of our neural architecture. We don't like inequalities. And we, individually, will strive to alter or overcome them in our own favor or at least to the point of rough equality.

Such is the engine of social competition in both the market and political sub-arenas. It is the engine that drives our free market system. It works for us—up to a point.

But there are dangers to the system when the tensions or inequalities permitted for production and supply become excessively cumulative and extreme. Our society becomes unstable. The economically or politically disenfranchised, or excluded, become motivated to change—through crime, riots, and other forms of disobedience and violence.

Ideally, to avoid excessive behavioral tension which translates into social unrest, the inequalities necessary to incent a free market economy should be held within the range approaching dynamic balance. Also, like the moment-by-moment, day-by-day tug-and-pull of the Ego and Empathy circuitries, the inequalities should be temporary and shifting.

If both conditions hold, the behavioral tension or inequality will be neither extreme nor cumulative in its effects. And if the market exchange system and the politico exchange system are allowed to interact and self-correct freely, the overall system driven by behavioral tension will tend to dynamic balance.

Social institutions and practices which impede this self-corrective tendency—like undue influence by powerful special interest groups—will skew the dynamic to the extremes and create behavioral tension and inequalities in the society.

This, of course, translates into social discontent and unrest. The behavioral tension underlying the discontent motivates efforts toward social change in the direction of a better balance.

The Practical Question

The foregoing has concentrated on establishing the scientific foundations for understanding the socio-political issues facing us. For practical purposes, of course, we must come down to a much lower level of analysis. The specific measures we take to correct imbalances in the system will always be situational and specific. They will require careful analysis, thought, planning, and execution—in the previously cited words of nobelist Thomas Sargent—they will require *intelligent design.* That is the practical challenge to be met.

22 Conclusion

At the beginning of this book I set out to explore the linkages between economic biology and behavioral economics. To accomplish this I accepted the challenge to present the proof and power of the biological Mecca of Alfred Marshall.

As proof, I sought to challenge the sole primary motive of self-interest and the still current Newtonian plus mid-nineteenth-century appropriated physics foundations of general equilibrium theory (GET). As noted in the introduction, both self-interest and GET have been dubbed crown jewels of economics. The biological analysis has effectively demonstrated that the so-called crown jewels are flawed gems.

At the turn of the millennium Mark Perlman and Charles McCann, in their magisterial two-volume work, *The Pillars of Economic Understanding* (1999, 2000), suggest that later in the twenty-first century scholars will understand more of the workings of the brain as the source of individual and social decision-making (2000: 325; see also Kirman 2006: 275). That is, in their view, understanding of how the brain works could lead to new and more profitable directions for economics. This has been demonstrated.

The Conflict Systems Neurobehavioral (CSN) model of our mammalian neural architecture, developed from the two biological disciplines of evolutionary neuroscience and physiology, identifies the homeostatically regulated dual motives (not single) of Ego and Empathy, or self- plus other-interest, as the foundation for human social exchange. In other words, in our evolved mammalian neural architecture we have an organic or biological foundation for a dual motive equilibrium in social exchange rather than a semi-mystical, Newtonian, or other physics-based mechanical foundation.

I might even suggest that the homeostatic nature of our social exchange neural architecture may well have provided subliminal motivation or validation for the search for a Newtonian-like equilibrium of forces. That is, we seek or perceive intuitively the tendency for balance or justice in social exchange. The more recent emergence of neuroeconomics, based primarily on new imaging technology, holds the promise of helping to detail more completely the underlying neural circuitry.

DOI: 10.4324/9781003303190-25

The physico-mathematical approach that dominated economic theory for the past century or more led us down the wrong path using the wrong mathematics. As one economist noted we became slaves to the wrong mathematics (Kirman 2006: 275).

In presenting the CSN model and its applications, I have used the standard economic methods of rhetoric (or presentation)—modeling, mathematics, and everyday language. By doing so, I hope to have made it accessible to a wide range of readers.

In the attempt to become a positive science in the manner of physics, economics abandoned Adam Smith's intuited dual motives of self-interest and sympathy for the single self-interested motive of Mandeville and Hobbes. The discovery and definition of the mammalian architecture of our brain driving self- and other-interest, Ego and Empathy, show that Adam Smith, without knowledge of evolutionary brain science, intuited it right. Social or market exchange is not driven by some mystical or physico-mathematical force of nature. It is motivated by a dual motive organic, behavioral dynamic wired into our brain over millions of years of mammalian evolution.

Economics can now hopefully move forward along this new path in fulfilling its promise for a better society. There is much work yet to be done.

But That's Not All

I like to think of DMT not only as fulfillment of the biological Mecca insight of Alfred Marshall, but also perhaps the correction and fulfillment of neoclassical theory rather than a challenge to replace it. I feel that if Marshall had access to the biological sciences of today he would almost certainly have incorporated them into his synthesis.

Moreover, a full grasp of the biological perspective anticipated by Marshall allows economics to come nearly full circle from the days of Adam Smith. From its origins as a moral or normative science, through its failed transition to a purely positive science, the revised theory emerges as a mixed positive-normative science. It is a positive science because it is anchored firmly in the fundamental biological sciences. It is a normative science because what we have come to cognitively call our moral choices, expressed so forcefully in the present-day social demands for equality and justice, emerge from and are mandated by our physiology—the homeostatic, dynamically balanced function of our evolved dual motive mammalian neural architecture. Therefore, from the positive emerges the normative. There is no separation of the two.

It follows, therefore, that Equality and Justice in economics and the other social sciences can no longer be considered as solely ethical, philosophical, religious, cultural, or even "learned" considerations.

They are, scientifically: inborn—genetically evolved—neuro-physiological imperatives.

They are imperatives that we urgently need to understand and facilitate in all areas of social, economic, and political exchange.

They are, further, the genetically evolved imperatives that move humanity, slowly and falteringly, toward the end of tribalism and the eventual social unification of our species.

References

Abiotiz, F. & Montiel, J. 2012. "From Tetrapods to Primates." Progress in Brain Research, 195: 3–24.

Ackerman, F. 1999. "Still Dead After All These Years: Interpreting the Failure of General Equilibrium Theory." Global Development and Environment Institute. Working Paper No.00.01.

Alexander, R. 1987. The Biology of Moral Systems. Aldine de Gruyter.

Appadurai, A. (ed.) 1986. The Social Life of Things. Cambridge.

Arrow, K. & Debreu, G. 1954. "Existence of an Equilibrium for a Competitive Economy." Econometrica, 22: 265–290.

Arrow, K. & Hahn, F. 1971. General Competitive Analysis. North-Holland Publishing.

Axelrod, R. 1984. The Evolution of Cooperation. Basic Books.

Axelrod, R. & Hamilton, W. 1981. "The Evolution of Cooperation." Science, 211: 1390.

Baal, J. van. 1975. Reciprocity and the Position of Women. Amsterdam: Van Gorcum, Assen.

Barfield, T, ed. 1997. The Dictionary of Anthropology. Blackwell.

Batson, C. 1991. The Altruism Question: Toward a Social-Psychological Answer. Lawrence Erlbaum.

Beauregard, M. & O'Leary, D. 2007. The Spiritual Brain. Harper One.

Becker, G. 1987. "Economic Analysis and Human Behavior." In Advances in Behavioral Economics, Volume 1. Edited by L. Green & J. Kagel. Ablex Publishing, 3–17.

Becker, L. 1986. Reciprocity. Routledge and Kegan Paul.

Bendor, J. & Swistak, P. 1997. "The Evolutionary Stability of Cooperation." American Political Science Review, 91(2): 290–303.

Bentham, J. 1907 [1789]. An Introduction to the Principles of Morals and Legislation. Reprint. Oxford Clarendon Press.

Berger, S., Kouzarides, T., et al. 2009. "An Operational Definition of Epigenetics." Genes & Dev., 23: 781–783.

Berridge, K. 2003. "Comparing the Emotional Brains of Humans and Other Animals." In Handbook of Affective Sciences. Edited by Davidson, R.J., Scherer, K.R. & Goldsmith, H.H. et al. Oxford, 25–51.

Bianchi, M. 1993. "How to Learn Sociality: True and False Solutions to Mandeville's Problem." History of Political Economy, 25(2) (summer): 209–240.

Blair R. 2003. "Facial Expressions, Their Communicatory Functions and Neurocognitive substrates." Philos Trans R Soc Lond B Biol Sci., 358: 561–572.

Blaug, M. 1990. Economic Theories, True or False? Edward Elgar.

Blaug, M. 1980. The Methodology of Economics. Cambridge.

Blumberg, M., Freeman, J. & Robinson, S. 2010. Oxford Handbook of Developmental Behavioral Neuroscience: Introduction. Oxford University Press.

Boehm, C. 1999. Hierarchy in the Forest: The Evolution of Egalitarian Behavior. Harvard.

Bohannon, P. 1963. Social Anthropology. Holt. Rinehart and Winston.

Bowles, S. & Gintis, H. 1998. Recasting Egalitarianism. Verso.

Braudel, F. 1982. Civilization and Capitalism 15th–18th Century. Trans. by S. Reynolds. Harper & Row.

Breggin, P. 2008. Brain-disabling Treatments in Psychiatry. Springer.

Brownell, H. & Martino, G. 1998. "Deficits in Inference and Social Cognition: The Effects of Right Hemisphere Brain Damage on Discourse." In Right Hemisphere Language Comprehension: Perspectives from Cognitive Neuroscience. Edited by M. Beeman and C. Chiarello. Lawrence Erlbaum, 309–328.

Buss, D. 1999. Evolutionary Psychology. Allyn and Bacon.

Butler, A. 2009. "Triune Brain Concept: A Comparative Evolutionary Perspective." Encyclopedia of Neuroscience. Elsevier, 1185–1193.

Butler, A. & Hodos, W. 2005. Comparative Vertebrate Neuroanatomy. 2nd edn. Wiley.

Cacioppo, J.T., Berntson, G.G., Adolphs, R., Carter, C.S., Davidson, R.J., McClintock, M.K., McEwen, B.S., Meaney, M.J., Schacter, D.L., Sternberg, E.M., Suomi, S.S. & Taylor, S. E., eds. 2002. Foundations in Social Neuroscience. MIT, 1st Edition.

Cannon, W. 1932. The Wisdom of the Body. Norton.

Cannon, W. 1929. Bodily Changes in Pain, Hunger, Fear, and Rage. D. Appleton & Co.

Carter, C.S., Ahnert, L., Grossmann, K.E., Hrdy, S.B., Lamb, M.E., Porges, S.W. & Sachser, N. 2006. Attachment and Bonding: A New Synthesis. MIT.

Carter, C. & Keverne, E. 2002. "The Neurobiology of Social Affiliation and Pair Bonding." In D. Pfaff (ed), Hormones, Brain, and Behavior. Academic Press, 299–337.

Carter, C., Lederhendler, I. & Kirkpatrick, B. eds. 1997. The Integrative Neurobiology of Affiliation. NY Academy of Sciences, Volume 807.

Chalupa, L.M., Berardi, N., Caleo, M., Galli-Resta, L. & Pizzorusso, T. 2011. Cerebral Plasticity: New Perspectives. MIT.

Chan, Y-G; Cory, G.; Luo, J. 2008. "The Tri-Oriented Approach and Dual Motive Theory." Annual Conference IFSAM, Shanghai, China, July 27–29.

Chan Y-G.; Cory, G.; Rajaram K. 2007. "Neuroeconomics and Dual Motive Theory: Can East Meet West? Bridging Eastern and Western Economics." Paper presented at Pacific Rim Conference, WEAI, Guanghua School of Management, Peking University, China, 17–21.

Cheal, D. 1988. The Gift Economy. Routledge.

Clinard, M. 1990. Corporate Corruption: The Abuse of Power. Greenwood.

Clower, R. & Howitt, P. 1997. "Foundations of Economics." In Is Economics Becoming a Hard Science? Edited by A. d'Autume & J. Cartelier. Edward Elgar, 17–34.

Cory, G. 2012. Consilience, Brains, and Leadership. International Technological University.

Cory, G. 2010a. Consilience, Brains, and Markets. International Technological University.

Cory, G. 2010b. Consilience and Spirituality. International Technological University.

Cory, G. 2009. "Let's Stop Teaching Greed. Dual Motive Theory as a New Paradigm for Global Economics." Paper presented at the combined meeting of the International Association for Research in Economic Psychology (IAREP) and the Society for the Advancement of Behavioral Economics (SABE) held at Saint Mary's University, Halifax, Nova Scotia, July 7–10.

Cory, G. 2006a. "Physiology and Behavioral Economics: The New Findings from Evolutionary Neuroscience." In Handbook of Contemporary Behavioral Economics: Foundations and Developments. Edited by M. Altman. ME Sharpe, 24–49.

Cory, G. 2006b. "A Behavioral Model of the Dual Motive Approach to Behavioral Economics and Social Exchange." The Journal of Socio-Economics. 35(4) (August): 592–612.

Cory, G. 2004. The Consilient Brain: The Bioneurological Basis of Economics, Society, and Politics. Kluwer Academic/Plenum.

Cory, G. 2003. "MacLean's Evolutionary Neuroscience and the CSN Model: Some Clinical and Social Policy Implications." In Human Nature and Public Policy. Edited by A. Somit & S. Peterson. Palgrave MacMillan, 161–180.

Cory, G. 2002a. "Reappraising MacLean's Triune Brain Concept." In The Evolutionary Neuroethology of Paul MacLean: Convergences and Frontiers. Edited by G. Cory & R. Gardner. Greenwood/Praeger, 9–27.

Cory, G. 2002b. "Algorithms of Neural Architecture, Hamilton's Rule, and the Invisible Hand of Economics." In The Evolutionary Neuroethology of Paul MacLean: Convergences and Frontiers. Edited by G. Cory and R. Gardner. Greenwood/Praeger.

Cory, G. 2000a. "From MacLean's Triune Brain Concept to the Conflict Systems Neurobehavioral Model: The Subjective Basis of Moral and Spiritual Consciousness." Zygon: Journal of Religion & Science, 35(2): 385–414.

Cory, G. 2000b. Toward Consilience: The Bioneurological Basis of Thought, Behavior, Language, and Experience. Kluwer Academic/Plenum.

Cory, G. 1999. The Reciprocal Modular Brain in Economics and Politics: Shaping the Rational and Moral Basis of Organization, Exchange, and Choice. Plenum.

Cory, G. 1992. Rescuing Capitalist Free Enterprise for the Twenty First Century. Center for Behavioral Ecology.

Cory, G. 1974. The Biopsychological Basis of Political Socialization and Political Culture. Ph.D. thesis. Stanford.

Cory, G. & Duffy, M. 2008. "Dual Motive Theory in India: An Analysis of Sen's Development As Freedom." Paper presented at the IAREP/SABE annual meeting, Luiss University, Rome, September 6–8.

Cory, G., Chan, Y-G. & Luo, J. 2008. "The Tri-Oriented Approach and Dual Motive Theory." Annual Conference IFSAM, Shanghai, China, July 27–29.

Cory, G. & Duffy, M. 2007. "Dual Motive Theory and Development: A Look at Sen's Development as Freedom through Brain Physiology." Paper presented at the Annual Meeting of the Society for the Advancement of Behavioral Economics (SABE), New York University, May 15–18.

Cory, G., Chan Y-G. & Rajaram, K. 2007. "Neuroeconomics and Dual Motive Theory: Can East Meet West? Bridging Eastern and Western Economics." Paper presented at Pacific Rim Conference, WEAI, Guanghua School of Management, Peking University, China, 17–21 January.

Cory, G. & Gardner, R. (eds) 2002. The Evolutionary Neuroethology of Paul MacLean. Convergences and Frontiers. Greenwood/ Praeger.

Cournot, A. 1929 [1838] Researches into the Mathematical Principles of the Theory of Wealth. Trans. by N. Bacon. Richard Irwin.

Damasio, A. 1999. The Feeling of What Happens. Harcourt.

Damasio, A. 1994. Descartes Error. Grosset/Putnam.
Darwin, C. 1964 [1859]. The Origin of Species. Facsimile of the First Ed. with intro. by E. Mayr. Harvard.
d'Autume, A. 1997. "What Space for Macroeconomics?" In Is Economics Becoming a Hard Science? Edited by A. d'Autume & J. Cartelier. Edward Elgar, 239–251.
Davidson, R., Scherer, K. & Goldsmith. H. (eds) 2003. Handbook of Affective Sciences. Oxford.
Davis, N. 2000. The Gift in Sixteenth Century France. Madison, Wisconsin. Oxford University Press.
Dawkins. R. 1982. The Extended Phenotype. Freeman.
Dawkins, R. 1976. The Selfish Gene. Oxford.
Decety, J. & Ickes, W. 2009. The Social Neuroscience of Empathy. MIT.
Derrida, J. 1992. Given Time: I. Counterfeit Money. Trans. by Peggy Kamuf. University of Chicago Press.
Descartes, R. "Rules." in Great Books of the Western World. Vol. 31. Edited by R. Hutchins & M. Adler. Encyclopedia Britannica.
Devinsky, O. & Luciano, D. 1993. "The Contributions of Cingulate Cortex to Human Behavior." In Neurobiology of Cingulate Cortex and Limbic Thalamus: A Comprehensive Handbook. Edited by B. Vogt, and M. Gabriel. Boston: Birkhauser, 527–556.
de Waal, F. 1996. Good Natured: The Origins of Right and Wrong in Humans and Other Animals. Harvard.
de Waal. Frans. 2002. "Evolutionary Psychology: The Wheat and the Chaff." Current Directions in Psychological Science, 11(6): 187–191.
Donaldson, Z. & Young, L. 2008. "Oxytocin, Vasopressin, and the Neurogenetics of Sociality." Science, 322(5903): 900–904 (Nov 7).
Douglas, M. 1990. "Foreword: No Free Gifts." In The Gift. Edited by M. Mauss. Trans. by W. Halls. Norton.
Duffy, M. & Cory, G. 2008. "Dual Motive Theory in India: An Analysis Of Sen's Development As Freedom." Paper presented at the IAREP/SABE annual meeting, Luiss University, Rome, September 6–8.
Dugger, W. 1996. "Four Modes of Inequality." In Inequality: Radical Institutionalist Views on Race, Gender, Class, and Nation. Edited by W. Dugger. Greenwood, 21–38.
Dunbar, R. 2016. Human Evolution. Oxford.
Dyson, F. 1999. Origins of Life. Cambridge.
Ebenstein, A. 2001. Frederich Hayek: A Biography. St. Martins.
Eckel, C. & Grossman, P. 1997. "Equity and Fairness in Economic Decisions: Evidence from Bargaining Experiments." In Advances in Economic Psychology. Edited by G. Antonides & W. F. van Raaij. Wiley, 281–301.
Edgeworth, F. 1881. Mathematical Psychics. Kegan Paul.
Eisenberg, N. 1994. "Empathy." In Encylopedia of Human Behavior. Edited by V. S. Ramachandran. Academic Press, 247–253.
Erdal, D. & Whiten, A. 1996. "Egalitarianism and Machiavellian Intelligence in Human Evolution." In Modelling the Early Human Mind. Edited by P. Mellars & K. Gibson. The Mc Donald Institute, Cambridge, 139–150.
Etzioni, A. 1988. The Moral Dimension: Toward a New Economics. MacMillan.
Evans, G. & Honkapohja, S. 2005. "An interview with Thomas J. Sargent." Macroeconomic Dynamics, 9: 561–583.

Evans, S. 2000. "General Discussion II." In Evolutionary Developmental Biology of the Cerebral Cortex. Edited by G. Bock & G. Cardew. Wiley, 109–111.

Fehr, E. & Gachter, S. 2000. "Fairness and Retaliation: The Economics of Reciprocity." Journal of Economic Perspectives, 14(3): 159–181.

Feiwel, G, ed. 1987. Arrow and the Ascent of Modern Economic Theory. Macmillan.

Fennell, L. 2002. "Unpacking the Gift." In The Question of the Gift. Edited by M. Osteen. Routledge, 85–101.

Fioriti, L., Myers, C., Huang, Y.-Y., Li, X., Stephan, J. S., Trifilieff, P., Colnaghi, L., Kosmidis, S., Drisaldi, B., Pavlopoulos, E. & Kandel, E. R. 2015. "The Persistence of Hippocampal-Based Memory Requires Protein Synthesis Mediated by the Prion-like Protein CPEB3" Neuron, 86(6): 1433–1448, 17 June 2015.

Flyvbjerg, B. 2001. Making Social Science Matter: Why Social Inquiry Fails and How It Can Succeed Again. Cambridge.

Force, P. 2003. Self-Interest Before Adam Smith. Cambridge.

Frank, R., Gilovich, T. & Regan, D. 1993. "Does Studying Economics Inhibit Cooperation?" Journal of Economic Perspectives, 7(2) (Spring): 159–171.

Frank, R. 1988. Passions Within Reason: The Strategic Role of the Emotions. Norton.

Freud, S. 1961 (1920). "Beyond the Pleasure Principle." Trans. by J. Strachey. Norton.

Freud, S. 1915–1917. Introductory Lectures. Psychoanalytic Training Institute.

Friedman, M. 1962. Capitalism and Freedom. University of Chicago Press.

Fuentes, A. 2012. Biological Anthropology: Concepts & Connections, 2/e. New York: McGraw Hill.

Fuentes, A. 2014. "Human Evolution, Niche Complexity, and the Emergence of a Distinctively Human Imagination." Time and Mind, 7(3): 241–257.

Fukuyama, F. 1992. The End of History and the Last Man. Free Press.

Fulton, J. 1951. Frontal Lobotomy and Affective Behavior. Norton.

Fuster, J. 2008. The Prefrontal Cortex (Fourth Edition) Academic Press.

Fuster, J. 1980. The Prefrontal Cortex: Anatomy, Physiology, and Neuro psychology of the Frontal Lobe. Raven Press.

Gehring, W. 1998. Master Control Genes in Development and Evolution. Yale.

Gérard-Varet, L.-A, Kolm, S.-C & Mercier Ythier, J. (eds) 2000. The Economics of Reciprocity, Giving, and Altruism. St. Martin's Press.

Ghiselin, M. T. 1974. The Economy of Nature and the Evolution of Sex. University of California Press, Berkeley.

Ghiselin, M. T. 1989. Intellectual Compromise: The Bottom Line. Paragon House.

Gintis, H. 2000. "Strong Reciprocity and Human Sociality." Journal of Theoretical Biology, 206: 169–179.

Glimcher, P. 2003. Decisions, Uncertainty, and the Brain: The Science of Neuroeconomics. MIT.

Gloor, P. 1997. The Temporal Lobe and the Limbic System. Oxford: Oxford University Press.

Godelier, M. 1999. The Enigma of the Gift. Polity Press.

Goldin-Meadow, S. et al. 2008. "The Natural Order of Events: How speakers ofdifferent languages represent events nonverbally." Proceedings of the National Academy of Sciences, July 8.

Gouldner, A. 1960. "The Norm of Reciprocity: A Preliminary Statement." American Sociological Review, 25: 161–178.

Gray, J. 1987. Fear and Stress. 2nd edn. Cambridge,

Greenough, W. & Chang, F. 1989. "Plasticity of Synapse Structure and Pattern in the Cerebral Cortex." In Cerebral cortex: Vol. 7. Edited by A. Peters & E. Jones. Plenum, 391–440.

Gregory, C. 1982. Gifts and Commodities. Academic Press.

Gregory, T. 1928. An Introduction to Tooke and Newmarch's History of Prices and the State of the Circulation from 1792 to 1856. P. S. King and Son.

Gribbin, J. 2004. Deep Simplicity: Bringing Order to Chaos and Complexity. Random House.

Hameroff, S. & Penrose, R. 1996. "Orchestrated Reduction of Quantum Coherence in Brain Microtubules: A Model for Consciousness." In St Hameroff, A. Kaszniak & A. Scott, eds, 1996. Toward a Science of Consciousness: The First Tucson Discussions and Debates. MIT Press, 507–539.

Hamilton, W. 1964. "The Genetical Evolution of Social Behavior, I & II." Journal of Theoretical Biology, 7: 1–16, 17–52.

Harel, D. 1987. Algorithms: The Spirit of Computing. Addison-Wesley.

Harrington, A. ed. 1992. So Human a Brain. Boston: Birkhauser.

Hayek. F. 1991. Economic Freedom. Basil Blackwell.

Hayek. F. 1988. The Fatal Conceit. Chicago. University of Chicago Press.

Hayek. F. 1973, 1976, 1979. Law, Legislation, and Liberty. 3 vols. Chicago. University of Chicago Press.

Hayek. F. 1944. The Road to Serfdom. Chicago. University of Chicago Press.

Heller, W., Nitschke, J. & Miller, G. 1998. "Lateralization in Emotion and Emotional Disorders." Current Directions in Psychological Science, 7(1): 26–32.

Henry, J. & Wang, S. 1998. "Affects of Early Stress on Adult Affiliative Behavior." Psychoneuro-endocrinology, 23(8): 863–875.

Herbert, J. & Schulkin, J. 2002. "Neurochemical Coding of Adaptive Responses in the Limbic System." In Hormones, Brain and Behavior. Edited by D. Pfaff. Academic Press, 659–697.

Hicks, J. 1939. Value and Capital. Oxford. Oxford University Press.

Hobbes, T. 1971/1651. Leviathan. Pelican Classics. Penguin.

Hobhouse, L. [1906] 1951. Morals in Evolution: A Study in Comparative Ethics. Chapman & Hall.

Hodgson, G. 1993. Economics and Evolution. Polity Press.

Hoffman, M. 2000. Empathy and Moral Development. Cambridge. Cambridge University.

Hoffman, M. 1981. "Is Altruism Part of Human Nature?" Journal of Personality and Social Psychology, 40: 121–137.

Homans, G. 1961. Social behavior: Its Elementary Forms. Harcourt Brace and World.

Homans, G. 1950. The Human Group. Harcourt Brace Jovanovich.

Housepian, E. 1998. "Bilateral Frontal Resection for Psychoses Revisited." Medical Review, 5(2) (Fall).

Hubisz, M. & Pollard, K. 2014. "Exploring the Genesis and Functions of Human Accelerated Regions Sheds Light on Their Role in Human Evolution. Current Opinion in Genetics & Development, 29:15–21.

Humphrey, N. 1976. "The Function of the Intellect." In Growing Points in Ethology. Edited by P. Bateson & R. Hinde. Cambridge, 303–317.

Hunt, R. 2002. "Economic Transfers and Exchanges: Concepts for Describing Allocations." In Theory in Economic Anthropology. Edited by J. Ensminger. Altamira Press, 105–118.

Iidaka, T., Terashima, S., Yamashita, K., Okada, T., Sadato, N. & Yonekura, Y. 2003. "Dissociable Neural Responses in the Hippo-campus to the Retrieval of Facial Identity and Emotion: An Event-related fMRI Study." Hippocampus, 13: 429–436.

Ingrao, B. & Israel, G. 1990. The Invisible Hand: Economic Equilibrium in the History of Science. Trans. by Ian McGilvray. MIT.

Isaac, G. 1978. "The Food-sharing Behavior of Protohuman Hominids." Scientific American, 238: 90–108.

Jaffe, W. 1983. William Jaffe's Essays on Walras. Ed. D. Walker. Cambridge.

Jevons, W. 1888. The Theory of Political Economy. MacMillan.

Jevons, W. 1905. Essays of Economics. MacMillan.

Johnson, G. 1986. Research Methodology for Economists. Macmillan.

Jones, E. 2007. The Thalamus. 2nd Ed. Cambridge.

Kahneman, D., Diener, E. & Schwarz, N., eds. 1999. Well-Being: The Foundations of Hedonic Psychology. Russell Sage.

Kaku, M. 2014. The Future of the Mind: The Scientific Quest to Understand, Enhance, and Empower the Mind. Doubleday.

Kandel, E., Schwartz, J., Jessell, T., Siegelbaum, S. & Hudspeth, A.J. 2013. Principles of Neural Science. 5th edn. McGraw-Hill.

Kandel, E., Schwartz, J. & Jessell, T. 2000. Essentials of Neural Science and Behavior. Appleton & Lange.

Kemp, T. 2016. The Origin of Higher Taxa. Oxford & Chicago.

Kirman, A. 2006. "Demand Theory and General Equilibrium: From Explanation to Introspection, a Journey down the Wrong Road." History of Political Economy 38 (annual suppl): 246–280.

Knauft, B. 1991. "Violence and Sociality in Human Evolution." Current Anthropology, 32: 391–428.

Knauft, B. 1994. "Culture and Cooperation in Human Evolution." In L. Sponsel & T. Gregor, eds. The Anthropology of Peace and Nonviolence. Lynne Rienner, 37–67.

Kohlberg, L. 1984. The Psychology of Moral Development. Vol. 2. Harper & Row.

Kolb, B. 1995. Brain Plasticity and Behavior. Erlbaum.

Kolb, B., Gibb, R. & Robinson, T. 2003. "Brain Plasticity and Behavior." Current Directions in Psychological Science, 12(1) (February): 1–5.

Kolb, B. & Gibb, R. 2011. "Brain Plasticity and Behaviour in theDeveloping Brain." Journal of the Canadian Academy of Child and Adolescent Psychiatry, 20(4) (November): 265–276.

Komter, A. 2005. Social Solidarity and the Gift. Cambridge. Cambridge University Press.

Krugman, P. & Wells, R. 2013. Microeconomics. Third Edition. World Publishers.

Lambert, K. & Gerlai, R. eds. 2003. "A Tribute to Paul MacLean: The Neurobiological Relevance of Social Behavior." Physiology and Behavior, 79(3).

Landsburg, S. 2002. Price Theory and Applications. Southwestern.

Lasley, E. 2009. "A Road Paved by Reason." Cerebrum 2009. Edited by D. Gordon. Dana Press.

Lederman, L. & Teresi, D. 1993. The God Particle. Houghton Mifflin.

Leh, S.E., Petrides, M. & Strafella, A.P. 2010. "The Neural Circuitry of Executive Functions in Healthy Subjects and Parkinson's Disease." Neuropsycho-pharmacology, 35(1) (January): 70–85.

Leven, S. 1994. "Semiotics, Meaning, and Discursive Neural Networks." In Neural Networks for Knowledge Representation and Inference. Edited by D. Levine. Lawrence Erlbaum, 65–82.

Levi-Strauss, C. [1949] 1969. The Elementary Structures of Kinship. Eyre and Spottiwoode.

Levine, D. 2006. "Neural Modeling of the Dual Motive Theory of Economics." Journal of Socio-Economics, 35(4) (August).

Levine, D. & Yani, N. 2002. "Toward a Neural Network Theory of the Triune Brain." In The Evolutionary Neuroethology of Paul MacLean: Convergences and Frontiers. Edited by G. Cory & R. Gardner. Praeger.

Lieberman, P. 2000. Human Language and Our Reptilian Brain. Harvard.

Liebersohn, H. 2011. The Return of the Gift. Cambridge. Cambridge University Press.

Loonen, A. & Ivanov, S. 2016. "Circuits Regulating Pleasure and Happiness: the evolution of the amygdalar-hippocampal-habenular connectivity in vertebrates." Front Neurosci, 10: 539.

Loye, D. 2007. Darwin's Lost Theory. Benjamin Franklin Press.

Luo, J., Chan, Y-G. & Cory, G. 2008. "The Tri-Oriented Approachand Dual Motive Theory." Annual Conference IFSAM, Shanghai, China, July 27–29.

Lynne, G. 2006. "Toward a Dual Motive Economic Theory." Journal of Socio-Economics. 35(4) (August).

MacLean, P. 1990. The Triune Brain in The Triune Brain in Evolution: Role in Paleocerebral Functions.

Malinowski, B. 1926. Crime and Custom in Savage Society. Kegan Paul.

Malinowski, B. 1922. Argonauts of the Western Pacific. Routledge & Kegan Paul.

Mandeville, B. de. 1714. Fable of the Bees.

Mansbridge, J. ed. 1990. Beyond Self-Interest. Chicago. University of Chicago Press.

Margulis, L. 1998. Symbiotic Planet. Basic Books.

Marshall, A. 1947 (1920). Principles of Economics. Eighth Edition. MacMillan.

Marshall, A. 2003 (1892). Elements of Economics of Industry. Simon Publications.

Martini, F.H., Nath, J.L. & Bartholomew, E.F. 2015. Fundamentals of Anatomy & Physiology. Tenth Edition. Pearson Education.

Mauss, Marcel. 1990. The Gift. Trans. by W. Halls. NY: Norton

Mauss, Marcel. 1954. The Gift. Trans. by Ian Cunnison. Norton.

Maynard Smith, J. 2002. "Equations of Life." In It Must be Beautiful: Great Equations of Modern Science. Edited by G. Farmelo. Granta Books, 193–211.

Maynard Smith, J. 1982. "The Evolution of Social Behavior–a Classification of Models." In Current Problems in Sociobiology. Edited by King's College Sociobiology Group. Cambridge, 28–44.

McQuaig, L., 2001. All You Can Eat: Greed, Lust and the New Capitalism. Penguin Books.

Mirowski, P. 1989. More Heat than Light. Cambridge. Cambridge University Press.

Moore, B. 1978. Injustice: The Social Basis of Obedience and Revolt. M.E. Sharpe.

Morgane, P., Galler, J. & Mokler, D. 2005. "A Review of Systems and Networks of the Limbic Forebrain/Limbic Midbrain." Progress in Neurobiology, 75: 143–160.

Morishima, M. 1992. "General Equilibrium Theory in the Twenty-First Century" in The Future of Economics. Edited by John D. Hey. Oxford: Blackwell.

Nadeau, R. 2003. The Wealth of Nature. Columbia University.

Nash, J. 1953. "The Two Person Cooperative Games." Econometrica, 21: 405–421.

Nash, J. 1951. "Non-Cooperative Games." Annals of Mathematics, 54: 286–295.

Nash, J. 1950. "The Bargaining Problem" Econometrica, 18: 155–162.

Nelson, R., 2000. An Introduction to Behavioral Endocrinology. 2nd edn. Sinauer.

Neumann, J. von & Morgenstern, O. 1944. Theory of Games and Economic Behavior. Second edn. Princeton.

Newman, J. & Harris, J. 2009. "The Scientific Contributions of Paul D. MacLean 1913–2007." Journal of Mental and Nervous Disease, 197(1).

Newmarch, W. 1861. "The Progress of Economic Science During the Last Thirty Years: An Opening Address [before Section F]." Journal of the Statistical Society, XXIV, Part IV (December): 451–467.

Numan, M. & Insel, T. 2003. The Neurobiology of Parental Behavior. Springer.

O'Brien, M.J. & Laland, K. 2012. "Genes, Culture, and Agriculture: An Example of Human Niche Construction." Current Anthropology, 53(4): 434–470.

O'Callaghan, M. & Carroll, D. 1982. Psychosurgery: A Scientific Analysis. MTP Press.

Odling-Smee, F.J., Laland, K.N. & Feldman, M.F. 2003. "Niche Construction: The Neglected Process in Evolution." Monographs in Population Biology 37. Princeton University Press.

Osteen, M. 2002. "Gift or Commodity." In The Question of the Gift. Edited by M. Osteen. Routledge, 229–247.

Panksepp, Jaak. 2004. Textbook of Biological Psychiatry. Wiley.

Panksepp, Jaak. 2002. "Foreword." In The Evolutionary Neuroethology of Paul MacLean: Convergences and Frontiers. Edited by G. Cory & R. Gardner. Praeger.

Panksepp, Jaak. 1998. Affective Neuroscience. NY: Oxford.

Panksepp, Jaak & Panksepp, Jules. B. 2000. "The Seven Sins of Evolutionary Psychology." Evolution and Cognition, 6: 108–131.

Parry, J. and Bloch, M. (eds) 1989. Money and the Morality of Exchange. Cambridge. Cambridge University Press.

Parsons, T. 1960. "Pattern Variables Revisited." American Sociological Review, 25: 467–488.

Parsons, T. 1951. The Social System. Free Press.

Patlolla, B. 2008. "The Neuro-Physiological Foundations of Dual Motive Theory: A Review of the Brain Model set forth in Wilson and Cory's The Evolutionary Epidemiology of Mania and Depression." Paper presented at the IAREP/SABE annual meeting, Luiss University, Rome, September 6–8.

Penrose, Roger. 1994. Shadows of the Mind. London: Oxford.

Penrose, R. 1991. The Emperor's New Mind. Penguin.

Perlman, M. & McCann, C. 1999, 2000. The Pillars of Economic Understanding. 1 & 2. Michigan.

Pfeiffer, U. 2013. "Oxytocin – Not Always a Moral Molecule." Frontiers in Human Neuroscience, 7: 10.

Piaget, Jean. [1932] 1965. The Moral Judgement of the Child. Free Press.

Piketty, T. 2020. Capital and Ideology. Harvard.

Piketty, T. 2014. Capital in the Twenty-first Century. Harvard.

Pinker, S. 1997. How the Mind Works. Norton.

Plant, R. 1992. "Enterprise in its Place: The Moral Limits of Market." In The Values of the Enterprise Culture: The Moral Debate. Edited by P. Heelas & P. Morris. Routledge, 85–99.

Plato. 1982 [c 380 B.C.]. The Republic. Trans. by G. Grube Indianapolis, IN: Hackett.

Polanyi, K. 1944. The Great Transformation. Farrar & Rineheart.

Pollard, K. 2009. "What Makes Us Human?" Scientific American, 300(5): 44–49.

Porges, S. 1998. "Love: An Emergent Property of the Mammalian Autonomic Nervoussystem." Psychoneuroendocrinology, 23: 837–861.

Porter, T. M. 1986. The Rise of Statistical Thinking, 1820–1900. Princeton.
Pressman, J. 1998. Last Resort: Psychosurgery and the Limits of Medicine. Cambridge. Cambridge University Press.
Pribram, K. & Luria, A. (eds) 1973. Psychophysiology of the Frontal Lobes. Academic Press.
Prigogine, I. & Stengers, E. 1984. Order out of Chaos: Man's New Dialogue with Nature. New Science Library.
Przewlocki, R. 2002. "Stress, Opiod Peptides, and their Receptors." In Hormones, Brain, and Behavior. Edited by D. Pfaff Academic Press, 691–733.
Pyyhtinen, O. 2014. The Gift and its Paradoxes. Ashgate.
Reiner, A. 1990. "Review of MacLean's The Triune Brain in Evolution." Science, 250 (October 12): 303–305.
Rizzolati, G. 2011. "The Mirror Mechanism: New Findings." Keynote Address: Annual Conference American Psychological Society. Washington, D.C. May 26–29.
Robbins, L. 1952. An Essay on the Nature & Significance of Economic Science. Second edn. MacMillan.
Rolls, E. 2016. Cerebral Cortex: Principles of Operation. Oxford. Oxford University Press.
Ross, D. 2010. "Neuroeconomics and Economic Methodology" (May 30, 2010). In The Elgar Handbook of Economic Methodology. Edited by J. Davis & W. Hands. Forthcoming.
Saarela, M.V., Hlushchuk, Y., Williams, A.C. de C., Schürmann, M., Kalso, E. & Hari, R. 2006. "The Compassionate Brain: Humans Detect Intensity of Pain from Another's Face." Cerebral Cortex, doi: 10. 1093/cercor/bhj 141
Sagan, C. 1977. Dragons of Eden. Ballantine Books.
Sahlins, M. 1976. Culture and Practical Reason. Chicago. University of Chicago.
Sahlins, M. 1972. Stone Age Economics. Aldine-Atherton.
Sahlins, M. 1963. "On the Sociology of Primitive Exchange." in The Relevance of Models for Social Anthropology. Edited by M. Banton. Tavistock, 139–236.
Samuelson, P. 1947. Foundations of Economic Analysis. Harvard.
Santiesteban, I., Banissy, M.J., Catmur, C. & Bird, G. 2012. "Enhancing Social Ability by Stimulating Right Temporoparietal Junction." Current Biology, 22(23) (4 Dec): 2274–2277.
Sargent, T. 2008. "Evolution and Intelligent Design." American Economic Review, 98(1): 5–37.
Say, J-B. 1855. A Treatise on Political Economy. Trans. by C. Princep. Lippincott.
Scheidel, W. 2017. The Great Leveler. Princeton. Princeton University Press.
Schlefer, J. 2012. The Assumptions Economists Make. Belknap Press of Harvard.
Schumpeter, J. 1954. History of Economic Analysis. NY: Oxford.
Schumpeter, J. 1947 [1942]. Capitalism, Socialism, and Democracy. Harper & Brothers.
Schulkin, J. 2002. "Hormonal Modulation of Central Motivational States." In Hormones, Brain, and Behavior. Edited by D. Paff. 1. Academic, 633–657.
Sen, A. 1997. On Economic Inequality. Expanded Edition. Clarendon Press.
Sen, A. 1979. "Rational Fools: A Critique of the Behavioral Foundations of Economic Theory." In Philosophy and Economic Theory. Edited by F. Hahn and M. Hollis. Oxford. Oxford University Press.
Seymour-Smith, C. 1986. Dictionary of Anthropology. Boston: G. K. Hall & Co.
Shaw, C. & McEachern, J. 2001. Toward a Theory of Neuroplasticity. Psychology Press.
Sherman, S. & Guillery, R. 2001. Exploring the Thalamus. Academic Press.

Sherman, D.K., Kim, H.S. & Taylor, S.E. "Cultural and Social Support: Neural Bases and Biological Impact." In Cultural Neuroscience: Cultural Influences on Brain Function. Edited by J. Chiao. Progress in Brain Research. 178. Elsevier, 227–237.

Sherwood, C., Bauernfeind, A., Bianchi, S. & Raghanti M. 2012. "Human Brain Evolution Writ Large and Small." Progress in Brain Research 195: 237–254.

Simmel, G. 1950. The Sociology of Georg Simmel. Trans. by K. Wolff. Free Press.

Singer, T. 2006. "The Neuronal Basis and Ontogeny of Empathy and Mind Reading." Neuroscience and Biobehavioral Reviews, 30: 855–863.

Skoyles, J. & Sagan, D. 2002. Up from Dragons: The Evolution of Human Intelligence. McGraw-Hill.

Smith, Adam. 1977[1740–90]. "The Correspondence of Adam Smith (1740–90)." In Vol. 6 of The Glasgow Edition of the Works and Correspondence of Adam Smith. Edited by E. Mossner & T. Ross. General editing by D. Raphael and A. Skinner. Oxford: Clarendon Press.

Smith, Adam. 1982 [1790]. The Theory of Moral Sentiments. 6th edn. Edited by D. Raphael & A. Macfie. Liberty Press.

Smith, Adam. 1937[1776]. The Wealth of Nations. Edited by E. Cannan. Modern Library.

Smith, Adam 1986 [1776]. The Wealth of Nations, Books I–III. Penguin Classics.

Stallen, M., et al. 2012. "The Herding Hormone. Oxytocin Stimulates In-Group Conformity." Psychological Science. 23(11) (November): 1288–1292.

Stapp, H. 1972. "The Copenhagen Interpretation." American Journal of Physics, 40(8): 1098–1116.

Stigler, G. 1976. "The Successes and Failures of Professor Smith." Selected Papers no. 50, Graduate School of Business. University of Chicago.

Stigler, G. 1971. "Smith's Travels on the Ship of State." History of Political Economy, 265.

Stigler, G. 1952. The Theory of Price. MacMillan.

Stuss, D. & Knight, R. 2002. Principles of Frontal Lobe Function. Oxford. Oxford University Press.

Tankersley, D., Stowe, C., Huettel, S. 2007. "Altruism is Associated with an Increased Neural Response to Agency." Nature Neuroscience, 10(2) (February): 150–151.

Taylor, S. 2002. The Tending Instinct. Time Books.

Taylor, T. 2012. The Instant Economist. Plume (Penguin).

Tett, G. 2009. Fool's Gold: How the Bold Dream of a Small Tribe at J. P. Morgan was corrupted by Wall Street Greed and Unleashed a Catastrophe. Free Press.

Thurnwald, R. 1932. Economics in Primitive Communities. Oxford. Routledge.

Tickell, C. 1993. "The Human Species: A Suicidal Success." Geographical Journal, 159: 219–226.

Teitelbaum, H. 1956. "Homeostasis and Personality." Archives of Neurology and Psychiatry 76(3), 317–324.

Thompson, D. 1993. "Mediated Corruption: The Case of the Keating Five." The American Political Science Review, 87(2) (June): 369–381.

Titmuss, R. 1972. The Gift Relationship: From Human Blood to Social Policy. Pantheon.

Tooke, T. & Newmarch, W. History of Prices and the State of the Circulation from 1792 to 1856.

Tomer, J. 2012. "Brain Physiology, Egoistic and Empathetic Motivation, and Brain Plasticity: Toward a More Human Economics," World Economic Review, 1: 2012.

Trivers, R. 1981. "Sociobiology and Politics." In Sociobiology and Human Politics. Edited by E. White. Heath & Company, 1–44.

Trivers, R. 1971. "The Evolution of Reciprocal Altruism." The Quarterly Review of Biology, 46: 35–57.

Tucker, D., Luu, P., Phan, P. & Pribram, K. 1995. "Social and Emotional Self-Regulation." Annals of the New York Academy of Sciences, 769: 213–239.

Valenstein, E. 1986. Great and Desperate Cures: The Rise and Decline of Psychosurgery and Other Medical Treatments for Mental Disorders. Basic Books.

Van Baal, J. 1975. Reciprocity and the Position of Women. Van Gorcum.

Vaughan. G. (ed.) 2007. Women and the Gift Economy. Inanna Publications.

Vaughan, G. 1997. For-Giving. Plain View Press.

Vinogradova, O.S. 2001. "Hippocampus as comparator: role of the two input and two output systems of the hippocampus in selection and registration of information." Hippocampus, 11(5): 578–598.

Von Bertallanfy, L. 1968. General Systems Theory. Revised Edition. George Braziller.

Walker, D. (Ed.) 1983. William Jaffe's Essays on Walras. Cambridge. Cambridge University Press.

Walras, Léon. 2010 (1936). Studies in Social Economics Trs. Edited by J. van Daal & D.A. Walker. Routledge.

Walras, Léon. 1954. Elements of Pure Economics. 4th edn. Trans. by W. Jaffe. Richard D. Irwin, Inc.

Ward, L. 2013. "The Thalamus: Gateway to the Mind." WIREs Cognitive Science, 4(6):609–622. doi: 10.1002/wcs.1256

Wells, J. & Stock, J. 2007. "The Biology of the Colonizing Ape." American Journal of Physical Anthropology, Supplement: Yearbook of Physical Anthropology 134(Supplement 45): 191–222.

Whittaker, R.A., Levin, S.A. & Root, R.B. 1973. "Niche, Habitat, and Ecotope." American Naturalist 107: 321–338.

Wiener, N. 1948. Cybernetics. John Wiley.

Wiest, G. 2012. "Neural and Mental Hierarchies." Frontiers in Psychology, 3: 516.

Wilson, D. 2006. "The Evolutionary Neuroscience of Human Reciprocal Sociality: A Basic Outline for Economists." Journal of Socio-Economics, 35(4) (August).

Wilson, D. 1992. "Evolutionary Epidemiology." Acta Bio-theoretica, 40: 87–90.

Wilson, D. & Cory, G. 2008. The Evolutionary Epidemiology of Mania and Depression. Mellen Press.

Wilson, E. 1998. Consilience: The Unity of Knowledge. Knopf.

Wilson, E. 1993. "Analyzing the Superorganism: The Legacy of Whitman and Wheeler." In The Biological Century. Edited by Barlow, R., Dowling, R. & Weissman, G. Harvard, Harvard University Press, 243–255.

Witter, M. & Groenewegen, H. 1992. "Organizational Principles of Hippocampal Connections." In The Temporal Lobes and the Limbic System. Edited by Trimble, M.R. & Bolwig, T.G. Wrightson Biomedical Publishing, 37–60.

Wilson, E.O. 2012. *The Social Conquest of Earth*. W W Norton & Co.

Wood, R.C., Levine, D.S., Cory, G.A. & Wilson, D.R. 2015. "Evolutionary Neuroscience and Motivation in Organizations." Pp. 143–167 in Organizational Neuroscience. Edited by D. Waldman and P. Balthazard. Emerald, 37–60.

Zak, P. 2012. The Moral Molecule. Dutton.

Zimmer, C. 2014. The Tangled Bank: An Introduction to Evolution. Second edn. Roberts and Company.

Index

Note: Page numbers in *italics* indicate figures on the corresponding pages.

Ackerman, F. 94
A-Complex 21
adults, egoistic behavior in 42
affect 34; flat 34
affection 36
Affective Neuroscience 30
algorithms of social behavior: algorithmic neural dynamic 41; First Rule, Egoistic Range 41–42; organic 59–60; origins of 4–5; physics, genes, and 61–62; in price theory 104–106; Second Rule, Empathetic Range 42–44; Third Rule, Range of Dynamic Balance 44; transaction and 73–74
al-Khowarizmi, M. 40
alliances 161
altruism 43–44, 71, 142–143, 148, 154–156
American Journal of Sociology 67
American Scientist 15
amniotes 13, 18–19, 26
amoral economics 144
Anglo-American thinking, stiff upper lip in 148, 149
Appadurai, A. 72
applied science 56
Archives of Neurology and Psychiatry 54
arginine vasopressin 35–36
Arrow, K. 93
art of selling 79–80
Assumptions Economists Make, The 94
Attachment and Bonding: A New Synthesis 30
axiomatization 92–93

Bargaining Problem, The 132
Beautiful Mind, A 127
Becker, G. 115
behavior 26–27; altruistic 43–44, 71, 142–143, 148, 154–156; dynamic balance range 38; egalitarian 88–89; egoistic range 36–37, *37*; empathetic range *37*, 37–38; energy or activation level escalation and de-escalation 38–39; ethology of 152; external and internal conflict 27; global-state circuits in 27; interconnected neural networks subjectively driving objective, observable 33–34; major ranges of reciprocal, conflict 36–39, *37*; in the market 88; physics, genes, and 61–62; predictability of 46; *See also* algorithms of social behavior
behavioral empathy 123–124
behavioral tension (BT) 27–28; driving transaction 74–75; equation 53–54, 101, 108–112; frustration as expression of 103; as generic regulator of social architecture 50; incentives, productivity, and 167–168; mitigated by courtesy 69; motivating price change 103; reciprocity and 69; stratification as structured 158; transaction and 73–74
behavioral wave function 62–63
behaviorism, radical 148
Bem, D. 31
Bernard, C. 47
Bertalanffy, L. v. 47
biological linkages 12
Biopsychological Basis of Political Socialization and Political Culture, The 137
Blaug, M. 2
Bloch, M. 85
Boehm, C. 68, 88–89
Bohannan, P. 72

brain: Conflict Systems Neurobehavioral (CSN) Model 3, 4, 31–32; Ego and Empathy and (*See* Ego and Empathy); evolutionary psychology and 153; executive centers of 50; executive circuitry and language 30–31; executive circuitry and neural networks 33–36; gating of dual motives 34; homeostatic variability and 50; hormones and neurotransmitters and 27, 35–36, 139–140; lateralization vs. integration *32*, 32–33; neocortex 19, 33; phenotypic power of mammalian architecture and behavior and 151; as physiological organ 29; psychosurgery and 34–35; social nature of 3, 8, 29–31; temporoparietal junction (TPJ) 34; triune brain theory (*See* triune brain theory)
Braudel, F. 85
bribes, gift as 73
Butler, A. 3, 14, 19–21, 25, 32, 138

Cannon, W. B. 47
Cantillon, R. 144
chaos/complexity theory 57
Cheal, D. 84
children, egoistic behavior in 42
choices and meaning 30
Civilization and Capitalism 85
Civil Society rules 121
cognitive integration 31
Common Amniote Formation 21
competition, market 123
computers 48
conflict: external and internal 27; reciprocity through 44
Conflict Systems Neurobehavioral (CSN) Model 3–4, 31–32, 159, 169–170; avoiding future minor technical disagreements 32; as functional representation of physiological circuits 31–32; major ranges of 36–39, *37*; predictability and 46; sources of probability and 60; zero at or below extremes of ego or empathy and 57–58
consilience 2, 20; neuroeconomics and 137–138
Consilience, Brains, and Leadership: The Emergence of Human Alliance 137
Consilience, Brains, and Markets: Saving the Free Enterprise Market for a Global Society 30, 137
Consilience and Spirituality: the Scientific Foundations for the Choice to Believe or Not to Believe 137
Consilience: The Unity of Knowledge 2
Consilient Brain: the Bioneurological Basis of Economics, Society, and Politics, The 137
constant case, equilibrium equation 108–111
cooperation 154–155
cooperative games 131–132
Copenhagen Interpretation 63
corruption through gifts 72–73
Cournot, A. A. 56
courtesy 69
creative destruction: innovation and 124–125; sustainability, inequality, and 125
creativity in the market 124–126
customer service 79
Cybernetics 47
cybernetics, information theory, and homeostasis 47–48

Darwin, C. 142–143, 153, 161
Davis, N. 71
Dawkins, R. 149–150, 151
death, zero equals 54
Debreu, G. 93
deception of self-interest 80
deduction in economics 144, 145
Demand and Supply 5–6, 72, 83–84, 97–102, 163; demand curve 98, *98*; dynamic balance in 100–101; equilibrium price 107–109, *108*, 165, *165*; expanded social equation and 101; homeostatic, self-correcting market dynamic and 101–102; homeostatic equation and "haggle" range and 101; Invisible Hand and 83; market equilibrium and 100, *100*; price theory and 102, 104–106; supply curve *99*, 99–100
democracy: necessary conditions for market exchange system in 167; preventing undue interference or obstruction in 167; socio-political participation and pressures for equality in 160
Derrida, J. 71–72
Descartes, R. 130
Descartes' Error: Emotion, Reason, and the Human Brain 30
desire for conquest 142
de Waal, F. 68
Dictionary of Anthropology, The 72
diffuse reciprocity 69
divergence: to extremes due warning of survival danger 55; magnitude of 54

Donaldson and young 36
Douglas, M. 89
Dragons of Eden 17, 22
dual motives 34, 89, 115–116; electrochemical physiology of 35–36; psychosurgery and 34–35
Dugger, W. 158
Durkheim, E. 70
dynamic balance range 38; algorithmic neural dynamic 44; Demand and Supply 100–101

economics: Anglo American stiff upper lippedness in 148, 149; attempts to apply physics to 76, 90–91, 144; Charles Darwin on survival, self-interest, and altruism and 142–143; deduction in 144, 145; dual motives in (*See* dual motives); emergence of amoral 144; epicyclic patchwork in 147; gift economy vs. market economy and 84–87, *86*; gift-giving and 70; induction in 144–145; Judeo-Christian tradition in 141–142; laws of, as tendencies 60; making of "scientific" 143–148; as moral enterprise 143; negative social side effects in 148; neoclassical 90; new, as mixed positive-normative science 96; reciprocity and 67; self-interest in 76–77; selfish gene and 149–150; "silo" effect of departmented academia in 141; Social Darwinism and 143; uncertainty in 93; *See also* neuroeconomics
Edgeworth, F.Y. 113
egalitarian behavior 88–89
Ego and Empathy 3–6, 8, 25, 170; all-inclusive, hedonic approach to 146; BT equation 53–54; clarification of 35; death at extremes of 57–58; Demand and Supply and 83–84, 97–102; dynamic balance range 38; egoistic range 36–37, *37*; empathetic range *37*, 37–38; energy or activation level escalation and de-escalation 38–39; family connection 45; flat affect and 34; interconnected neural networks and 33–34; lateralization vs. integration and *32*, 32–33; limits to variability and 51; optimal functioning and 55; pragmatism and 95–96; present-day mismatch and importance of socialization and education 45; reciprocity and 68; scale of inclusiveness 45; as sources of all motives 36–39, *37*
egoistic range 36–37, *37*; algorithmic neural dynamic 41–42; in children vs. adults 42
electrochemical physiology of dual motives 35–36
empathetic range *37*, 37–38; algorithmic neural dynamic 42–44; altruism 43–44; gift-giving and reciprocity 43; thank you expressions 43
empathy 117–118; accommodating self-interest and 132–133; behavioral 123–124; explicit 131–132; implicit 121, 131–132; as implicit in Nash equilibrium 130–133; improving survival odds of self *plus* others inclusively 155–156; in the marketplace 79–80; as preference or taste 116–117; structural 123–124; *See also* Ego and Empathy
endocasts 12
energy or activation level escalation and de-escalation 38–39
enlightened self-interest 147
epicyclic patchwork in modern economics 147
epigenetics 23–24
equilibrium price (EP): constant case 108; elaborated equation 108–109; as a function 109–111; nonconstant case 111–112; unit change above/below 107–108, *108*
Essai sur le Don 70
ethology 152
Evans, G. 95
evolutionary biology 153
evolutionary brain science 12–13; amniotes in 13, 18–19; cautionary pitfalls in 22–23; common amniote formation or A-complex 21; concept of niche in 24–25; epigenetics and 23–24; evolved networked brain and behavioral conflict and 26–28; in higher primates and Homo Sapiens 14–18, *17*; interconnected triality in 18–19; MacLean's Reptilian Brain model in 14–19; neocortex and greater complexity of behavior in 19; parental care and social bonding in 14, 19, 26; phenotypic power of mammalian architecture and behavior and 151; replacement generalization 20–22; *scala naturae* and 23; self-preserving mechanisms and 25–26; self-survival phase in 13–14; Stem Mammalian Formation 21; Therian Formation 21

Evolutionary Epidemiology of Mania and Depression, The 30
evolutionary neuroethology: empathy improving survival odds of self *plus* others inclusively and 155–156; ethology as study of animal behavior and 152; evolutionary biology and evolutionary psychology and 153; humans as information processors and 152; inclusive fitness and 154–155
Evolutionary Neuroethology of Paul MacLean: Convergences and Frontiers 15
evolutionary psychology 153
executive circuitry: language and 30–31; neural networks and 33–36
existence 93–94
Extended Phenotype, The 150
external conflict 27

Fable of the Bees 81, 126
failure, market 125–126
family 45; natural affection in 69; as social system 162, *162*
Fatal Conceit, The 119
features vs. benefits empathy 79–80
feedback 48
fellow-feeling *See* sympathy
Fennell, L. 71
feudal systems 87
flat affect 34
Foundations in Social Neuroscience 30
Foundations of Economic Analysis 92
Friedman, M. 88, 123
Future of the Mind, The 16

Gardner, R. 15
gating of dual motives 34
general equilibrium theory (GET) 2, 8, 89, 145, 169; axiomatization and top-down formalization of 92–93; disillusionment with 94–95; distortions of physics and Plato and 92; existence, uniqueness, and stability in 93–94; initially off on the wrong foot 91; Léon Walras and full establishment of 91–92
General Systems Theory (GST) 47
genes: continuity and 18; development and learning interacting with 61; genetic variation and 60; physics, and behavior precision vs. statistical probability 61–62; selfish 149–150
Ghiselin, M. 43–44
Gift, The 70, 89
gift economy: as based on feminine perspective 84; evolutionary sequence from gift to exchange and 85; social exchange and 85–87; as total social system 84; transition to market economy 85
gift-giving 43; as bribery 73; deconstructive logic applied to 71–72; economic and political consequences of 70; as empathetic act 69–70; expanded literature on 71; pervasive reciprocity in 70; that corrupts 72–73; transition evolved from 72; universality across cultures 71
Glimcher, P. 137
global-state circuits 27
Gloor, P. 38
God Particle, The 140
God's model 5, 95
Gouldner, A. 67
granite of self-interest 113
Graunt, J. 144
Gray, J. 38
Great Transformation, The 85
Greenspan, A. 83
Gregory, C. 72
Groenewegen, H. 38
groping 102

"haggle" range 101
Halls, W. D. 70
Hameroff, S. 63
Hamilton, W. D. 154–155
Handbook of Affective Sciences 30
Harel, D. 41
Hastings, W. 73
Hayek, F. 6–7, 158; hopefulness and wishful thinking of 122; on moral instincts 120–122; resolving the Hayekian conflict and 122; on spontaneous order 120, 121–122, 125–126; works by 119
hedonic approach 146
hierarchical exchange 88–89
hierarchy, social 161; instability of 161
History of Prices and the State of the Circulation from 1792 to 1856 144
Hobbes, T. 120, 142, 143, 146, 170
Hobhouse, L. T. 67
Hodgson, G. 11
homeostasis 3, 47–48; cybernetics, information theory, and 47–48; Demand and Supply and 101–102; feedback and 48; limits of variability and 51; neural

plasticity, learning, and variability in 50; of social architecture 48–49; success of human social life 51–52
homeostatic equation: constant case 108–111; elaborated equation 108–109; nonconstant case 111–112; unit change above/below equilibrium price 107–108, *108*
homo arrogance 30
homo economicus 115–116
Honkapohja, S. 95
hormones 27, 35–36, 139–140
HPA (hypothalamic-pituitary-adrenal) axis 38
Human Evolution 30
human nature 142, 147
Human Species: A Suicidal Success?, The 52
Hume, D. 143
Hunt, R. 72
hunting, gathering, and sharing 30
Hutcheson, F. 81, 143

implicit empathy 121
incentives 167–168
inclusive fitness 154–155
inclusiveness, scale of 45, 89
individual learning 61
induction in economics 144–145
inequality: creative destruction and 125; social brain equation as metric of socio-behavioral tension and 157–161
Ingrao, B. 91
innovation, market 124–126
Insel, T. 16
Integrative Neurobiology of Affiliation, The 30
Intelligent Assist 95–96
intelligent design 95, 168
interconnected triality 18–19
internal conflict 27
Invisible Hand 5–6, 101; Adam Smith and 81–83; Bernard de Mandeville on 81; Demand and Supply and 83–84; spontaneous order vs. 120, 125–126; in structure and behavior of the marketplace 87–89
Israel, G. 91

Jevons, W. S. 113, 145–147
Journal of Economic Perspectives 114
Judeo-Christian tradition 141–142

Kahneman, D. 146
Kaku, M. 16
Kemp, T. S. 22
Kennedy, D. 31
kinship reciprocity 72
Kirman, A. 94
Kohlberg, L. 61
Krugman, P. 103, 113–114

language and executive circuitry 30–31
lateralization vs. integration *32*, 32–33
Law, Legislation, and Liberty 119
learning, individual 61
learning differences 60
Levi-Strauss, C. 67, 71
linkage rules 12
Locke, J. 81, 142
logical positivism 148
Lorenz, K. 152

MacLean, P. 3, 14–19, 25, 138, 161; evolutionary neuroethology and 153–154; *See also* triune brain theory
magnitude of divergence or convergence 54
Malinowski, B. 67, 71
Mandeville, B. de 81, 126, 170
market, the: behavior in 88; bottom-up approach to development of 85; creativity and innovation in 124–126; customer service and 79; dealing with complete strangers in 74; deception in 80; Demand and Supply in (*See* Demand and Supply); evolution of 68–69, 85, *86*; extension of the scale of inclusiveness and universalization of dual-motive values in 89; features vs. benefits empathy and art of selling in 79–80; incentives, productivity, and behavioral tension in 167–168; Invisible Hand and 5–6, 81–84, 87–89; moral instincts and 120–122; negative side effects of overemphasis on self-interest in 78–79; not based on laws of physics 76, 90–91; pragmatism vs. ideology and failure of 125–126; preventing undue interference or obstruction in 167; schizophrenic duality of 97–102, *98*, *99*, *100*; social standard for necessities and 166; structure of 87–88, 123; *See also* transaction
Marshall, A. 1–2, 60, 101, 170; on biology as "Mecca" of economics 11; metaphors vs. linkages and 12; as synthesizer not innovator 12
Marx, K. 92

mathematics: algorithms 41–44; mystique of 127–129; platonic 128; representation of symbolic reality in 53–54, 128; in social sciences 55–56; social sciences and mystique of 129
Mauss, M. 70–71, 89
McCann, C. 169
metaphors 3, 12
Mirowski, P. 90–91
Montesquieu 91–92
moral instincts 120–122; conscious pursuit of social justice and 121; implicit empathy and 121; as primitive necessity 120; self-interest as market rule of conduct and 120
Moral Molecule, The 139
Morgenstern, O. 92
Morishima, M. 94
mystique of mathematics 127–129; social sciences and 129

Nash, J. 7, 127; on the bargaining problem 132
Nash equilibrium 7; accommodating self-interest and empathy 132–133; appeal of 129; conditions, assumptions, and axioms in 130; empathy as implicit in 130–131; implicit vs. explicit empathy and 131–132; mystique of mathematics and 127–129; practical wisdom vs. obfuscation in 134; pre-gravity and 129; shortfalls of 133–134; social equation as causal dynamic in 130
natural selection 143
negative social side effects 148
neoclassical economics 90
neocortex 19, 33; gating of dual motives 34
neural architecture 27; avoidance of inequality and 159; commonality of 61; evolution of fundamental homeostatic logic of equality and 159–160; evolution of market and 85, *86*; God's model of 5, 95; mathematics in social sciences and 55–56; neural social equation 56–58; self-corrective tendency vs. social stratification and 159; third form of neural dynamic 53–55
neural networks and executive circuitry 33–36
neural plasticity 50
neural social equation 56–58
neuroeconomics: challenge and promise of 138–139; consilience and 137–138; defined 137; noteworthy exception in 139–140
neuroethology *see* evolutionary neuroethology
neuroreceptors 35–36
neurotransmitters 27, 35–36, 139
Newmarch, W. 60, 144–145
Newton, I. 11, 90, 144
niche 24–25
nonconstant case, equilibrium equation 111–112
noncooperative games 131
nonlimbic pallium 21

objectively, observable behaviors 33–34
opioids 36
optimal functioning 55
organic algorithms 59–60
organic death: thermodynamic equilibrium as 57; zero equals 54
original sin 142, 143, 148; in biology 149–150
Origin of Species, The 142–143
Osteen, M. 85
other-interest 25, 31; balanced with self-interest 77
others-over-self 38
oxytocin 35–36, 139–140

Palley, T. 94
Panksepp, J. 26–27
parental care, evolution of 14, 19, 26
Parry, J. 85
Parsons, T. 67
patron-client relations in feudal systems 87
pay for play 73
Penrose, R. 63
perfectly competitive market (PCM) 123; empathy in 123–124
Perlman, M. 169
Petty, W. 144
Pfeiffer, U. J. 139
physics: behavioral wave function similarities with quantum 62–63; genes, and behavior precision vs. statistical probability 61–62; market not based on laws of 76, 90–91; statistics laws compared to 60; uncertainty in quantum 93; Walras and distortions of 92
Physiology and Behavior 16
physiology of social behavior *See* homeostasis
Piaget, J. 61

Piketty, T. 2
Pillars of Economic Understanding, The 169
Pinker, S. 15–16, 138
Plato 92
platonic mathematics 128
Polanyi, K. 85
politico-legal exchange 163–165, *165*
politics and gift-giving 70, 73
positivism, logical 148
practical science 56
pragmatism 95–96, 125–126
predictability and CSN Model 46
predictions of social dynamic 166–167
pre-gravity and Nash equilibrium 129
Pribram, K. 15
price: behavioral tension motivating change in 103; as endogenous variable 102–103; equilibrium 107–109, *108*, 165, *165*; social demand and excess 165–166; social equation and 103; *tâtonnement,* groping, and the auctioneer 102; unit change above/below equilibrium 107–108, *108*
price theory 102; calculus and neural algorithms in 104–106; schizophrenic condition in 114
Prigogine, I. 54
probability: physics, genes, and behavior precision vs. 61–62; sources of 60
productivity 167–168
prolactin 35–36
psychosurgery 34–35
pure science 56
Pyyhtinen, O. 71

quantum physics 62–63; uncertainty in 93

radical behaviorism 148
"Rational Fools" 80
reciprocity 43; gifts and 69–70; Hamilton's rule and 155; kinship 72; literature on 67; mixed evolutionary thought on 68; social dynamic effects and diffuse 69; specified/quantified in transaction 74; suspected biological origin of 68; through conflict 44
Reiner, A. 20
replacement generalization 20–22
Reptilian Brain 14–19
Rescuing Capitalist Free Enterprise for the Twenty-First Century 41
Ricardo, D. 92
Road to Serfdom, The 119

Sagan, C. 16–17, 22
Sahlins, M. 85
Samuelson, P. 92
Sapolsky, R. 43
Sargent, T. 5, 95, 168
Say, J.-B. 55–56
scala naturae 23
scale of inclusiveness 45, 89
Schlefer, J. 94
Schumpeter, J. 124–125
Science 15, 20, 138
self-correcting market dynamic 101–102
self-corrective tendency of neural architecture 159–160
self-interest 2, 5–6, 8, 25, 31; accommodating empathy and 132–133; Adam Smith on 76–77, 142, 170; balanced with other-interest 77; Charles Darwin on 142–143; deception of 80; in economics 76–77; egoistic range 41–42; empathy as preference or taste and 116–117; enlightened 147; enshrinement of ideology of 113–114; first principle or faulty ideology of 113; granite of 113; logical positivism and radical behaviorism and 148; as market rule of conduct 120; naïve and native skepticism of 114–115; negative side effects of overemphasis on 78–79; reciprocity through conflict and 44; shift to self-reference 6, 116, 117; as sole primary motive the market 76; territorial defense and *homo economicus* 115–116; William Jevons on 145–146
Selfish Gene, The 149–150
self-over-others 37
self-preservation 25–26, 31, 142; major ranges of reciprocal, conflict behavior and 36
self-reference 6, 116, 117
self-sacrifice 43
self-survival 13–14
Sen, A. 6, 80
serotonin 35
Shaftesbury, Lord 143
"silo" effect 141
Simmel, G. 67
Smith, A. 2, 4–7, 11, 88, 96, 120, 143, 144, 146; on the Invisible Hand 81–83, 126; misinterpretation of motives of 76–77, 141; roots of misinterpretation of 78; on self-interest 76–77, 142, 170; on sympathy 78, 82; *Theory of Moral*

Sentiments 4, 77–78, 81, 82, 113; *Wealth of Nations* 2, 4, 76, 90, 113
social architecture 49–50
social behavior: egoistic range 41–42; empathetic range 42–44; homeostasis and 47–48; range of dynamic balance between contending motives 44; reciprocity through conflict 44; scale of inclusiveness 45
social bonding: evolution of 14, 19, 26; oxytocin and vasopressin in 35–36
social brain 3, 8, 29–31; choices and meaning 30; countering market system failures balancing out 164; equation of, as metric of socio-behavioral tension and inequality 157–161; evolution of the modern market and 68–69; executive circuitry and language 30–31; higher cognitive integration 31; hunting, gathering, and sharing 30; price theory and 102, 104–106; reciprocity and 67–68; Supply and Demand as expressions of 83–84
social competition 161
social context 159
Social Darwinism 143
social demand 164; excess price and 165–166
social exchange 85–87; market or economic exchange system and 163; politico-legal exchange system and 163–165, *165*; predictions of social dynamic and 166–167; social stratification and 157–161; society as overarching system for 162, *162*
socialization 61
social justice 121, 159
social sciences: mathematical mystique and 129; physics envy in 144
social standard for necessities 166
social stratification 157–161; conflict resolution and instability of hierarchy of 161; emergence of social competition, alliances, and hierarchy in 161; instability of 161; self-corrective tendency vs. 159
social system, gift economy as 84
socio-behavioral tension metric 112, 157–161
Spencer, H. 12
spontaneous order 120, 121–122, 125–126
stability 93–94
statistics 60, 61–62; induction and 144–145
Stem Mammalian Formation 21
stiff upper lippedness 148, 149
Stigler, G. 2, 94, 113
Stone Age Economics 85
stress, behavioral 28
structural empathy 123–124
structure, market 87–88, 123
structured Empathy 89
supply curve *99*, 99–100; *See also* Demand and Supply
survival and evolution 142–143, 155–156
survival limits 55
sustainability and creative destruction 125
sympathy 78, 82
synapsid line 14

tâtonnement 102
Taylor, T. 114
Teitelbaum, H. 54
temporoparietal junction (TPJ) 34
tendencies, economics laws as 60
testosterone 35
Textbook of Biological Psychiatry 30
thank you expression 43, 69
Theory of Games and Economic Behavior 92
Theory of Moral Sentiments, The 4, 77–78, 81, 82, 113
Theory of Political Economy, The 145–146
Therian Formation 21
thermodynamic equilibrium as organic death 57
third form of neural dynamic 53–55
three-brains-in-one 16–17, *17*
Thurnwald, R. 67
Tickell, C. 52
Tinbergen, N. 152
Titmuss, R. 71
Tomer, J. 50
Tooke, T. 144
Toward Consilience: The Bioneurological Basis of Thought, Behavior, Language, and Experience 137
transaction: avoiding the behavioral tension of obligation 73–74; behavioral tension driving 74–75; defining the contrast between gift and 72; evolved from gift 72; reciprocal specified/quantified in 74; social exchange and 85–87
Triune brain in Evolution: Role in Paleocerebral Functions, The 138
triune brain theory 14–15, 32; Butler's revised version of 19–20; faulty reviews of 15–16; interconnected three-phase

human brain and 16–17, *17*; mismeasure of 15; replacement generalization 20–21; resurgence of interest in 16
Two-Person Cooperative Game 132

uncertainty 93
uniqueness 93–94
utility theory of value 92

van Baal, J. 67
vasopressin 35–36
Vaughan, G. 84
violence 51
von Frisch, K. 152
von Neumann, J. 92, 94

Walras, L. 56, 91–92, 101, 145; utility theory of value 92
Wealth of Nations, The 2, 4, 76, 90, 113
Wells, R. 103
Wiener, N. 47
Wilson, Ed 137
Wilson, E. O. 2, 12, 25, 31; on cooperative behaviors 43
Witter, M. 38
World Economic Review 50

your're welcome expression 69

Zak, P. 36, 139–140
zero equaling death 54, 57–58